MARK TWAIN

MARK TWAIN

A Collection of Critical Essays

Edited by
Eric J. Sundquist

Prentice Hall, Englewood Cliffs, New Jersey 07632

Library of Congress Cataloging-in-Publication Data

Mark Twain : a collection of critical essays / edited by
  Eric J. Sundquist.
       p. cm.—(New century views)
     Includes bibliographical references (p.).
     ISBN 0-13-564170-5
     1. Twain, Mark, 1835-1910—Criticism and interpretation.
  I. Sundquist, Eric J.   II. Series.
  PS1338.M275 1994
  818'.409—dc20   93-2348
                                                    CIP

Acquisitions editor: Alison Reeves
Editorial assistant: Heidi Moore
Copy editor: Liz Pauw
Editorial/production supervision and
  interior design: Joan Powers
Cover design: Karen Salzbach
Prepress buyer: Herb Klein
Manufacturing buyer: Robert Anderson

© 1994 by Prentice-Hall, Inc.
A Paramount Communications
Englewood Cliffs, New Jersey 07632

Printed in the United States of America
10 9 8 7 6 5 4 3 2 1

ISBN 0-13-564170-5

Prentice-Hall International (UK) Limited, *London*
Prentice-Hall of Australia Pty. Limited, *Sydney*
Prentice-Hall Canada Inc., *Toronto*
Prentice-Hall Hispanoamericana, S.A., *Mexico*
Prentice-Hall of India Private Limited, *New Delhi*
Prentice-Hall of Japan, Inc., *Tokyo*
Simon & Schuster Asia Pte. Ltd., *Singapore*
Editora Prentice-Hall do Brasil, Ltda., *Rio de Janeiro*

Contents

MARK TWAIN

Introduction

Eric J. Sundquist

> If we can liken life, for a moment, to a furnace, then freedom is the fire which burns away illusion.
>
> —James Baldwin, *Nobody Knows My Name*

"It makes me dizzy to think of the Vatican—of its wilderness of statues, paintings and curiosities of every description and every age." There are "acres and acres" of artwork on the walls and ceilings, and the "old masters," Mark Twain mockingly laments in *The Innocents Abroad* (1869), "fairly swarm there." The rhetorical puncturing of Old World artistic or intellectual sublimity in this passage from his first book and most popular travelogue was Twain's early stock in trade. No American writer so often celebrated America's independence by ridiculing the surfeit and stagnation of European custom. Whereas Washington Irving, James Fenimore Cooper, Margaret Fuller, and Henry James, for example, employed study of the Old World as a cautious measure of American exceptionalism, Twain characteristically declared the lessons of the "old masters" bankrupt, at best the material of his own profitable standup comedy on the lecture circuit or the point of departure for travel books and novels whose frontier boisterousness and Yankee egotism overwhelmed any tribute to the culture and geography of another world.

There is, then, less irony than might first appear in the fact that to a significant number of today's American readers Mark Twain has himself become one of the "old masters." He remains a giant in the canon of American letters and cultural history, to be sure, but for that very reason he is viewed with suspicion in some quarters. Insofar as Twain was preoccupied with the mechanisms of human "mastery" in its whole range of forms—from chattel slavery to industrial exploitation to national imperialism to his own careful cultivation of a public persona and complex psychological theories of guilt, dependence, and delusion—he would no doubt have appreciated the peculiarity that *Adventures of Huckleberry Finn* (1885), the book thought by a century's worth of readers to be not only his finest achievement but also one of the great documents of American racial equality and freedom, has at the end of the twentieth century become among some critics an object of contempt and censorship for its arguable racism. For Twain, however, freedom was no abstraction of cross-cultural harmony or idealized promise of post-Revolutionary equality; nor, in his view, did it have much tangible proof in the previous history of humankind. Rather, the law of history *was* slavery, no less

1

in America, finally, than among the corrupt ideas of the Old World or the dusty antiquity of the Holy Land.

Born in Florida, Missouri, in 1835, the son of Jane Lampton Clemens and John Marshall Clemens, a farmer, slaveholder, failed businessman, and sometime lawyer and judge, Samuel Langhorne Clemens grew up on the banks of the Mississippi River in the port town of Hannibal, which he recreated in his best-loved books as the idyllic village of St. Petersburg. As though in tune with a cosmic cycle that he had foreseen, Halley's Comet appeared for Twain's birth and returned for his death in 1910. Not least because his creative energies swung constantly between the golden nostalgia of smalltown childhood and the punishing pessimism most evident in his late allegorical work but nonetheless present from the outset, the life between those dates fittingly encompassed the creation of the modern United States: the Anglo-American advance toward the far western frontier, the nation's survival of a rebellion and bloody civil war over slavery and states rights, and, flowing from both these events, an enormous economic and technological expansion. The conquest of the West, a formative subject in Twain's writings from the tall-tale greenhorn comedy of *Roughing It* (1872) to his angry attacks on late nineteenth-century American imperialism such as "To the Person Sitting in the Darkness" (1901), fostered plausible arguments that America was, indeed, now independent of and superior to Europe; but it also left the nation poised on the edge of a less insular history, its own military strength and insatiable political appetite, so Twain argued, a key part of the nightmare of modernity. In Twain's self-consciously representative American life, the North-South axis of the Mississippi River and the East-West axis of pioneering expansion toward and beyond the Pacific coast intersected in an imagined territory that took the shape of the nation's own compromised destiny.

By the time he published his wonderful recollection of his own early steamboating days as part of *Life on the Mississippi* (1883), the transit of King Cotton along a corridor entangled in African American slavery had given way to the magnified power of the railroad—the transcontinental railway was completed in 1869—whose allure comprised new western lands, the chance of sudden mineral wealth, and industrialization on a grand scale. Yet Twain's imagination went back again and again to an antebellum world of romance commingled with the horrors of slavery and southern lawlessness—not because the world represented by the old days on the Mississippi was dead but because it remained so much alive, a sustaining force in the post-Reconstruction decimation of black civil rights and in the new national consensus of expansion. Grounded in theories of Anglo-Saxon manifest destiny and popularized in the real life of Theodore Roosevelt, as well as the fictive hero's lives drawn by Owen Wister, Richard Harding Davis, and numerous dime novelists, imperial adventure, Twain maintained, was analogous to slavery in the moral burden that it imposed upon the nation and the sacrifice of humanity it made under the banner of American freedom. Not that Twain himself stood outside responsibility for that sacrifice: nothing is more clear than his recognition of authorial complicity in virtually every crime and frailty his essays and books condemn. As much Tom Sawyer as Huck Finn, and always the public performer fascinated by power, fame, and wealth, Mark Twain was also his own object of study not simply for reasons of egotism but because everything he loathed in the bleak world of the past reappeared enmeshed in his own writing life. "I have despised [the practical joker] as I have despised no other criminal," Twain would write late in his life (in the work published posthumously in 1924 as his *Autobiography*), "and when I am delivering my opinion about him the reflection that I have been a practical joker myself seems to increase my bitterness rather than modify it." Whether living comfortably in his mansion in Hartford, Connecticut, built with the large proceeds from his early books and lectures, or traveling on one of several later speaking tours at home and abroad calculated to recoup his losses in various financial boondoggles, the adult Mark Twain still had the Mississippi River, and the whole complex fate it implied, running in his heart.

Perhaps because of his troubled recollections of his father as a modest slaveholder, Twain's sympathies with the cause of the South in the Civil War were scant compared to those of most of his southern compatriots. But neither did he openly identify himself with the cause of the Union. A slaveholding state that happened also to produce the most notorious constitutional endorsement of black inequality in early American history, the 1856 Supreme Court case of *Dred Scott* v. *Sandford*, whose chilling renunciation of African American humanity figures in both *Adventures of Huckleberry Finn* and *Pudd'nhead Wilson* (1894), Missouri was nevertheless on the margin of the South and remained outside the Confederacy. Twain too was a renegade mix of West and South—so much so that, although he joined a Confederate militia unit in 1861, he quickly deserted and later burlesqued his service in a light sketch entitled "The Private History of a Campaign that Failed" (1885). Twain was famous enough by the time the piece was published that it could be included in the important (and otherwise militarily serious) *Century Magazine* series "Battles and Leaders of the Civil War," but his attenuated relation to the vainglory of the Old South, or the delusive trappings of virtually any moral idealism, is just as apparent in the sketch as it is in his story of the white boy Huck Finn and the black slave Jim, which was also finally published after years of struggle and interruption in 1885. Concluding from his brief Civil War service that he "knew more about retreating than the man that invented retreating," Twain magnified his ambivalence about the South by renouncing its cause and went west with his brother Orion Clemens, newly appointed as Secretary to the Nevada Territory. There he exchanged his early career as a steamboat pilot on the Mississippi River (he was licensed in 1859 after a two-year apprenticeship) for work as a journalist, travel writer, and aspiring public storyteller in Nevada and California.

Adopting in 1863 the pen name of "Mark Twain"—a steamboat call for measuring the depth of a river passage—Clemens began to cultivate the authorial persona that allowed him to write with the combined independence and self-examination that would typify all his best work. It can be argued as well that his pseudonym was a useful psychological disguise for a man who—anticipating Huck Finn's lighting out for the territory at the end of his narrative—had fled the bloodshed of the Civil War in favor of prospecting, gambling, carousing, and writing in the far West. Perhaps, as William Dean Howells would later claim, Twain was the "Lincoln of our literature." Nevertheless, the western spirit, popular acclamation, linguistic facility, and broad moral vision that they shared—and not excluding some measure of ambivalence about full racial equality—may also have served in Twain's case only to repress until a later moment in his career, but certainly not to erase, whatever guilt he felt about having suffered so little personal loss in the war against slavery. By the time of the surrender at Appomattox and Lincoln's assassination, Twain had become a skilled newspaper satirist; his first comic masterpiece, "Jim Smiley and His Jumping Frog," appeared in the autumn of 1865 and made him famous across the country. After honing his skills as an increasingly popular public speaker—he based his entertaining lectures on western adventures, both autobiographical and borrowed, and on an 1866 tour of the Sandwich Islands (Hawaii)—Twain moved to New York, where, commissioned as a travel writer for the San Francisco *Alta*, he set sail on a cruise for Europe and the Holy Land in 1867.

When the letters and sketches resulting from his trip were formed into *The Innocents Abroad* two years later, Twain was widely enough known that the great success of the volume was no surprise. As in the case of *Roughing It*, which was based on his travels in the far West and the Pacific, the subject of his first book was, finally, Mark Twain himself—a professional writer whose unique mix of journalistic observation, outright invention, and piercing cynicism made the hoax a philosophical principle, lying an art form, and comic bragging about American "innocence" the perfect vernacular of the postwar American Adam. In a prose voice nurtured by slang and well rehearsed in platform performance, Twain seems to have answered Walt Whitman's call, in his 1855 Preface to *Leaves of Grass*, for a new language that was rough, energetic, and expansive enough to distinguish the great poem of the United States from its European roots. For Twain, too, American vernacular was forged of the comic energy of rebellion that Whitman celebrated in "Slang in America" (1885): "Considering Language then as some mighty potentate, into the majestic hall of the monarch ever enters a personage like one of Shakespeare's clowns, and takes a position there, and plays a part even in the stateliest ceremonies." When the King and the Duke, frontier frauds and conmen of the highest order, board Huck and Jim's raft in *Adventures of Huckleberry Finn*, the groundwork for their bombast—as well for Huck's own celebrated voice—had already been laid in the performative speech and deflating satire of Twain's lectures and travel books.

Revelling in protest against linguistic traditions of the European past as well as the inherited conventions of genteel writing that still ruled American culture in the first half of the nineteenth century, Twain steadily pushed his colloquial voice toward the melange of the salesman's harangue and the tyrant's fulminations that constitutes Hank Morgan's language in *A Connecticut Yankee in King Arthur's Court* (1889). It is no surprise, therefore, that in *The Innocents Abroad* Twain would lace his own significant rendering of aesthetic and cultural detail with outrageous asides about the seeming cheapness and demoralization of the Old World. In his early prose, the sober pragmatism and light color of the travelogue give way almost unnoticeably, for example, to moments in which he delineates the history of the Roman Coliseum by reprinting a supposed playbill of gladiatorial combat and a dramatic review of the performance, or contrasts to it the "playful" and "soothing" tortures of the "enlightened, civilized" Inquisition. Working in counterpoint to this ironic traveler's voice one also finds, not surprisingly, a pessimism about the lessons of history that was to remain at the very center of his moral philosophy. Intermingled everywhere with famous architectural monuments and the imposing works of great artists is the reek of death, which reaches a pitch in Twain's description of the catacombs of the Capuchin Convent: "Evidently the old masters had been at work in this place. . . . There were shapely arches, built wholly of thighbones; there were startling pyramids, built wholly of grinning skulls; there were quaint architectural structures of various kinds, built of shinbones and the bones of the arm; on the wall were elaborate frescoes, whose curving vines were made of knotted human vertebrae, whose delicate tendrils were made of sinews and tendons, whose flowers were formed of kneecaps and toenails." To travel even further backward toward the beginnings of western time is to discover little more of value than the mysterious but barren loneliness of the Sphinx or, in the Holy Land itself, a world of disease and impoverishment. Well before his obsessive ridicule of the South's destructive indulgence in fabricated codes of chivalry and his later, more disturbing speculations about the microbiological origins of human existence, then, Twain's imagination was itself sinewed with the prospect of decay.

The Old World was an easy target for the vernacular artist, but Twain's burlesque also concealed within it weapons ready to be trained upon the domestic scene. Twain at once energetically boosted American ingenuity, democracy, and technological promise, and yet subjected his nation's arrogant exceptionalism to merciless critique. Even as he became a publically loved personification of frontier character and mildly risque middlebrow taste, Twain came also to understand that both his fame and his country's fresh spirit of enterprise were as liable to go bust as the dreamy gold and silver claims he wrote about in *Roughing It*, his own self-promoting manufacture and marketing programs for his books, or the fantasized reenactment of a democratic republic that Hank Morgan, the American "boss," undertakes in the backward medieval world of *A Connecticut Yankee*. Like speculation and like democracy itself, writing was a promising but inherently risky enterprise, governed in Twain's case by cycles of debt, prosperity, inflation, and collapse.

Whereas *The Innocents Abroad* might be best understood in relation to the antiquarian travel literature popularized by Irving and other lesser figures, a genre which Twain improved by parody, his points of departure in *Roughing It* were the exotic western sketches of Bret Harte and, in contrast, the grandiose prose found in romantic idealizations of the West such as Charles Henry Dana's emigration guide, *The Garden of the World; Or, the Great West* (1856), which focused attention on the continuity between the Puritan errand into the wilderness and the contemporary force of manifest destiny: "The *Land of Promise*, and the *Canaan* of our time . . . broadens grandly over the vast prairies and mighty rivers, over queenly lakes and lofty mountains, until the ebb and flow of the Pacific tide kisses the golden shores of the El Dorado. . . . O, the soul kindles at the thought of what a magnificent empire the West is but the germ, which, blessed with liberty and guaranteeing equal rights to all, shall go on conquering . . . until the whole earth shall resound with its fame and glory." Dana's overweening rhetoric, a staple of midcentury proclamations about the promised land of the West, remained present in imperialist literature on through the century. For Twain, both the myth of the frontier and the beneficence of American empire were fool's gold of the kind he turned up as a naive prospector in Nevada and later dreamed up in similarly doomed money-making schemes.

The West proved a fine crucible for an art that depended on creating a plausible illusion and then exposing it as fraudulent, whether the fabrication in question is Hank Morgan's republic of baseball and newspapers, Jim's forty dollars' worth of freedom, David Wilson's solution to the mystery of racial identity through the new science of fingerprinting, or, as Twain came to believe, the deluding fantasia of human consciousness itself. In *Roughing It* the El Dorado of the far West evaporates into a near chaos of corruption, banditry, and frequent violence; enchantment and deceit, heroism and vulgarity, are in the end nearly equivalent. Written from a distance after Twain had settled in Hartford—and written, obviously, for profit in the days before his grand mansion was yet in reach—the book's exacting entanglement of innocence and cynicism replaces plot with a retrospective satire on his own gullibility. *Roughing It* may be read as an experiment in the darker comedy to follow in *A Connecticut Yankee* and *Adventures of Huckleberry Finn*, but in this case too some passages backfire. Twain's vicious portrait of the "Goshoots Indians," for example, is meant to trash the comforting liberal myth of the Noble Savage and elicit the reader's "Christian sympathy and compassion," but by depicting the Indians as little more than dirty, village-less beggars whose Great Spirit is whiskey, Twain altogether loses control of his morality play. The same, of course, might be said of the evident "racism" that periodically overtakes Jim's characterization in *Adventures of Huckleberry Finn*. Throughout his work, though, Twain was governed by a sadistic logic that required him to drive his audience (in his day mostly white) into confrontation with its fundamental prejudices and fears. That he must have shared such prejudice and fear in some degree, to recall his remark about practical jokes, seems to have increased rather than modified his bitterness.

Although late, posthumously published works[1] such as *The Mysterious Stranger* and "The Great Dark" attempt to construct a more cogent theory of pessimism, Twain's imaginative logic of annihilation had already reached a climax in *A Connecticut Yankee*, in which anti-imperialism and the frontier travelogue are superimposed upon his excoriation of the European past. The considerable debate as to whether the novel is an attack upon the feudal world of Camelot alone or also turns back upon its American hero in a critique of technological progress and capitalism misses the point that the two intentions are hardly incompatible. Inspired in part by the anti-aristocratic message of Andrew Carnegie's *Triumphant Democracy*, *A Connecticut Yankee* also summons up contemporaneous dystopian predictions such as Ignatius Donnelly's *Caesar's Column* and assaults on America's own moneyed aristocracy such as Henry Demarest Lloyd's Standard Oil exposé, *Wealth Against Commonwealth* in which he argued that "our barbarians come from above" and that American private enterprise is "more cruel than Russian despotism." Twain stops short of so outright an attack—but not far short. In the homespun philosophy of the Yankee machinist, arms merchant, and entrepreneur Hank Morgan, "unlimited power *is* the ideal thing when it is in safe hands." But the "civilization nurseries" and "man factories" he creates in order to replace superstition and slavery with modern democracy cannot overcome the regressive forces of medievalism. Hank Morgan's power to engineer a new society fades in near ratio to his own transformation into a carnival showman and tyrant until at last his reduced army is trapped within an enormous circular bunker of enemy corpses—a "homogenous protoplasm, with alloys of iron and buttons," created by the Yankee's superior but self-defeating technology of Gatling guns and electrified fences.

Twain would later claim, in his autobiographical writing, that *A Connecticut Yankee* was his attempt to show modern civilization in favorable contrast to the past—"if we leave out Russia and the royal palace of Belgium." At the same time, however, the distinction appears to remain more hypothetical than certain. Twain had hoped to finish *A Connecticut Yankee* by the day in 1888 when the Paige Typesetting machine, in which he invested a fortune in hopes of even greater wealth, was to undergo its first test run. Neither the book nor the machine was ready; on the heels of the failure of his own publishing firm, the eventual failure of the typesetting venture left Twain bankrupt by 1894, at which point he renewed his world travel as a lecturer to regain solvency. In *A*

---

[1]Twain's late unpublished writings, most of which are now deposited in the Mark Twain Papers of the Bancroft Library at the University of California, Berkeley, have been published in a number of volumes, including *Mark Twain: Letters from the Earth*, ed. Bernard De Voto (New York: Harper and Row, 1962); *Mark Twain's "Which Was the Dream" and Other Symbolic Writings of the Late Years*, ed. John S. Tuckey (Berkeley: University of California Press, 1966); *Mark Twain's "Mysterious Stranger" Manuscripts*, ed. William M. Gibson (Berkeley: University of California Press, 1969); *Mark Twain's Fables of Man*, ed. John S. Tuckey (Berkeley: University of California Press, 1972); *What Is Man? and Other Philosophical Writings*, ed. Paul Baender (Berkeley: University of California Press, 1973); and *The Devil's Race-Track: Mark Twain's "Great Dark" Writings*, ed. John S. Tuckey (Berkeley: University of California Press, 1979).

Connecticut Yankee his seeming premonition of technological disaster is joined to his more obvious ridicule of the era's anti-modernist fad of medievalism (exemplified in Brooks Adams's *The Law of Civilization and Decay*) in the consummate metaphor of Hank Morgan's armor, a human trap that accumulates sweat, insects, and bodily filth while ultimately guaranteeing death in the modern combat of which Hank is master. The corrupting whirlwind of postwar economic speculation, whose feverish promise and catastrophic risk provided Twain and his co-author Charles Dudley Warner the era's defining label in their novel *The Gilded Age* (1873), has become appropriately, and ruefully, autobiographical by the time of *A Connecticut Yankee*. The robust voice of the Boss's democractic boosterism seldom slackens in the novel, but its self-conscious representation of Twain's own public clowning only heightens apprehension that the staged world of Camelot and the American alternative are not so far apart. Twain's evocative image of history itself—the "stratified record" of excrement left by the medieval nobility, supposedly enchanted into the form of pigs—argues that Hank Morgan's own republican dreams are soon to be buried. At length, Twain's anatomy of the corruptions of political power would evolve into his portrait of Belgium's Leopold II in *King Leopold's Soliloquy* (1905), where the voice of the huckster and the voice of the mad tyrant, with its frenzied attempt to create a passible public relations account of bloody atrocities in the Congo, are indistinguishable.

A *Connecticut Yankee* looks forward, quite skeptically, to the captains of industry portrayed by Theodore Dreiser, Frank Norris, and Robert Herrick, to the theories of labor and manufacturing efficiency promoted by Frederick Winslow Taylor, and to Thorstein Veblen's glorification of the modern engineer, in whose combination of scientific expertise and bureaucratic psychology society might find its utopia. The book is closer in spirit, finally, to Twain's later manuscript rendering of the "Battle Hymn of the Republic" as an imperialist march ("Mine eyes have seen the orgy of the launching of the Sword . . .") or, in the unpublished "Letters from the Earth," a scathing dissection of the Bible, his dismissal of the Beatitudes as "immense sarcasms . . . giant hypocrisies." But the novel also looks backward in the American tradition, and one might read it as a paranoid sendup of Ralph Waldo Emerson's thesis in "The American Scholar" (1838): "If there is any period one would desire to be born in, is it not the age of Revolution; when the old and the new stand side by side and admit of being compared . . . when the historic glories of the old can be compensated by the rich possibilities of the new era?" Along with *Pudd'nhead Wilson* and his less successful (and more obviously mercenary) travel writings, *A Tramp Abroad* (1880) and *Following the Equator* (1897), the novel has a simultaneous enthusiasm for, and ennervating weariness of, invention—invention both in its technological and literary senses. The key to Emerson's passage follows not in an answer but in a caveat: "This time, like all times, is a very good one, if we but know what to do with it." Hank is a man of the Revolution born too late for it in America.

Left only with jokes and terrible weapons once his philosophy fails, he retreats into brutality and dream.

Twain's vision of a medieval past in *A Connecticut Yankee*, written and published after both *Life on the Mississippi* and *Adventures of Huckleberry Finn* had appeared, was screened through his repeated assertion that the American South was haunted by feudal dreams, and he based his portrayal of slavery in Camelot on descriptions in an 1837 slave narrative by Charles Ball entitled *Slavery in the United States*. The conjunction of aristocratic arrogance and racism that permeates *Adventures of Huckleberry Finn* and *Pudd'nhead Wilson* leaves little doubt that Twain rightly saw the collapse of Reconstruction and the rise of an oftentimes more virulent racial prejudice to be the responsibility primarily of the New South. Without question, the economic and political reunion of North and South in the decades following the Civil War required northern complicity through judicial, legislative, scholarly, and cultural means in handing over the "Negro problem" to the states of the South. Yet the rapid escalation in the abridgment of African American rights, both within and outside the law, was fueled principally by southern reaction to Reconstruction, and the manifold forms of segregation that became possible in the wake of the landmark case of *Plessy* v. *Ferguson* (1896) largely separated the neo-Confederate South from the rest of the nation for more than another half century.

After he has concluded the downstream voyage recounted in *Life on the Mississippi* Twain remarks: "I missed one thing in the South—African slavery." The irony of the double entendre lies not just in the mock nostalgia. Coming as it does in a chapter purportedly on "Uncle Remus" (that is, on Joel Chandler Harris) and George Washington Cable but mostly devoted, in fact, to southern lawlessness and vigilantism, the suggested nostalgia for the Old Days on the part of many white southerners is authentic; and it is therefore a reminder as well that what Twain's unpublished black revenge tale "Which Was It?" would speak of as the "second slavery" continues in force. Or, as Pudd'nhead Wilson's calendar puts it: "It was wonderful to find America, but it would have been more wonderful to miss it." Just so the slaveholding South, which Twain's canny irony said was vigorously alive in repetitious reminiscences about the war, in the gaudy paraphernalia of a "sham' civilization" in which the world of Sir Walter Scott and the Confederacy remain one, and in blood sports like the cockfighting that Twain turns transparently into a miniature race war: "The big black cock plunged instantly at the little gray one and struck him on the head with his spur. . . . [at length] the dying creatures would totter gropingly about, with dragging wings, find each other, strike a guess-work blow or two, and fall exhausted once more. . . . We heard afterward that the black cock died in the ring, and fighting to the last." The crowd's "frenzies of delight"—probably aroused more by the blood itself than by the scene's subliminal allegory of the postwar South, reaching from Reconstruction into an imagined future and swirling with imagery of sexual retribution—are simulacra of the public dimension of race hatred, where lawlessness took on the trappings of theater. Although Twain would speculate in his notebooks about a future moment of black supremacy in the United States, the real future of the post-Reconstruction South showed only unhindered white violence against blacks. The cockfighting scene's grim prophecy was borne out during the era of Jim Crow in the rise of heinous, often spectacular and methodical lynchings. At length, the whole nation became prone to a new kind of racial lawlessness, Twain would argue in "The United States of Lyncherdom" (1901), one that bred "a mania, a fashion; a fashion which will spread wider and wider, year by year, covering state after state, as with an advancing disease."

Statistically, lynching in America had already peaked by the time of Twain's despairing essay—*Pudd'nhead Wilson* and "Those Extraordinary Twins" theorize its proliferation in figurative as well as physical forms—but in the South its brazen and frequently ritual character would not fully abate for another thirty years. In *Life on the Mississippi*, as in his greatest novels of the middle years, Twain chose to approach American racial violence obliquely, by arch symbolism and by an autobiographical journey into the past that, like the first-person narrative of Huck Finn, also told the story of the nation. Although its early chapters are a sign of the Mississippi's role as the lifeline of an economy based on slavery—a river whose national function only came into being, ironically, after the black overthrow of slavery in Haiti, an event which led directly to the Louisiana Purchase—*Life on the Mississippi* was primarily a journey into the vanished past of Twain's youth and into his own authorial past, whose classic formulation, itself an archetype of nostalgia, was *The Adventures of Tom Sawyer* (1876). But in *Life on the Mississippi* Twain also strove to make his life one with the national life, an intention clarified in the geographical excerpt from *Harper's Magazine* which is featured as an epigraph to the volume. Entitled "The Body of a Nation," the excerpt from an 1863 editorial column favorably compares the Mississippi River valley to other great river valleys such as the Amazon and the Ganges. In its original context, the editorial had employed the metaphor of the "body" to argue for the necessity of retrieving the nation's organic unity from the destructive strife of civil war. As Twain utilizes it, the editorial serves less to call attention to the restored Union than to remind us of the continued fracturings of his postwar vision and his text: the steamboat has now given way to the railroad in the national economy; the famous passage from "Old Times" in which the cub pilot finds the beauty of the river's "wonderful book" of language erased by the mere utility of his trade is here doubled in the fact that Twain's idyllic recollection of the independence of the pilot has been subsumed into the work of the profiteering author, Mr. "Mark Twain," now collecting material for his book; and even if the reunion of South and North has been provisionally effected, the union of the races is for that very reason far from complete.

As in *Adventures of Huckleberry Finn*, so in *Life on the Mississippi* nation and book thus reconstruct themselves by absorbing the past into the present—but in such a way as to measure the post-Reconstruction world's continued immersion in antebellum mythology. The set of sketches detailing his days as a cub pilot that were first published in the *Atlantic Monthly* in 1875 are incorporated bodily into the longer book and therefore framed by the contemporary account. Similarly, *Life on the Mississippi* may be said to be incorporated, as it were, into *Adventures of Huckleberry Finn*—not just because it includes the raftsman's passage deleted from the novel but more importantly because the writing and publication of the whole text intervened into Twain's composition of Huck's story, which he broke off in 1876 and worked at only sporadically until 1883, when he rapidly finished a first draft, choosing to evade Huck Finn's further virtuous wrestling with his conscience through Tom Sawyer's humiliating liberation of Jim. The steamboat's destruction of the raft in *Adventures of Huckleberry Finn* fuses the two books—in a forecast, one might say, of the Siamese twinship Twain exploited in *Pudd'nhead Wilson*—as though both his disillusionment with modernity and the South's strangling nostalgia had produced in Twain a despair whose only cure lay in the nightmare antics by which Tom, reluctantly joined by Huck, appeals to chivalric authorities and mockingly frees the already free Jim. In 1876, Twain had already murdered his "lord and master," his conscience, in "The Facts Concerning the Recent Carnival of Crime in Connecticut": Huck's comparable struggle, though it is no less powerful for the fact, is rendered moot by Tom's racist torment of Jim, much as the significant advances in black rights that followed from the Civil War Amendments and the Civil Rights Act of 1875 were rendered moot by such legal sanctions as the Supreme Court's retreat in *Civil Rights Cases* (1883) and its refusal to intervene in the problem of mob violence against blacks in the South.

"No Huck and Jim, no American novel as we know it," Ralph Ellison has argued in a 1970 *Time* magazine essay entitled "What America Would Be Like Without Blacks." "For not only is the black man a co-creator of the language that Mark Twain raised to the level of literary eloquence, but Jim's condition as American and Huck's commitment to freedom are at the moral center of the novel." The first part of this claim echoes Ernest Hemingway's famous assertion in *Green Hills of Africa* that "all modern American literature comes from one book by Mark Twain," while the last part is likewise familiar in the now forbidding library of criticism devoted to *Adventures of Huckleberry Finn*. But Ellison's focus on the African American contribution to Twain's vernacular is only today beginning to receive the attention it deserves. In a brilliant and innovative argument that Twain's source for Huck's voice was not just the white boy Twain recalled from Hannibal, Tom Blankenship, but a black boy whose extraordinary speech Twain had admired in an 1874 *New York Times* essay called "Sociable Jimmy," Shelley Fisher Fishkin has raised a striking set of questions for Twain scholars. Whether or not such a perspective will weigh persuasively against the increasing number of well-argued critiques of Twain's reliance on the stereotypes of minstrelsy and his casual recourse to racial epithets remains to be seen. Does Twain's reproduction of the era's typical white colloquial racism when he spoke of Jimmy as a "guileless little darky boy" undermine everything he may have learned from Jimmy? Or, one might ask, did Twain's quiet financial help for a black student at Yale Law School sufficiently counteract his propensity for racist jokes on the lecture circuit?

No author, particularly one who intentionally places himself so much in the public arena, can entirely escape judgments whose premises must change over time. By Twain's choice of an ironic denouement, Jim is forever locked in the cabin of slavery, as much a prisoner of white psychology as Harriet Beecher Stowe's hero in *Uncle Tom's Cabin* or Lucas Beauchamp in William Faulkner's *Intruder in the Dust*. Jim's cabin is nothing less than the cabin of American culture in its canonical formulation. And in its ironic complexities: Joel Chandler Harris's storytelling hero Uncle Remus, to take a signal example, was more quickly to become as much a byword for racialist mis-characterization as Stowe's Uncle Tom, but his voice, decidedly black in many of the animal tales he delivers to his post-Reconstruction audience, is fre-quently more provocative than Jim's. Yet however much it strands him somewhere between the post-Reconstruction South's denigrating interpreta-tion of the "new negro" (as he was imagined by authors such as Thomas Nelson Page and Thomas Dixon) and the rise of an empowering African American philosophy of the New Negro (as it was articulated by W. E. B. Du Bois, Alain Locke, Claude McKay, and others), Twain's penetrating vision into the moral collapse of post-Civil War promises of black equality still leaves Jim every inch a man—dignified, compassionate, and wise. The question of Twain's racism, however, is best evaluated neither by excusing it nor by highlighting it. Rather, it must be seen as a product of all of Twain's own self-lacerating complexities, his outrage against the crude racism of his day joined to his seeming inability to escape its effects completely. There is no question that *Adventures of Huckleberry Finn* will never again have the unquestioned place it once had in the schooling of young American readers; to recognize that the book must be taught with care is not censorship but an act of moral consciousness.

The appropriate way to read *Adventures of Huckleberry Finn*, in any event, is not in a cultural vacuum but rather within the antagonistic contexts of both the history and literature of the Jim Crow South and the works of nineteenth-century African-American writers, beginning with the various slave narratives that Twain himself drew on. His attack on the failure of Reconstruction appears in a different light when read alongside Frances Harper's *Iola Leroy*. Charles Chesnutt picks up elements of *Pudd'nhead Wilson* in his political masterpiece *The Marrow of Tradition*, and Twain's dream allegories and his theory of multiple selves find important corre-spondence not just in the theories of William James but also in Pauline Hopkins's Afrocentric imperialist parable *Of One Blood* or Du Bois's classic,

The Souls of Black Folk, which has an originating presence in the African-American canon comparable to that of Huck Finn's story in the traditional canon. By the same token, Huck and Jim's voyage down the Mississippi River is all but canceled as an American cultural icon in Henry Dumas's "Ark of Bones," a haunting evocation of the middle passage laid upon the river's burden of death in the domestic slave trade. In a broader sense, Twain's vernacular should be set alongside that of Zora Neale Hurston, Langston Hughes, or, more recently, Albert Murray, whose young hero Scooter in *Train Whistle Guitar* and *The Spyglass Tree*, like Huck Finn, creates a beautiful fictive reality compounded of resonant folk language, haunting but sometimes sardonic innocence, and complex racial awareness.

Twain's tropological investigation of the relationship between racial division, sectional opposition (or reunion), and the capitulation of federal law to states rights would have its most exhaustive hearing in the frantic doublings of *Puddn'head Wilson*, a novel in which the force of law is made to participate in the racism of custom. His parabolic account of the decay of the Fourteenth Amendment concludes in a state of moral paralysis from which there seemed no exit but in dream-like speculations, allegorical sketches of depravity such as "The Man That Corrupted Hadleyburg" (1899), or the passionate diatribe of Twain's various anti-imperialist writings, the most remarkably inventive of which is *King Leopold's Soliloquy*. Apparently exhausted by the demands of conscience and goaded by debt, Twain returned to minstrelsy in *Tom Sawyer, Detective* (1895) and *Tom Sawyer Abroad* (1894), the latter a burlesque travel book in which, for instance, the "darky" Jim professes absurd humility at visiting the land of Egypt and Moses, surveyed from a hot-air balloon: "En dah's de river dat was turn' to blood, en I's looking at de very same groun' whah de plagues was . . . Ole Jim ain't worthy to see dis day." Whatever the moral imperative of Twain's farce, the ugliness of such a scene, given the inestimable power of the Exodus in African American cultural history, is severe.

The imagination that could produce both *The Adventures of Tom Sawyer* and *The Prince and the Pauper* (1882), texts of shimmering innocence, and *The Mysterious Stranger* and *What Is Man?* (1906), manic rehearsals for the eclipse of human conscience, could, it seems, contain anything. No wonder that the most compelling work of Twain's late period involves truly bizarre narrative assumptions—in "Three Thousand Years Among the Microbes" a speaking voice that emanates from a cholera germ named "Bkshp" (Blankenship) or "Huck," who parasitically inhabits the Mississippi River-like veins of a tramp not unlike Pap Finn, or in "The Enchanted Sea-Wilderness" a becalmed maritime universe where "no compass has any value," a cosmic trap where the "stillness was horrible" and time is a pageant of ghost ships: "Where one day is like another, why record them? What is there to record? The world continues to exist, but History has come to an end." The universe of Twain's late work is one of fright and blankness, a fantastic wilderness of inchoate existentialism in which his earlier taut balance between imaginative invention and a perilous loss of control at last breaks down. After producing a body of work whose moral complexities replicated those of the nation, Twain's art reached the point at which genius and despair, vision and betrayal were one, and true freedom the fire that burned away any illusion to the contrary.

A Hero with Changing Faces

Louis J. Budd

Mark Twain had established a streak of grassroots affection surprisingly early. In 1878 a ne'er-do-well managed to travel free from Cincinnati to Washington, D.C., by charming two railroad conductors and a "boss workman" with a note written to him by Twain. About that time, a book agent let a "dirty, ragged clothed" boy look at her prospectus for peddling *The Adventures of Tom Sawyer*: " 'Oh, that's Tom! Isn't it?' And he looked with delight, talking on, 'I've been wantin' dad to buy me one, and he said he would if he had more money than he knowed what to do with. . . . Some boys told me about Tom Sawyer—said he and some other fellers went to their own funerals; gol! musn't that a been fun.' "[1] Such fans admired the author himself. In a still unpublished memoir Twain set down the tribute from a sturdy, cocky adolescent who forgave all his adult ignorance because he had written *Adventures of Huckleberry Finn*. No such boy, we hope, justified the fears of prim librarians about the influence of Twain's novels and grew up into the Bowery bum who shouted, "Hello, Mark!" Of course that book agent found a spread of customers including a black barber who ordered the most expensive binding because "dat Mark Twain's done a heap of good to dese United States."

Contemporaries with inside knowledge of how celebrity works realized, however, that he had gone far beyond depending on the appeal of his books. One obituary called him the "architect of his own reputation," and the *St. Louis Globe-Democrat* observed that he "had a subtle sense of commercialism in his own line, and not even Sarah Bernhardt surpassed him in making himself of continued interest to the public." When a magazine posed him a pious question in 1898 about "books which have most influenced my life," he brassily listed his own, surely creating much more amusement and attention than offense. Among the many later judgments of his showman side, Carl Van Doren's is the most succinct: "He created many characters, but none of them is greater than himself." Robert Frost, his closest modern rival at elevating the man of letters into a popular hero, still counted mainly on the well educated and never approached Twain's ability to snarl traffic on Fifth Avenue.

With varying degrees of reproach, critics have lately deepened a gap between the private Samuel L. Clemens who created masterpieces and a

Reprinted from *Our Mark Twain: The Making of His Public Personality* (Philadelphia: University of Pennsylvania Press, 1983), pp. 19–29. Copyright © Louis J. Budd. By permission of the author.

[1]Anon., *Facts/By a Woman* (Pacific Press, 1881), pp. 45–46. Copy in the Library of Congress.

Mark Twain who hungrily sought applause. Although the mind and psyche that guided the working author were just as real as those for the showman—a supportive point for anybody depressed by Frost's biographers—it is time to move on from that gap and appreciate the operative images of Twain, who, incidentally, could sign letters as just Mark and respond to either half of his pseudonym. Actually, while the Clemens within the bosom of family life sometimes regretted his public face, the indecision sprang from differing circuits of mood that in his later years often flowed together. His force and lasting power as an attractive personality would argue that major psychic confluences were pushing forward. During the 1880s, especially, and between 1898 and 1903 he achieved firmer unity of action and feeling than most of us can deliver in far less treacherous contexts. Furthermore, whatever the sufferings of an upstaged Clemens or a harassed Twain, American society has benefited intellectually as much as emotionally from the self presented before and, finally, to it.

That self was much richer than Twain's literary reputation, which of course played its evolving part. While many readers pictured with unusual vividness the author behind the page, these images made spreading circles that thinned out beyond the measurable or overlapped with extra-literary sources. Because of these complexities, analysis had better confine itself for now to the United States, though the implications of his career apply to at least the industrializing democracies and though his charm abroad, if only by correcting notions of New World uniqueness, helps to clarify his cohering image; the mere fact of that charm certainly increased his eminence at home, starting with his triumphs in England during the early 1870s. Analysis of only his American career still incurs four especially challenging yet enlightening problems, which can help to judge the authority of alleged culture-heroes.

First, printed sources seldom reflect opinion passively. Besides the subjectivity of any observer, the spokesmen for the genteel tradition, for example, pulsed with eagerness to elevate taste. Without necessarily aiming to denigrate Twain, their estimates of his current standing carried a strong desire to shape it; their book reviews hid sermonettes on what readers ought to like. Likewise, most editors of magazines and newspapers believed in their mission to inculcate social orthodoxy and proper behavior. Ironically, Twain may have gained more than he lost from their bias, which gave him a firm pattern against which to define himself more vividly. Second, hard analysis of "the public" splinters it into always smaller pieces. By 1899 Twain's case taught a professor at Columbia University that "there are many publics,—as many in fact as there are different kinds of taste." What passes for dominant attitudes often applies solely to that cohort of the populace which feels the right or duty to speak up or merely reacts to a cue from a hired scout. Public opinion as a measurable force was invented late in the nineteenth century with literary polls leading the way during the 1880s. Its reification blurs the fact that Twain was gifted in all varieties of humor, some with vastly different audiences. Third, most people absorb the ruling culture passively if not defensively or at least assume that nobody of consequence cares to know what they think, much less to read their letters to newspapers. Twain's own defense against the elite, "my audience is dumb; it has no voice in print," recognized this pattern. He can demonstrate better how mass adulation works than it can explain him. More specifically, his career encourages friendly suspicion toward those always poised to tell us what our esthetic preferences are.

The fourth problem is unique to Twain among authors because a sizable part of his late constituency had read little if any of his writing, had never heard one of his lectures or the speeches given mostly before select audiences. For millions he functioned primarily as a celebrity, somebody who is unquestionably popular aside from concrete accomplishments. For the leading media of the time his casual doings rated as priority news. This coverage turned his personality into common property that was haphazardly discussed on the horsecar or the front porch among fluid groups, which included members unable or too lazy to read who had formed an opinion by hearsay and so took their part in the bonding conversation. Twain became prime fodder for the "human interest" stories or just the floating paragraphs that filled out the typical newspaper page and served as the broadest level of popular literature before the comic strip. Partly because he lived so long he reached the momentum of a to-be-continued serial. Although high culture may shudder at the quality of the content, the spear carriers for Twain were choosing materials for their frame of values and were absorbing judgments from their peers about what counted in their day-to-day society. Their casual reactions flickered beyond the sensors of any scientific instrument. Still, they mounted up towards tens of millions and deserve the attention of any democratic approach to culture.

The widest circle of admirers that has fair distinctness covered the readers of the lightweight magazines and the newspapers—especially the metropolitan dailies and, above all, those of New York City, which filtered outside their area of revenue and set the tempo for small-town editors wanting to rise above provinciality. It would be fatuous to presume to codify the attitudes among that sea of admirers who responded to Twain as their hero. The values of an articulate layer should not be extrapolated to cover tens of millions, many speaking broken English. The total circulation of the dailies peaked here at one-third of the population. Even the specialists in American Studies have used the term of "culture" loosely, jumping "from the 'literate public' to everyone," although the "imputation of collective beliefs is an extraordinarily complex empirical procedure."[2] Twain's public offered such divergent responses that abandoning analysis might seem wisest except for the fact that his career so undeniably held meaning for it.

Increasingly, different impulses within any extended public can pick clashing heroes, from Albert Schweitzer to Marilyn Monroe, can adulate both an

---

[2]Bruce Kuklick, "Myth and Symbol in American Studies," *American Quarterly* 24 (Oct. 1972): 444–46. Karl R. Popper, *Conjectures and Refutations* (1962), p. 341, warns against "naive collectivism" that easily assumes the existence of "social wholes."

embodiment of the consensus and one of its lively critics, functioning seemingly as a vicarious threat but perhaps in fact as a safety valve. To reach full stature the same hero almost must be claimed by opposing sides. If Twain's freewheeling ways appealed to those who were discontent with modernization and its bureaucracy and the other daily repressions it brought, he could stride forth elsewhere as the champion of official values because of his competitiveness, his thinking in national rather than local terms, his patriotism, his commitment to technology, his gusto for financial speculation, and even his delight in romantic landscape. John G. Cawelti argues that a popular novel (or hero) satisfies a "variety of cultural, artistic, and psychological interests" and, more generally, formulaic attitudes while introducing elements of change and thus achieving a "transition between old and new."[3] Much of the later disagreement about Twain springs from emphasis on either his rebelliousness or his conformities. Furthermore, those who admire his nonconformity refuse to grant that it carried some safe attitudes for ballast and that its acceptance depended on signs that it had limits and, in a basically optimistic culture, did not "oppose everything."

A balanced analysis soon sketches too many on-the-other-hands. That effect brings the temptation to settle for shaped models such as the Trickster, borrowed from cultural anthropology. But Twain's America could not pass for an oral, face-to-face community. Most of his audience engaged his presence through print or even less direct ways. A worse flaw of neat models is that his image changed steadily and, before his career ended, changed qualitatively at least twice. That fact undermines other inviting paradigms based on elemental human nature, though societies large and small do seem to need the privileged jester—Twain liked to claim he was "God's Fool"—who releases collective discontent by offering himself up to ridicule or comically belittling the sacred or personifying freedom through a madcap deviance. On the primitive antisocial level, the id of some admirers wallowed in Twain's joking about bad smells, itches, body noises, and furtive habits that polite discourse wants to ignore. However, he also encouraged more complicated rebellion than that.

Lately, *homo ludens* has aroused a fresh round of theory in which the play instinct is celebrated as not only the escape from routine but the insistence upon emotive and mental willfulness. Twain is a leading exemplar. In composite his career fits the four great archetypes—*homo ludens, homo agonistes* enduring pain and competing heartily, *homo aleator* gambling, and *homo fraternalis* advancing the common good.[4] So far, his lasting appeal verifies such universal frames of reference or others. But his works and personality also directly support our sense that shape-shifting reality overruns tidy ideas.

3John G. Cawelti, *Adventure, Mystery, and Romance: Formula Stories as Art and Popular Culture* (1976), pp. 30, 36. This strikes me as more workable than the thesis in Wyn Wachhorst's excellent *Thomas Alva Edison: An American Myth* (1981) that the culture hero always "functions to resolve mechanically contradictory" values.
4Edwin H. Cady, *The Big Game: College Sports and American Life* (1978), pp. 46–57, expounds these archetypes extremely well.

That proposition applies in turn to analyses of Twain, who bursts through any pattern that systematizes him. Though he belonged to *homo sapiens* and though his career was rooted in history, any set of abstract terms starts to dull a magnificently particular individual, a homegrown mind that could jeer at "that kind of so-called 'housekeeping' where they have six Bibles to one corkscrew."

Likewise, the universal models distort Twain's relationships with his era. For example, with the sense of community ebbing as industrial capitalism displaced the issues from local to national elections, heroes were needed to revivify the feeling of a concretely shared culture; along with inventing and exploring (in both of which Twain dabbled), literature was a less divisive sphere of activity in which to locate them. Or, from economic history it can be argued that the tenseness of a laissez-faire marketplace created a demand for the frothy entertainer that Twain knew how to be, as when he joked about smoking only one cigar at a time. Much humor depends on the social context, dominated then by a middle class that was dedicated to making good but chafed under the required discipline, that liked to pound itself on the back for individuality but was guiltily aware of its hypocrisies. From religious history it can be argued that the easing of orthodoxy opened a chance for secular entertainment that knew just how far it could dare to go with comedy about the spirit as well as the flesh. Socio-history can show that the urban masses, cut off from the gossip of the small town, were ripe for vicarious intimacy with celebrities, preferably associated with such reminders of the fading pasts as the village or the frontiers. Twain had one of the richest stocks of pasts available, whether by region or occupation. Finally, the undying wish to behold in person the true American, the new man in the New World, called for a fresh supply of candidates. Only a combination of such needs can explain the extent of Twain's triumph. Nevertheless, they cannot tell us why he and not somebody else became their supreme vehicle.

The best way of tying his uniqueness to abstract patterns, of making Twain belong to his times without shrinking him to an effect of them is to trace the evolving impact of his role. The clever hero can serve as a favorite American type who makes a fool of his righteous enemies and thus gratifies the democratic pleasure of seeing pretense leveled down.[5] But his function can grow grittier, more complicated. The revered jester may either relieve pressure damaging to social stability or divert tensions into nonsense. Comic self-assertion can encourage spontaneity in others or simply assure them that the ideal of resistance marches on even while they are knuckling under. On balance, Twain encouraged his public to reach out for autonomy and authenticity. In a subtler message, he achieved by 1900 a heartening degree of frankness about his image-building, a frankness that more than makes up for

---

[5] I have benefited especially from the ideas of Orrin E. Klapp in *Symbolic Leaders: Public Dramas and Public Men* (1964); also "The Creation of Popular Heroes," *American Journal of Sociology* 54 (Sept. 1948): 135–41; "The Clever Hero," *Journal of American Folklore* 67 (Jan.– March 1954): 21–34; *Heroes, Villains, and Fools: The Changing American Character* (1962).

his moments of fakery. As early as 1863 he openly warned that he had "a sort
of talent for posturing."

That posturing operated in and on a relatively new context—the world of
commercialized print and the burgeoning industry of publicity. The industry
is now so visible that we tend to overestimate its dominance over competing
interests. Normally a hero takes up little of an admirer's total life. But we
underestimate the self-awareness of both parties in the transaction, at least
during Twain's century. The hero was deliberately indulged as an alternative
to personal concerns, as the star in a welcomed public drama: a sequence of
actions before an audience that participates with some consciousness that "it's
only a play." As a writer Twain started from western attitudes based in the
newspaper office rather than the book and frankly allied to the trades of
publicity and staged entertainment. In his early lectures the deadpan style,
punctuated by mock perplexity at the laughter it brings, already proved his
skill at establishing a mutual recognition that he was posing. A kindred spirit,
P. T. Barnum had risen to fame during the 1850s "not simply because of his
enterprise and energy, but because of a special outlook on reality, a peculiar
and masterly way of manipulating other people and somehow making them
feel grateful for being the subjects of his manipulation." He delighted in
telling reporters about his ploys because he not only counted on the "national
tolerance for clever imposture" but understood that audiences could cheer-
fully gather for "something they suspected might be an exaggeration or even a
masquerade."[6] Like Barnum, Twain improved on the confidence man by going
legitimate and got credit for his shrewdness in managing to do that so openly.
For an early fan of "camp," he was parodying the asides that actors shared with
the audience of a melodrama; more fundamentally he parodied the Victorians'
veneration of sincerity. His posturing increasingly became a shared put-on of a
decreasing pool of outsiders. In Twain's late speeches the game of revealing
his tactics verged on infinite regression—genially warning that he always lied
about himself and so must be doing just that in admitting it. The larger point
of that game is that he never wore out his welcome through merely rehashing
the old routines. Rather he turned his herohood into a self-feeding process
that rose from notoriety to images so vitally attractive that they have swept
over the ordinary barrier of taste between generations. Seventy years after his
death, admen can use his figure without wasting space to identify it, though a
white suit often acts as a cue.

During Twain's forty-year performance the dominant quality was his irreverence, which flashed from *The Innocents Abroad* like an electric storm.
Inconsistently, he could support reverential absolutes, particularly about
womanhood and the family. But he insisted he had been "born irreverent—

6Neil Harris, *Humbug: The Art of P. T. Barnum* (1973), pp. 56, 61–62. The best statement of
this point with reference to Twain is in Martin Green, *Re-Appraisals: Some Commonsense
Readings in American Literature* (1965), pp. 113–18. W. D. Howells commented in "The Country
Printer," *Scribner's Monthly* 13 (May 1893): 548–49, that the "printing-office of former days had
so much affinity with the theatre, that compositors and comedians were easily convertible."

like all other people I have ever known or heard of."[7] Confident while in such a mood that he was appealing to a gut instinct he mocked cherished values— Sunday school theology, decorum in dress, parlor wisdoms, electoral politics, or the literalist conscience. Irreverence is always needed to challenge the status quo, which entrenches itself in sacred tradition, and to strip away the clichés that cover up evil or just insensitivity. It had an immediate force for the later nineteenth century. When Twain burlesqued Tennyson's *Idylls of the King* or quipped, "Heaven for climate, and hell for society," he was not merely deriding conventional ideas but striking at the social foundations of the age.

At its best his irreverence worked through comedy and gained privileges of frankness from it. We can only guess at the diagram of his psychic grid, and no theoretician—except perhaps Freud—has tracked humor on a persuasive level of sophistication without paradoxically eroding its base in illogicality or instinct. Whatever the buried sources of Twain's gift its reception by others joined it to a common "mental process, a distinctive feature of the social consciousness." These phrases come from a still respected essay, "The Psychology of Humor," that appeared during his lifetime.[8] It contends that the mainspring within us as audience is the pleasure of liberation from the taut consciousness we need in order to cope with reality. For a tumultuous moment we can transcend the laws of nature. Humor is the "only objective fact in our experience that dares to defy the world order with impunity, that can violate ruthlessly, without pain and without apology, the manifold human contrivances, social customs and relationships and thereby not only creates the sense of freedom, but also assures us that we may temporarily escape from the uniformities and mechanisms of life." It "bids us look behind the scene where luck, chance, spontaneity and life operate." Without naively assuming that Twain's audience had tenser psyches than ours or resented more the rigidities of economic efficiency, we can feel sure that monotony lurks everywhere and its victims welcome expert resistance to it. Whether just resistant through childlike play or reconstructive through irreverence that constantly threatened to "go too far," Twain's humor operated as a liberating force.

Still, the most important social fact about Twain was not humor but Twain as humorist, a likable personality who expanded into a comic hero. No theory accounting for a class or group can cover his mixture of creating books, lecturing, writing for the newspapers and magazines, public speaking, posing for cameras and interviews, manipulating the press, and expanding his word-of-mouth fame all the way down to passersby who had asked why a crowd was

---

7Quoted in the introduction to Franklin J. Meine's edition of *1601* (Chicago, 1939). As late as Apr. 1920 (*Atlantic Monthly*) Gamaliel Bradford fretted at length that Twain's "irreverence" might sway the "average ignorant reader of democracy." Morton Gurewitch, *Comedy: The Irrational Vision* (1975), pp. 56–59, capably praises "cynical wit" as an enemy of social and economic oppression.

8L. W. Kline, *American Journal of Psychology* 18 (1907): 421–41. D. H. Munro's balanced *Argument of Laughter* (1951), pp. 177–81, regards Kline as still quite cogent. Kline named as his main forerunner a French essay of 1893.

gathering. Hobbes's argument for the "sudden glory" of feeling superior to others can fit only that aspect of Twain which exploited hostility with suspicious ease. Most of the members of most of his publics learned to look to him for a more positive effect and then for personification of the comic spirit.

Usually billeted with drama, the comic hero can win applause at rising levels of cerebration.[9] As a buffoon he leaves us committed to the side of vitality and pleasure, released from intellectuality (as some of Twain's detractors did complain), and hopeful that a happy-go-lucky spirit will beat the odds. When raised to psychiatric significance he can fake paranoia as a screen for releasing energy, celebrating the gross body, and gratifying chaotic fantasies. Or, conceived sociologically, he wages war against rules and systems, delighting the many who would join him if they dared. In his time Twain was particularly admired for his touch for and quickness to radiate mock violence. When most intellectual, the comic hero earns his stature by "courageous perseverance, resourceful intelligence, and a more or less conscious acceptance of the inevitable risks that he chooses to run in his wilfully comic challenge to the deadly seriousness of his world." The personae of Twain's travel books approached this last standard. Some of his later sketches and essays met it; so did his public self after the mid 1890s even if snatches of the buffoon and the sham paranoiac would reappear until his death. It is nevertheless a blunder to peg the finest Twain at any of these levels. His genius stands out in his unsurpassed gift for so many kinds of comedy—from crude, even cruel joking (about the "hare-lip" girl in *Huckleberry Finn*) to irony as chilling as interstellar space.

Twain emerged, however, as not only a comic but also a popular hero. Broadening his constituency that far leads into the heart of a lively debate over terminology. Some would like to divorce "popular" from "mass," which turns pejorative in many contexts or suggests the technicalities of social dynamics. As for "folk" hero, though illiterates enjoyed Twain's image, the backbone of his audience could grasp the articles written about him. On the other hand, it was larger than "midbrow" or "midcult," which could carry the point that the middle class, by 1850 dictating the sanctions of taste, eventually granted Twain a crucial, validating degree of respectability. Likewise—depending on whether the cheap book, the penny newspaper, the entertaining magazine, or the audio-visual complex qualifies as the crucial artifact—different dates can be named as the time when a popular culture reached a density that makes it reasonable to call somebody a genuine national hero with followers in all strata of the society. For Twain's career, anyway, the decisive changes occurred during his boyhood and brought a huge jump in literacy that in turn compounded the kinds of publishing he would exploit. More specifically, his rise as public hero is inseparable from that of the newspapers that sold lively reading, which very much included

9See Anthony Caputi, *Buffo: The Genius of Vulgar Comedy*; Maurice Charney, *Comedy High and Low*; and Robert M. Torrance, *The Comic Hero*—all three published in 1978.

fillers, columns, and then picture-spreads on interesting personalities. As an insider, Twain understood this linkage better than we have, so far. Furthermore, he expanded it constructively throughout his lifetime. Aside from the gratifications of being a celebrity, he needed and used immediate interaction with his audience to find out how he was going over. This interaction was often mediated by the newspapers, which collectively gave him much better guidance than the scattered reviews in magazines or essays in books.[10]

Well before his birth, intellectuals had begun worrying about the quality of popular culture. As Twain recognized uneasily, he became a focal point in the continuing debate, then centered ordinarily on printed literature. Although a few guardians of quality accepted him as a bridge to the demotic audience, most accused him of bringing down standards. Before rejecting popular culture, its critics still need to distinguish between a moralistic judgment that legislates taste and a psychological approach that empathizes with the human need for release or entertainment. Moreover they will do best to classify esthetic objects and activities not by their content but by the use being made of them. To feel that Renoir's "Boating Party" looks great in an ad for beer hardly equals gusto for the Impressionists. Conversely, many of those who ridicule mass culture consume slabs of it. A devotee of elitist poetry may roar around in one of Detroit's showiest models; users of television and the glossy magazines dip into materials they condemn in principle. In fact too many explications of *Huckleberry Finn* cannot bear to admit its debts to Twain's training as a newspaper humorist.

Popular culture once differed substantially in practice and ideals from that of today, when the youth scene sets the beat while the hucksters follow so well that they lead. For 1870, for example, it is defensible to set up a line between mercilessly exploiting taste and satisfying it in good faith. Although Twain's self-promotion could slide into hokum, a loyalty to his origins and his early experiences saved him from condescending toward popular standards or sneering at the blunders of upward cultural mobility. During the nineteenth century the gap between low and high esthetics did not look so steep or even desirable to as many as it does now. The genteel leadership claimed a mission to recruit the millions in the expanding school system. While elective officials tried to act humble, they also thought it safe to come across as well read because, in turn, the populace had a strong ideal of self-improvement. Twain worried whether his lyceum talks had proved informative and not merely entertaining. During the 1890s, the decade when he mounted into hero-hood, big-scale entrepreneurs began to envelop popular culture. But for a while much was still oriented toward the realistic world and a social context interwoven with the traditions of its consumers. With Twain's help

---

[10]Henry Nash Smith, in *Mark Twain: The Development of a Writer* (1962), p. 107, suggests that "both the best and the worst of his work derived from the popular culture." In *Harvests of Change* (1967) Jay Martin begins by declaring Twain was "incredibly sensitive to the shifting, unpredictable mass mind" (p. 166).

while also to his benefit it could still offer both worthwhile stimulus and satisfactions.[11]

Romanticizing popular culture would be foolish. Its audience can demand trite patterns, then suddenly stampede after a fad; its ultimate sanction, applied quickly, is salability. But it can pay for vibrant work and seems able to preserve a populist strain that resists corporate deadness, either head-on or through a loyalty to liveliness that turns no wheels but just spins for fun. Twain did his part. Increasingly he also met the more general criterion implied by Richard Hoggart's *Uses of Literacy* (1957). Reared in the British working class, Hoggart neither disowns his roots nor regrets that education along with higher wages has brought the reading habit to the bottom of the social ladder. Yet he is appalled by the "self-indulgence" preached through the mass media and by the "trivial" entertainments that "make it harder for people without an intellectual bent to become wise in their own way." Sometimes a noisy echo, Twain much more often encouraged an earthy self-knowledge.

Still alive in his writings today, this stimulus once flowed at least as strongly from his personality. Skeptics, probing for false legends, brush away his image as a smoke screen and condescend to the public Twain who did fall short of perfect integrity—as any account must that is not a fairy tale. But if heroes on a human scale can happen, Twain qualified as ultimately authentic, deserving of accolades more than an exposé. To imply that he should have acted very differently is to forget that he fashioned one of the prized characters of our culture, that his unique élan overrode any posing. His climb to herohood took shrewdness, courage, toughness, and perseverance. Achieving it loosened the grip of editors anxious to enforce the reigning literary conventions. How much would we care about him now if hackwork for the magazines had drained his energies?

Today our political health is threatened by the image building used by candidates, from the county to the national level, to evade tough issues, and posturing always threatens the self-respect of anybody trying to stay honest. Twain suffered from his self-contempt. Furthermore, success breeds its own problems. Like the hustler in Budd Schulberg's *What Makes Sammy Run?* Twain learned how much effort it takes to hold the lead against the endless string of contenders and to try topping each previous triumph. As an unexpected cost, his control over the public increased his depressing suspicion that the damn fools hold a majority anywhere. But whatever the psychic strains, he projected the ideal of autonomy, which can subvert clichés, idols, habits, ideas, and systems that have outlived reality. In positive terms he

---

[11]See Oscar Handlin, "Comments on Mass and Popular Culture," pp. 63–70, in Norman Jacobs, ed., *Culture for the Millions?* (1961). Herbert Gans, *Popular Culture and High Culture* (1974), is particularly good at challenging arguments for the prima-facie superiority of elite tastes and the harmful effect of lowbrow ones. John G. Cawelti, "Recent Trends in the Study of Popular Culture," *American Studies: An International Newsletter* 10, no. 2 (Winter 1971), is still cogent, especially for his sensitivity to basic definitions.

dramatized an incorrigibly spontaneous individualist who tacitly accepted the need for social forms but drove them toward renewed vitality. We can admire those dramatics without conceding that they conjured up a fake Twain. Like George Santayana, I believe that "our deliberate character is more truly ourself than is the flux of our involuntary dreams."[12] More truly ourself, also, than the elevated feelings and ideas we keep private.

[12]Quoted approvingly in Erving Goffman, *The Presentation of Self in Everyday Life* (1969), p. 57.

The Writer's Secret Life: Twain and the Art of Authorship

Susan K. Gillman

The process of literary creation confronted Mark Twain in business, in the law, in publishing, and in performing, with graphic divisions between authorship and control. Although never a particularly programmatic or self-conscious theorist, Twain responded to the pressures of the literary marketplace by addressing the broad issue of authorial control through a series of related tropes: the artist as passive amanuensis / unconscious plagiarist, as unwilling midwife / proprietor / father, and finally as the unconscious. These scattered metaphors suggest that, unlike some literary men, Twain experienced creativity not through the model of the pen-penis disseminating its writings on the virgin page, but rather as illegitimately sexualized, a threateningly uncontrollable power. Amanuensis to plagiarist to midwife to father: the relationship of author to text is envisioned as increasingly intimate, entangled, complicit.

The first set of metaphors figures the author as distant from and as passively related to his literary creations as possible. Sometimes the "books would go gaily along and complete themselves if I would hold the pen," Twain reminisced in 1906, and "as long as a book would write itself I was a faithful and interested amanuensis." But in practice the process of composition, like childbirth, often proved to be laborious, and so the pen-holding amanuensis resorted to a more mechanistic turn of phrase. The Mark Twain "literary shipyard" almost always had "two or more half-finished ships on the ways, neglected and baking in the sun," because "the minute that the book tried to shift to *my* head the labor of contriving its situations, inventing its adventures, and conducting its conversations, I put it away . . . [until it] was ready to take me on again as amanuensis." By accident, he says, during the year-long lull (in the mid-1870s) in producing *Tom Sawyer*, he discovered the reason—and new imagery—for his own fitful process of composition:

> My tank had run dry; it was empty; the stock of materials in it was exhausted . . .
> It was then that I made the great discovery that when the tank runs dry you've
> only to leave it alone and it will fill up again in time, while you are . . . quite

Reprinted from *Dark Twins: Imposture and Identity in Mark Twain's America* (Chicago: University of Chicago Press, 1989), pp. 31–52. Copyright © 1989 The University of Chicago. By permission of the publisher and the author.

unaware that this unconscious and profitable cerebration is going on. There was plenty of material now, and the book went on and finished itself without any trouble.[1]

As Justin Kaplan argues, this "basic tenet of Mark Twain's faith in himself as a writer" is framed in metaphors which reflect "both his mechanistic turn of mind and his frontier assumption of endless forests and numberless buffaloes."[2] But I would add that this is an oddly self-compromising tenet of faith. The tank will fill up again, but the writer, "unaware" and "unconscious," denies himself any control over the process. For Twain to authorize his art means, it seems, to qualify his authority over it. What is jeopardized, then, by the process of artistic production is, to extend [Walter] Benjamin's terms, not simply the "authority" of the "object," but the "authenticity" of the self that produces the object.

Just how problematic this conception of creativity is may be gauged from a related metaphor: the author as plagiarist. Unlike the Walt Whitman poet, an "original," "the Me myself," Twain rejected the possibility of originality in art. Even thoughts are not self-generated, he argued in a letter to Helen Keller on St. Patrick's Day, 1903:

> As if there was much of anything in any human utterance, oral or written, *except* plagiarism! The kernal, the soul—let us go further and say the substance, the bulk, the actual and valuable material of *all* human utterances—is plagiarism. For substantially all ideas are second-hand, consciously and unconsciously drawn from a million outside sources, and daily used by the garnerer with a pride and satisfaction born of the superstition that he originated them. (*MTL*, 2:731)

More than consciously drawing on sources, the notion of *unconscious* plagiarism, like the "unconscious cerebration" of the tank filling up, becomes a major trope in Twain's theorizing about creativity.

Both Twain's letter to Helen Keller and his *Autobiography* recall one striking case of unconscious authorial borrowing from the 1860s. So influenced was Twain (according to his own account) by reading a book of Oliver Wendell Holmes's poetry, *Songs in Many Keys,* that three years later Twain "stole" Holmes's dedication to the book when dedicating his own *Innocents Abroad.* Although Twain was later mortified that the gist of the dedication "was promptly mistaken by me as a child of my own happy fancy," Holmes assured the culprit (in Twain's paraphrase) that "there was no crime in unconscious

---

[1]This passage and all the others in this paragraph come from *Mark Twain in Eruption,* ed. Bernard De Voto (1940; rpt. New York, 1968), pp. 196–99; hereafter abbreviated *MTE.* Other abbreviations used in the text and notes are as follows: *MTL* = *Mark Twain's Letters,* ed. Albert Bigelow Paine, 2 vols. (New York, 1917); *MTHL* = *Mark Twain-Howells Letters,* ed. Henry Nash Smith and William M. Gibson, 2 vols. (Cambridge, Mass., 1960); *MTN* = *Mark Twain's Notebook,* ed. Albert Bigelow Paine (New York, 1935; *MTDW* = *Henry Nash Smith, Mark Twain = The Development of a Writer* (New York, 1967); *SSW* = *Selected Shorter Writings of Mark Twain,* ed. Walter Blair (Boston, 1962); *MTP* = *Mark Twain Papers,* Bancroft Library, University of California, Berkeley. See notes below for further abbreviations used in the text.

[2]Kaplan, *Mr. Clemens and Mark Twain* (New York, 1966), pp. 205, 73.

plagiarism." "No happy phrase of ours is ever quite original with us," but rather "all our phrasings are spiritualized shadows cast multitudinously from our readings."[3] If no originality is possible, still here *some* more intimate relationship than that of mere amanuensis is postulated between the writer and his "phrasings." Together the images of a child and spiritualized shadow, which conjure up writing for Twain in the case of the Holmes plagiarism, lead us to his most extended metaphors for creativity, those that link books to childbirth and to the shadows of the unconscious cast by dreams.

Responding in 1889 to George Bainton's request for a few words on authorial methods for a book to be called *The Art of Authorship,* Twain underscored the unconscious nature of his own creative process:

> If I have subjected myself to any training processes, and no doubt I have, it must have been in this unconscious or halfconscious fashion . . . This unconscious sort . . . is guided and governed and made by-and-by unconsciously systematic, by an automatically-working taste—a taste which selects and rejects without asking you for any help . . . Yes, and likely enough when the structure is at last pretty well up, and attracts attention, *you* feel complimented, whereas you didn't build it, and didn't even consciously superintend . . . So I seem to have arrived at this: doubtless I have methods, but they begot themselves, in which case I am only their proprietor, not their father.[4]

This theory of creativity should be read first in the context of Twain's general doctrine of determinism and the particular text *What Is Man?* (written 1898, published 1906), which Twain called his "gospel" and De Voto called "a plea for pardon."[5] *What Is Man?*'s mind-as-machine thesis explicitly formulates what the Bainton letter implies, that rejecting the notion of conscious taste (and hence of personal merit) is a prerequisite to abrogating any question of personal responsibility. But the letter addresses itself specifically to literary responsibility, disavowing any credit or blame for authorial "methods" that "begot themselves." The birth metaphor must strike us as odd, since it actually affirms some tie in the act of denying others, just as the distinction between proprietor and father begs the critical question of whether even a proprietary relationship does not entail significant claims and responsibilities.

The metaphor reflects, then, a paradoxical double desire with striking affinities to the contradictory divisions many have perceived in the Mark Twain-Samuel Clemens relationship. From Van Wyck Brooks's thesis that the writer was emasculated by the conflict between the forces of Puritanism and the frontier ("Mark Twain was an unworthy double of Samuel Langhorne Clemens")[6] to James Cox's contradictory view that Samuel Clemens channeled

---

[3]This account of the Holmes plagiarism is in *The Autobiography of Mark Twain,* ed. Charles Neider (New York, 1959), pp. 150–51. Twain also discusses various experiences with plagiarism in print in a piece entitled "Mark Twain on Thought-Transference," *Journal of the Society for Psychical Research* 1 (October 1884): 166–67.

[4]Twain's emphasis; first printed in *The Art of Authorship,* ed. George Bainton (New York, 1890); rpt. in *SSW,* 225–26.

[5] Bernard De Voto, *Mark Twain at Work* (Boston, 1967), p. 116.

[6]Van Wyck Brooks, *The Ordeal of Mark Twain* (New York, 1920; rpt. New York, 1955), p. 193.

his aggressions and found a literary identity in the comic personality of "Mark Twain," critics have been themselves divided over how Samuel Clemens relates to Mark Twain: in creative or destructive opposition? The critical division goes all the way back to the divided subject himself, who regarded his literary methods with similar ambivalence. No one, including the writer himself, can decide whether "Mark Twain" was a blessing or a curse for Samuel Clemens.

The cultural components of Clemens's self-creation as "Mark Twain" further remind us that the role of humorist evoked a popular image fraught with contradictions.[7] As "Mark Twain," he was indeed trapped by the split perceived in nineteenth-century America between the roles of humorist and litterateur, humor defined as part of "vernacular" or "low" culture and literature assigned to "high" culture. As early as the 1860s, purportedly the heyday of humor on the San Francisco "literary frontier," Twain exhibited a reluctance to accept his vocation as a humorist. Indeed, he appeared to share his contemporaries' low opinion of the humorist's calling—the opinion not merely of his later, genteel Hartford contemporaries but also of his fellow writers in the West. "Funny fellows are all right and good in their place," cautioned one California journalist, but "the sole supreme taste of the public ought not to be in that direction."[8] At the other end of the continent and of Twain's career, a similarly qualified "good" was similarly equivocally extended to humor. At a ceremonial banquet at Delmonico's on 5 December 1905, in honor of Twain's seventieth birthday, Professor Brander Matthews of Columbia University spoke of "the proper praise" to be paid him: "With Mark Twain, the humorist, his humor is always good, his humor is never irreverent, never making for things of ill repute."[9] While asserting the "good"-ness of Twain's humor, Matthews clearly felt obliged to distinguish Twain from those who indulged in "irreverent" humor, just as earlier the California journalist had praised "funny fellows" as "good in their place." When even praise for the art of humor betrays such unintended slights, and when those slights appear to be ubiquitous, part of western culture of the 1860s and of the eastern literary establishment at the turn of the century, we get a full sense of the deeply ambivalent treatment accorded the funny man throughout Twain's lifetime.

Given this cultural ambivalence, it is no wonder that in the letter to George Bainton, Mark Twain would rather envision himself as proprietor than father of his art, wanting to separate himself from the bulk of his writing, associated as it was—and as he was—with the taint of humor. He did not,

---

[7]On the issue of Mark Twain as a public figure, see Budd, *Our Mark Twain*, and Sara de Saussure Davis and Philip D. Beidler, eds., *The Mythologizing of Mark Twain* (Tuscaloosa, Ala., 1984). In the latter volume, see especially Henry Nash Smith, "Mark Twain, 'Funniest Man in the World,'" pp. 56–76, on the distortions and contradictions in "the image evoked by the name Mark Twain . . . in American popular culture" (p. 56).

[8]"A Glance at San Francisco Literature," *Grass Valley* (Calif.) *National*; rpt. in *Californian* 2 (11 February 1865).

[9]"Mark Twain's Seventienth Birthday. Souvenir of Its Celebration," Supplement to *Harper's Weekly*, 45 (23 December 1905), p. 1886; quoted in Smith, "'Funniest Man in the World,'" p. 62.

however, want to repudiate all of his literary offspring; such birth imagery as that of the Bainton letter crops up apparently only in relation to his fiction. The nonfiction—political articles, satiric pieces—and the fiction based on long distant fact—historical novels like *The Prince and the Pauper* or *Joan of Arc*—constituted a different, less revealing, more distanced and controlled kind of writing. Only imaginative writing was sufficiently threatening to be envisioned in images of unnatural or abortive or violent birth.

Literary creation is most strikingly associated with freakish birth in the preface to *Those Extraordinary Twins*, itself a farce about Siamese twins that evoked, if not gave birth to, the tragedy *Pudd'nhead Wilson*. Twain's flippant account of the composition of his twin novels unmasks how a "jackleg" novelist works: much like that of the amanuensis, his writing "goes along telling itself" until "it spreads itself into a book." A "tragedy" that first masqueraded as a "farce" during the long and tortuous composition, the finished novel exposed unwanted truths linking black and white genealogies through the institution of slavery—truths so unwanted that their author refused to acknowledge his own creation. His "original intention," he protests in the preface and afterword published with the two books, was to write an "extravagantly fantastic little story" about a "monstrous 'freak'"—a pair of Siamese twins. But when "it changed itself from a farce to a tragedy" and other new characters, among them "a stranger named Pudd'nhead Wilson," began "working the whole tale as a private venture of their own," Twain turned into a powerless bystander at an event beyond his control, with not one "but two stories tangled together." Moreover, between the "two stories in one" there was now "no connection . . . no interdependence, no kinship." The solution was violently to reassert his authorial control: "I pulled one of the stories out by the roots, and left the other one—a kind of literary Caesarean operation."[10]

Twain assists at this twin birth, more midwife than mother, attempting to sever himself from his progeny, whom he also severs from one another. Not only does he characterize the entire tragedy as an unwilled creation "intruding" into his authorial consciousness and "superseding" the farce that nurtured it, but also his chief character is a "stranger" in terms of the plot and perhaps to the author himself. Earlier, in the 1889 Bainton letter, the grudging admission of paternity ("Doubtless I have methods, but . . . I am only their proprietor, not their father") raises the spectre of the suspicious father, forced to assume paternal responsibility but unsure that the child is really his. The preface to *Pudd'nhead Wilson* retreats behind a similar veiled accusation of loose behavior in its suggestion that two such different siblings could not possibly share the same paternity. The midwife image, too, repudiates authorial responsibility. If, it implies apologetically, the tragedy seems as "monstrous" as the "grotesque" farce out of which it grew, the author is not implicated, for, like all his literary creations, "they begot themselves." The

---

[10]Mark Twain, *Pudd'nhead Wilson and Those Extraordinary Twins*, ed. Sidney E. Berger (New York, 1980), p. 119; further references to this work will be abbreviated *PW*.

Pudd'nhead Wilson preface thus conflates acknowledgment of the paternal responsibilities of authorship with denial. The question Twain begs in this literary family history, consisting almost entirely of denials of kinship, is whether the tragedy of the part-black Tom Driscoll is not as preposterous as the grotesquerie of *Those Extraordinary Twins*, so preposterous that it had to be represented as the unwilled product of the author's creative unconscious.

With this literary genealogy based on division rather than connection, Mark Twain tried to separate himself from possible charges of poor taste (in the "extravagant farce") and of immorality (in the racial tragedy). But at the same time the theory of unwilled creativity shook his confidence in his ability to "consciously superintend" his own art—a phrase, we remember, that appears, along with "proprietor," in the Bainton letter. The Whittier dinner speech and its aftermath raised similar fears. Howells's metaphor of "demoniacal possession" for Twain's performance at the dinner conjured an extreme image of the creator who cannot control his own creations, his demons. So, too, we remember, did Twain's own confession to Howells that he must have been "insane" when he wrote that speech. Echoing that confession, in Twain's formal letter of apology to Emerson, Longfellow, and Holmes he similarly castigates himself for not having exercised better control over his crude, but unconscious, impulses. "I ask you to believe that I am only heedlessly a savage, not premeditatedly," he wrote on December 27, 1877:

> I come before you, now, with the mien & posture of the guilty . . . If a man with a fine nature had done that thing which I did, it would have been a crime. . . but I did it innocently & unwarned . . . But when I perceived what it was that I had done, I . . . suffered as sharp a mortification as if I had done it with a guilty intent.[11]

If the real author of this crime is some savage, the logic goes, then Twain is paradoxically savage but guiltless, an innocent criminal. Ironically, each of these attempts, both Howells's and Twain's, to distinguish between willful and unintentional artistry, and thereby relieve the artist of any criminal complicity, envisions some kind of guilty association between artist and art: he is either demoniacally possessed or insane or savage. No matter what the metaphor, Twain's art seems fatefully conjoined to the illicit or the illegitimate.

In this context, Twain's choice of procreative metaphors for literary creation becomes particularly revealing, for he persistently associated creativity not with conventional, communally sanctioned sexuality but with violation of sexual taboos. In 1872 Twain thanked Howells for his favorable review of *Roughing It*: "I am as uplifted and reassured by it as a mother who has given birth to a white baby when she was awfully afraid it was going to be a mulatto" (*MTHL*, 1:10–11). This casually off-color joke more radically confuses boundaries than the *Pudd'nhead Wilson* preface; literary conception not only threat-

---

[11]Quoted in *MTDW*, 99–100. Letter in *Harvard Library Bulletin* 9 (Spring 1955): 164.

ens sexual taboos, it also crosses racial barriers. Twain fantasizes not merely that he is a woman but an adulterous woman who may be disgraced by bearing racially mixed offspring. We can see the perverse logic of the joke emerging if we remember that humor was indeed regarded as a kind of "mongrel" literature violating social and linguistic conventions. Humor also generates a crossbreeding of modes (farce, burlesque, satire), of purposes (serious, entertaining), of audiences (mass and elite), and it even, in the case of southwestern humor, generates a cross between oral and written traditions. In addition, Twain's humorous writings traversed the formal boundaries of journalism, travelogue, autobiography, and fiction. As a writer permanently confused over what category his work belonged to, divided over whether to write farce or tragedy, Twain imagined himself violating literary, racial, and sexual taboos.

The relationship of an author to his books thus did not so much convey to Twain an image of dividedness where there should be unity as it undermined the very notion of division itself. That is, the categorical divisions (between races, sexes, between self and other) on which definitions of identity depend seemed not to hold up in the context of Twain's creative process. The act of creation results in an intimate relation, yes, but a contaminated intimacy that blurs boundaries between self and other. Hence the increasing closeness and complicity of Twain's metaphors for creativity. His language suggests that a book is part of the self but also an alien other—in Faulkner's words the writer's "dark twin"[12] revealing unacceptable or forbidden knowledge— including self-knowledge of which even the self is unconscious. Any absolute separation between self and creation thus proves unstable as the control creator wields over creature breaks down—and the unconscious dimly emerges as the tie that binds the two. . . .

Dream analysis fascinated Mark Twain most of his life, and from early on he cultivated the habit of recording his own dreams. Probably the best-known example is a notebook entry in the late fall of 1884 containing the germ for *Connecticut Yankee:* "Dream of being a knight errant in armor in the middle ages. Have the notions & habits of thought of the present day mixed with the necessities of that" (*MTN*, 171). A less well known experiment with translating into writing the peculiar disjunctions of time experienced in dreams is "My Platonic Sweetheart," a short story written in 1898, published in the 1912 *Harper's Magazine* Christmas issue, and based on a recurrent dream of over forty-four years.[13] The dream is always the same: the narrator loves and loses his "Dreamland sweetheart," but each time his loss of her is mitigated by his knowledge that she will appear in another dream. The "platonic" nature of this unconsummated fantasy, like its transitory and elusive female figure, seems

12William Faulkner, *Mosquitoes* (New York, 1927), p. 251.

13Abridged version of "My Platonic Sweetheart" first published in *Harper's Magazine* (December 1912); rpt. in *The Mysterious Stranger and Other Stories* (New York, 1923). The complete holograph manuscript, from which I quote, is in *MTP*; further references to this work will be abbreviated *MPS*.

both to protect and to titillate the male dreamer / narrator. Indeed, the dream sequence is far less sexual than it is mournful, a recurrently rehearsed sensation of loss–loss of unsublimated, prelapsarian energies, whether sexual or artistic. . . .

In "My Platonic Sweetheart" he directly addresses the issue of who controls or "superintends" or "architects" his art and ends by broadly questioning the validity, even the reality, of both himself and his world. Emotional pain, for example, suffered in this recurrent dream of loss, transcends and therefore seems to question the validity of waking suffering,

> for everything in a dream is more deep and strong and sharp and real than is ever its pale imitation in the unreal life which is ours when we go about awake and clothed with our *artificial selves* in this vague and dull-tinted artificial world. When we die we shall slough off this cheap intellect, perhaps, and go abroad into Dreamland clothed in our *real selves*, and aggrandized and enriched by the command over the mysterious mental magician who is here not our slave, but only our guest. (Twain's emphasis; *MPS*, 37)

Structured in opposed pairs—dreaming / waking, real / unreal, cheap / rich, artificial selves / real selves—this passage confirms Twain's habit of articulating perception in binary terms. Dreams articulate themselves structurally through oppositions between various selves and various layers of experience. Furthermore, these dichotomies privilege dream over waking life. Twain's inverted hierarchy defines the "real selves" of "Dreamland" by their contrast to and precedence over the "artificial selves" in "this vague and dull-tinted artificial world." But the lines of authority are not so clearly drawn for the "mysterious mental magician," a commanding figure with an ambiguous relation to the dreamer. His authority seems to shift with the fine distinctions in his status, for he is defined equally as a guest to be hosted with courtesy and as a part of the self to be commanded but not enslaved. . . .

If all of these overlapping versions of the artist—amanuensis / plagiarist, midwife / proprietor, seer / superintendent, the unconscious / dream-self—represent the creative power of the imagination, then this power is ambiguous, wielded by shadowy agents with an uneasy relationship to the artist. Twain's ambivalence toward his own art frames itself particularly as a problem of power, of who assumes the dominant and who the submissive role—the artist or his superintendent.

In the sense, then, of our being agents of forces we do not control, literary creativity posed for Twain problems of mastery similar to those posed by sexuality. More important, though, both creativity and procreativity in some fundamental way violate the social and psychological boundaries they also help to enforce—boundaries between creator and creature, between maleness and femaleness, between dominance and submission. As Twain revealed in his comparison of himself, the male artist, to a white woman who fears her child may be a mulatto, the author may be betrayed by his own intentions, much as the social world divides itself along sharp racial and sexual lines that are readily, if covertly, crossed. And once the concept of authorial intentionality had thus been called into question, Twain began questioning the very nature, even the possibility, of a "self" in control of "reality." The late dream narratives repeatedly interrogate reality: "Which Was the Dream?"

All of these issues came together during 1898 in Twain's most sustained effort to work out a theory of the mind. What he called "the duality idea" framed his hypothesis, summarized in unpublished sections of "My Platonic Sweetheart" (written August 1898), but first and most fully formulated in a long notebook entry, to which I have already alluded, written a few months earlier, in January 1898.[14] This extended entry, actually a short essay of about 1,500 words, goes a long way toward filling out what seem sometimes merely to be incoherent fragments of thought in his fiction—epitomized by that figure of indeterminate identity, the writer / impostor in the Whittier dinner speech. For the long and complex January 1898 entry acknowledges explicitly that Twain himself recognized as his own lifelong project the inquiry into identity and that a cluster of apparently disparate issues and languages was continually brought to bear on the subject. Finally, this entry documents for us how the unconscious was not only a personal territory to which Twain lit out during the 1890s and afterwards, but also a late-nineteenth-century cultural terrain.

Playing the detective, Twain begins the entry, "Last Sunday I struck upon a new 'solution' of a haunting mystery." Like the detective fiction whose ratiocinative structure Twain draws upon here, the mystery of "our seeming duality" is conceived almost immediately as posing a threat to social order and control. The mystery of divided selves is for Twain a problem of divided control, the same mystery that resisted solution in his various metaphors for the artist. The relationship between detective and mystery meant more to Twain, though, than simply a representation of external social control; it also stood as a model for an internalized power struggle in which the criminal, antisocial self is constantly threatening the control of selfhood willed by the socialized self. As far back as 1877, Twain remembers, he had experimented with this detective-criminal model of the doubled psyche in "Facts Concerning the Recent Carnival of Crime in Connecticut":

> That was an attempt to account for our seeming *duality*—the presence in us of another *person*; not a slave of ours, but free and independent and with a character distinctly its own. I made my conscience that other person and it came before me in the form of a malignant dwarf and told me plain things about myself and shamed me and scoffed at me and derided me. This creature was so much its own master that it would leave the premises . . . and go off on a spree with other irresponsible consciences—and discuss their masters (no—their slaves). (*MTN*, 348)

Like Huck's "deformed conscience" internally berating him in the linguistic pieties of the dominant culture, Twain's dwarf serves as no ethical guide but

---

14*MTN*, 348–52. On the biographical and literary significance of this entry, see Kaplan, *Mr. Clemens and Mark Twain*, pp. 403–5, and John S. Tuckey, "Mark Twain's Later Dialogue: The 'Me' and the Machine," *American Literature* 41 (January 1970): 532–42.

instead dominates as an alien "creature" invading from without, as "master" to Twain's "slave." But the precise structure of roles in this internal power struggle eludes Twain, just as the division of power between the dreamer and his dream-artist ("the mysterious mental magician who is here not our slave, but only our guest") does in "My Platonic Sweetheart."

The conception of duality in "Carnival of Crime" as a conscious power struggle was "a crude attempt to work out the duality idea," Twain asserted later in 1898, in both his notebook and the "Sweetheart" story. By this time "Carnival" appeared lacking, especially in comparison to Robert Louis Stevenson's version of a similar duality (presented with "genius and power") in *Dr. Jekyll and Mr. Hyde* (1886) (*MPS*, 9). Stevenson's book was "nearer, yes, but not near enough" to Twain's own developing theory, he explained in his notebook: "J. & H. were the dual persons in one body, quite distinct in nature and character . . . the falsity being the ability of the one person to step into the other person's place, *at will*" (*MTN*, 348). Stevenson was wrong, Twain says, just as he himself was wrong "in the beginning" to theorize the conscience as man's conscious tormentor. On the contrary, "distinct duality" is unconscious: "The two persons in a man do not even *know* each other and . . . have never even suspected each other's existence." Twain's "*new* notion" of duality, then, led away from literary conceptions derived from popular fiction and toward contemporary experimentation in America and Europe with hypnosis, hysteria, thought transference, and dream analysis—all apparent avenues to the unconscious.[15]

Of these various bodies of research, Twain singles out "the French experiments in hypnotism ten or twelve years ago, and the investigations made by our Professor William James" (*MPS*, 9) as both shaping and confirming his own theory of personality:

> The French have lately shown (apparently) that that other person is in command during the somnambulic sleep; that it has a memory of its own and can recall its acts when hypnotized and thrown again into that sleep, but that *you* have no memory of its acts. (*MTN*, 349)

The fine points of this hierarchy are clarified in "My Platonic Sweetheart": "The subordinate person is always in command during somnambulic (not the common) sleep, therefore his chief is ignorant of what is happening and will have no recollection of it; but the somnambulic sleep can be reproduced by hypnotism" (*MPS*, 10). What "the French" have clearly contributed is an experimental vocabulary amenable to Twain's own earlier language of control, the dualisms of masters and slaves, power and subordination. . . .

---

[15]In addition to Dr. *Jekyll and Mr. Hyde*, Twain also mentions "Chamisso's striking tale of a century ago" (*MPS*, 9)—a reference to Adelbert Chamisso, *Peter Schlemihl's Wundersame Geschichte* (1835) [*The Shadowless Man; or, The Wonderful History of Peter Schlemihl*, (London, n.d.)]. On the copies (in German and English) that Twain owned, see Alan Gribben, *Mark Twain's Library: A Reconstruction*, 2 vols. (Boston, 1980), 1: 137–38.

The 1898 notebook entry indicates in small, then, what I want to argue is the characteristic development of Mark Twain's inquiry into identity: away from literal, external, and conscious forms toward the increasingly metaphysical, abstract, and speculative. That is, as we will see, the double conceived as a character or characters gives way to a structural conception of narrative doubling. In addition, the entry acknowledges how the curve of the whole enterprise took its shape from contemporary culture. Not until the 1880s and 1890s did contemporary interest in the "pseudoscience" of spiritualism and the "science" of psychology finally provide Twain with a body of knowledge through which he could directly address issues that had long, but elusively, concerned him. The many theories of the unconscious that entered the public domain—through debates over the insanity plea in criminal law or through controversial new conceptions of and treatments for mental illness or through efforts to authenticate psychic phenomena such as thought transference—focused attention on the structure of the personality and on the relationship between conscious behavior and unconscious motivation. For Twain, long restricted to modes of externalizing problems of identity, the result of this climate of thought was a frantic outpouring of a distinctly different kind of writing during the last two decades of his life. Whether one characterizes these late works as dream tales, science fiction, or fantasy, collectively they experiment with a new narrative structure that could articulate the instabilities of a divided psyche via an unstable relationship of author to text to reader.

If there is a cultural explanation for why dreams became such a presence only in Twain's late writing, similar explanations account for the other vocabularies and concepts in the 1898 notebook entry. I have noted how the terms "master" and "slave" and hierarchies of control pervade every aspect of the entry. These psychological issues of power have a social and political analogue in the institution of slavery, whose historical realities provided the major cultural context instrumental in forming Twain's views. "The skin of every human being," Twain wrote in his notebook, "contains a slave" (*MTN*, 393). In part this reflects his much-discussed (and often maligned) determinism, the view that the individual is enslaved by some combination of external forces and the internalized version of those forces. More particularly, though, Twain saw the institution of race slavery as an arena of subtle power reversals in which the ideology of white supremacy so dominated both groups, masters and slaves, that, for example, many whites were driven to deny that their skin did in fact mask some "black blood." Slavery thus engendered for both whites and blacks a problematic heredity that could not be legislated away.

The contradictions historically associated with slavery—its overt policies of racial classification and strict separation of the races subverted by covert crossing of racial and sexual lines—anticipated Twain's own unacknowledged link between race and sex as part of his otherwise deliberate theorizing about the self. The January 1898 notebook entry ends with a description—not an analysis—of one of Twain's own dreams that betrays unintentionally, through its presence in this entry, how the conjunction of race and sex is somehow conjoined with the rest of the meditation on the self. Twain dreams of "a negro wench," "not at all badlooking," who made a proposition to him, one that was "disgusting" yet "seemed quite natural." She sold him an apple pie— "a mushy apple pie—hot"—but neglected to provide a spoon, and Twain recounts his revulsion at her offer of her own tin teaspoon. "She took it out of her mouth, in a quite matter-of-course way, and offered it to me. My stomach rose—there everything vanished" (*MTN*, 352).

Twain's dream of black female sexuality merges with his perception of his conscience, his dream-self, and his unconscious. Aside from the fact that all of these figures appear together in one notebook entry, linked in a sort of free association that Twain called "the methodless method of the human mind,"[16] what does this amalgamation imply? To the notebook writer, each figure is marked by a paradoxically strange familiarity, somehow known, intimate, even a part of himself, yet at the same time distinctly other. The young black female's "disgusting" proposition, for example, does not surprise the dreamer, for in the dream he is also young "and it seemed quite natural that it should come from her." The alien intimacy of something disgusting yet natural repeats itself in the other figures in the entry, an intimacy further enforced by possessive pronouns: "my" conscience is a malignant dwarf; "my" dream-self is "my" other self "with the ordinary powers of both [body and mind] enlarged in all particulars" (*MTN*, 350–52). Throughout the entry this configuration of recognition and otherness constantly promises (or threatens) to dissolve so that the boundaries between the self and his other may be crossed, freeing (or forcing) him to confront his own desires for the forbidden. But none of the scenarios in the entry goes so far; instead each remains suspended on the border between promise and threat.

First, communication is thwarted in the case of the conscience, which Twain dismisses as an inauthentic representation of the other self ("It is not a separate person . . . merely a *thing* . . . whatever one's mother and Bible and comrades and laws . . . have made it"). Next, communication with the dream-self is also frustratingly incomplete. The waking dreamer, "dimly acquainted" with his dream-self, only partially remembers the dreams whose occasional "vividness" serve to remind him merely of his own distance from such powerful experiences ("Waking, I cannot create in my mind a picture of a room. . . but my dream self can do all this with the accuracy and vividness of a camera" [*MTN*, 350]).

And finally, Twain's dream ends similarly, just at the moment when he and the black woman are on the verge of eating together from the same spoon— that is, after the acceptable transaction of buying a pie from her (purchasing a suggestively sexual offering?), followed by the less acceptable "disgusting" proposition (the sexual suggestion is overtly offered?), the white male's fantasy of an undifferentiated sexualized nourishment from the "negro wench" / wet-

---

[16]Paine described Mark Twain's dictating his autobiographical reminiscences in his later years: "He went drifting among episodes, incidents, and periods in his irresponsible fashion; the fashion of table-conversation, as he said, the methodless method of the human mind" (*MTB*, 3: 1268).

nurse breaks off just before consummation. The dream's long moment of suspension between male self and female other is epitomized in the way he sees and the way she is clothed. He visualizes her body despite its being hidden from view: "She was about 22, and plump—not fleshy, not fat, merely rounded and plump; and. . . not at all bad-looking. She had but one garment on—a coarse tow-linen shirt that reached from her neck to her ankles without a break" (*MTN*, 350–52). That shirt marks the boundary that trembles, but remains unbroken, in the dream as in the rest of the entry.

Both the dream and the whole entry that contains it thus verge on the edge of violating a number of boundaries that are carefully maintained. Something illicit threatens in all of the figures—the Connecticut conscience, the dream-self, and the dreamer Mark Twain. But the notebook entry, structured around the rather finely calibrated hierarchy of waking, dream, and somnambulic selves, contains those threatening figures by bounding the illicit pleasures of dreams from the safe but dull waking world. Twain's hierarchy of selves is so confused and confusing, though, that while ordering the personality through division and classification, it calls attention to the possible weaknesses in its own foundation as an ordering system. Similarly, his fictional dream tales question such epistemological order by deliberately confusing the boundaries between dream and reality. They leave open the question posed by the title of one of them, "Which Was the Dream?" . . .

Ants at the Picnic: *The Innocents Abroad*

Richard Bridgman

The Innocents Abroad, Mark Twain's first travel book, which consolidated his fame and which has sustained its popularity, was on the surface his most conventional. Following a fixed itinerary, the tour ship, the *Quaker City*, took him along familiar touristic routes, ones so familiar, in fact, that earlier accounts of these standard sights became the targets of his mockery. Much of the book is a high-spirited, confident, and satirically inventive performance.

But there is another, more troubled, voice heard in it too. In the preface Mark Twain calls the *Quaker City* excursion "a pic-nic," and on the opening page, "a picnic on a gigantic scale" (19). Americans do characteristically start off on trips, parties, marriages, careers, and wars in a state of unbounded optimism, something Melville knew when he described the green troops of the Union "gayly" marching off to the first battle of Bull Run as if it were a "picnic party in the May."[1] But irony is always waiting in the wings, and for all Mark Twain's festive expectations, the *Quaker City* tour proved to be dominated by "many elderly people" (32). By the time the pilgrims returned home, Mark Twain played indignantly on that motif. The trip turned out to have been a "picnic of patriarchs." Three-fourths of the "passengers were between forty and seventy years of age! There was a picnic crowd for you!" (644).

The Innocents Abroad records multiple betrayals, beginning with the composition of the group with which Mark Twain signed on so expectantly. Worse, though, the world itself that he went to see for the first time turned out to be largely a sham, the nature of which had been meretriciously falsified by the travelers who had preceded him as well as by the guides on the spot. If the book begins in an expectant mood, or no worse than a calmly ironic one, it ends weary, rancorous, and exhausted. There were a number of reasons for this negative tone. Mark Twain had tired of expanding and revising his original newspaper letters for the book, so he composed the second half more cursorily and with his exasperation closer to the surface. That exasperation

Reprinted from *Traveling in Mark Twain* (Berkeley: University of California Press, 1987), pp. 14–29. By permission of the publisher. Copyright © 1987 The Regents of the University of California.

[1]"The March into Virginia," in *Collected Poems of Herman Melville*, ed. Howard P. Vincent (Chicago, 1947), 10–11.

centered on the pious, middle-aged Christian party in whose company he traveled, and it was heightened by plain fatigue from sightseeing. The whole party became "surfeited with sights" (582). Much more dispiriting than this, though, Europe, our old home, had proved to be decadent, and over the Middle Eastern cradle of civilization and spiritual resurrection, flies swarmed. If America was coarse and violent, the older worlds were deceitful, violent, and degraded.

Everywhere Mark Twain went on this trip, his attention was engrossed by imprisonment, torture, mutilation, and corpses. In effect, the tour led him to misery. Venal and idiotic guides took him deliberately to celebrated sites of suffering. Catholic art in particular was appalling to Twain, both in subject matter and in condition. Its subjects were martyred saints, skewered and writhing in pain, or the crucified Savior himself, hands mutilated, side pierced, body scourged and streaming with blood. And the paintings themselves were faded, patchy, cracked. Even at the *Quaker City's* first stop in the Azores, the cathedral could offer only "a swarm of rusty, dusty, battered apostles" who had suffered various kinds of damage, such as the loss of an eye, fingers gone, or "not enough nose left to blow" (57). Later, at Notre-Dame de Paris, Twain again observed a facade that was "clustered thick with stony, mutilated saints" (130).

The classical gods had suffered similar indignities—Cupid was noseless, Jupiter was missing an eye, Venus had "a fly-blister on her breast" (167). Even the most famous depiction, Leonardo's *Last Supper,* proved to be "battered and scarred . . . stained and discolored by time" (190). But even though the pictorial representations of Christianity were monotonously conventional and in bad shape, the tourists still praised them as if they were perfect. The authenticity of religion, always a central issue for Mark Twain, rested for the moment on surfaces. The deeper problem might merely be that Old World Catholic corruption was in league with New World fatuity.

The European world, though, was permeated by suffering. The cancan delighted Mark Twain, but it was no more than the twitching of a moribund civilization. In Paris, as part of the regular tour, he visited the morgue to view the corpse of a drowned man (132). At the Château d'If, he brooded over the idea of prisoners locked away in permanent solitary confinement, especially the Man in the Iron Mask (102–4). He viewed the dungeons and torture chambers of Venice and meditated in horror on the frescoes of the Council of Three with their "pictures of death and dreadful suffering!" (224). He listened to the story of a man hanged by his chin on an iron hook and tried to exorcise it with a scoffing humor (215). He was proudly brought to see a statue of a man flayed, "every vein, muscle, every fiber and tendon of the human frame, represented in minute detail." At this dreadful sight, Twain let down his guard for a moment, saying that he regretted he had seen it, that he was certain he would dream of it, sometimes as if it were leaning over his bed and looking at him with its dead eyes, sometimes "stretched between the sheets with me and touching me with its exposed muscles and its stringy cold legs" (175). That grisly fantasy yielded in turn to an account of returning late one night when a boy and deciding to sleep in his father's office. Gradually, he realized that a form lay stretched upon the floor. It was a corpse, its eyes fixed, stabbed to death. That figure too, Mark Twain says, he has seen "often, since then—in my dreams" (177).

The progress of this particular innocent was then through halls of horror, featuring painted depictions of martyrs and statues mutilated by time; underground through tombs and catacombs, past decaying, grinning mummies; even to a dungeon in Pompeii where two charred prisoners had been burned to death in the volcanic fires. This last was a situation of peculiar vividness for Mark Twain, for he believed that as a boy he had been responsible for the death of a prisoner in the local jail, one whose cell had caught fire shortly after Twain had passed him a match to light his pipe (178, 301–2, 329; *Life on the Mississippi*, 290).

Which is to say that Europe revived the worst terrors of a hideous death that Mark Twain had carried in his memory from boyhood. Such feelings or something even worse may account for a curious and otherwise unexplained sentence that occurs when Twain is at Lake Como. Dramatically isolated by separate paragraphing, it is neither expanded nor otherwise explained. Here it is in its frame:

> Then to bed, with drowsy brains harassed with a mad panorama that mixes up pictures of France, of Italy, of the ship, of the ocean, of home, in grotesque and bewildering disorder. Then a melting away of familiar faces, of cities and of tossing waves, into a great calm of forgetfulness and peace.
> After which, the nightmare.
> Breakfast in the morning, and then the Lake.
>
> (201)

Aside from that undescribed nightmare, many other things were happening to this brash young traveler abroad. He began to perceive the cant of the guidebooks. The aesthetic reverence of the tourists at first amused, then irritated him. He flirted with sexual possibilities, although his fervor was quashed when he inspected the fabled *grisettes* up close, for they were ungainly, homely, had mustaches, and ate garlic (151). Similarly, the tears he and his fellows had wasted on the sentimental love story of Héloise and Abelard proved fallacious, for Abelard turned out to be no more than "a dastardly seducer" who had abused the confidences of a young girl (147).

The fraudulence of Mark Twain's guides was especially significant to him. This despicable world contained no one who could be relied on for guidance, no Vergil or Beatrice to take one safely through this inferno. The guides were in fact doubly duplicitous, because they deceived their clients to line their own pockets and because they spoke out of manifest ignorance. Twain was lost—at least there in Europe—in a stinking swamp.

All these reactions are fused in that famous mock-serious refrain that Mark Twain and his youthful co-conspirators used when the guides mechanically recounted the story of Christopher Columbus, or any of a thousand other luminaries of the European past. "Is—is he dead?" they asked (295).[2] Of course, it was a joke. But *was* all they were asked to believe in, to revere, dead? The boldness of the explorers, the eternal love stories, the glories of the Renaissance painters, the greatness of the architecture, the histories of powerful men—were these all fraudulent, or if once genuinely inspirational, were they now without force? Were they no more than grinning skulls in a continental catacomb? Emerson had counseled Americans to free themselves from the dead hand of the past, but a generation later a nostalgia for the fathers had revived. There was a curiosity about sources and a thirst for cultural enlargement and continuity. But once discovered, was it all to prove dead?

Given such submerged apprehensions, one is not surprised to hear Mark Twain laud Napoleon III, for even when reviled, this emperor persisted in dreaming of a crown, until at last he rather improbably gained it. Moreover, having done so, he seemed to have brought commercial prosperity to France, and security to Paris. Twain particularly admired Napoleon's having eliminated the crooked cobblestone streets into which the mob could dodge, streets they could tear up when inflamed and hurl at his majesty's troops (128, 158). Twain may seem to be offering disconcerting praise for dictatorial efficiency, but one can see that it arises out of his revulsion at a poisonous, plotting, obstreperous world. Napoleon at least meant to modernize and control it. This brought Twain to praise the French railway system, whose efficiency he attributed to the practice of hanging someone for any accident that occurred (110). The same impatient motivation obtained when Xerxes had those contractors who had built a flimsy bridge beheaded. "If our Government would rebuke some of our shoddy contractors occasionally, it might work much good," Twain remarks (357). His exasperation moved one step further toward comic exaggeration when he later declared that he wished Russia would annihilate Turkey a little, because of "the inhuman tyranny of the Ottoman Empire" (443). Underneath all the joking one can see the attraction for him of strong social measures. Still, that solution was far from satisfactory. Although Twain would repeatedly revert to the idea of the strong man who could manage the otherwise perverse human animal, he ultimately suspected that the abuses rose from deeper sources, the key to which might be found at the heart of Western spirituality.

In the *Innocents*, the pivotal point between Europe and Asia is Greece. Its cultural riches were virtually denied the party, however, since the ship had just come from Italy where a cholera epidemic was developing; the passengers, therefore, were not to land until they had remained in quarantine for eleven days. Under penalty of imprisonment if caught, Mark Twain and three

---

[2]As David Sloane points out, in Artemus Ward's "The Greenlion and Oliver Cromwell" (1867), a London landlord asks: "And this Mr. Cromwell—is he dead?" (*Mark Twain as Literary Comedian* [Baton Rouge, La., 1979], 43).

others made a Tom Sawyerish expedition ashore at night. Although Twain was duly impressed by the Acropolis, two other eerie moments stand out in his account. Thirsty, the group picked some grapes "and were reaching down for more when a dark shape rose mysteriously up out of the shadows beside us and said 'Ho!' And so we left" (343). Although Twain would seem to be describing no more than someone protecting his vines from interlopers, the description itself has an unearthly quality. The "dark shape" is not specifically human, and its exclamation is more indefinite than a warning.[3] Even more disconcerting, when they reached the courtyard outside the Parthenon, where fragments of statues were strewn about, "it startled us, every now and then, to see a stony white face stare suddenly up at us out of the grass with its dead eyes" (347). The dead eyes are a new detail, for the original notebook entry merely reads: "Grim marble faces glancing up suddenly at you out of the grass at your feet" (*Notebooks and Journals,* I, 396).

The atmosphere of Greece was not one of European corruption but of a pale, shadowed, and essentially unavailable past. When they approached the Acropolis, the party passed "a row of open graves, cut in the solid rock." Now, in the moonlight, everything seemed spectral, "alive with ghosts," while Athens below them was "like some living creature wrapped in peaceful slumber" (344, 347, 348). Twain could only catch unearthly glints of whatever the classical world might have been supposed to represent.

Coming to Mars Hill where Saint Paul had disputed with the Athenians, Mark Twain said that he had tried to recollect what the Bible said of the matter, "but for certain reasons I could not recall the words" (349). He never attempted to explain the reasons for that memory lapse but said that he had since found the biblical account, which he then quotes. It concerns Paul's reproaching the Athenians for having an altar inscribed "TO THE UN-KNOWN GOD." Paul declares that he now brings that mysterious God into the light: "Whom, therefore, ye ignorantly worship, him I declare unto you" (Acts 17:23; 349). That is the end of the incident. The next paragraph begins: "It occurred to us after a while that if we wanted to get home before daylight betrayed us, we had better be moving." One cannot tell whether Twain consciously arranged this confrontation of cultures, but he highlighted the moment when it occurred, then passed on without further comment. But the idea that an unknown god, a hidden, mysterious, long-lost divinity, might finally be identified always had manifest attractions for Twain. Ironically, as he moved into the Middle East, the only God he had ever known began to lose his identity with distressing finality.

First, though, the party had to touch Turkey and Russia. What few illusions Mark Twain possessed about Turkey were swiftly dispelled. The boatmen in

---

[3]Mark Twain's notebook entry is a little more informative, but not much: "We made the trip! (stopped occasionally by savages armed with guns, who rose mysteriously up out of the shadows & darkness & said Ho! when we happened to be stealing grapes) . . ." (*Notebooks and Journals,* I, 389–90).

Constantinople were "the awkwardest, the stupidest, and the most unscientific on earth" (358). The city itself was "the very heart and home of cripples and human monsters" and "everybody" there "lies and cheats" (361, 370). Saint Sophia's "was the rustiest old barn in heathendom" and its floor was covered with "a complication of gums, slime, and general corruption" (362). Nor could a Turkish bath cleanse the corruption. It was all "a malignant swindle" (380).

Had there been a Hercules to clean the Augean stables of Constantinople, no doubt Mark Twain would have celebrated him as he did Napoleon III for bringing order to Paris. But Twain's ambivalence about earthly figures of power appeared when the ship moved on to Yalta. There the party met Alexander II. Twain was taken by his physical height, his courtesy, and his air of kindness. Most of all, he was impressed at the tremendous autocratic power the czar possessed over seventy million people, for all of them would at a nod "spring to his bidding" (395). But contemplating this epitome of political power, Twain reverted to democratic aggression. "Here was a man who could do this wonderful thing, and yet if I chose I could knock him down." Further, he avowed that if he could have, he would have stolen the czar's coat—just to have "something to remember him by" (395).

As the party finally approached the Holy Land, the commentary began to focus on Christianity in its early guises. Much of Mark Twain's reaction is satiric and skeptical. The Seven Sleepers of Ephesus, those Christian Rip Van Winkles, were thieves from the start; and after they awoke from their long sleep, they were profoundly distressed: "Our homes are desolate, our friends are dead. Behold, the jig is up—let us die" (428). That is how Twain's parodic resurrection concludes. No wonder that at the edge of the Holy Land, he makes the gray lizard the emblem of mockery of human vanity. It is "the color of ashes; and ashes are the symbol of hopes that have perished." When all the temples and palaces and empires have been built and fallen, the lizard will still survive them all. "You, who stand here and moralize over me: I will crawl over *your* corpse at the last" (489).

To be sure, a good portion of Mark Twain's animus toward organized Christianity was directed against his contemporaries, the aging pilgrims, who were vandals and souvenir hunters and who broke the spirit of religious law while keeping the letter of it; against the biblical commentators and the preachers who damaged their religion through obtuseness; and against all who would kill those who truly and fearlessly preached the reality of Christ (543, 451–52, 409, 462–63). Any idealist or imaginative human was prey for their malice. Twain remarks that when the elders saw Joseph, they "were glad. They said 'Lo, here is this dreamer—let us kill him'" (493). And the "image-breakers and tomb-desecrators" of the *Quaker City* were of a piece with such hard-eyed men (493).

By contrast, to Mark Twain's mind, there had once been a superior order of beings. For him, the authors of the Bible had the supreme capacity for telling their stories in simple language and without intruding their own personalities

(492). Christ himself had the gift of making the afflicted whole again with a word (475). But even in Christ's lifetime, oppressive layers of venality and stupidity smothered that freshness. In his notebook Twain burst out: "The people of this region in the Bible were just as they are now—ignorant, depraved, superstitious, dirty, lousy, thieving vagabonds" (*Notebooks and Journals,* I, 425). And there too, starkly, he made this entry: "Christ been once—never come again." (*Notebooks and Journals,* I, 449).

When his party passed through Shechem, a Samaritan community (now Nablus), Mark Twain concluded his remarks with what would appear to be a joke. He says that while there he purchased "a secret document" of "extraordinary interest" that he proposed to publish as soon as he had finished translating it (552). Presumably Twain meant to satirize new archaeological discoveries that were being oversold when announced to the public, but one also feels the desire that such potent secrets might become available, supposing they were translatable. In a sense, all Twain's travel reports were attempts to comprehend hidden meanings. Unfortunately, his interpretations were often so negative that he felt they could not be made available to the American audience. He told his notebook that the second coming was an illusion, but not his public.

Some of the Holy Land's illusory powers Mark Twain attributed to atmospheric effects. In reality the landscape was an ugly, dusty, rocky chaos, but under starlight or moonlight, it became a shimmering mystery (512–13). Still, "the magic of the moonlight is a vanity and a fraud and whoso putteth his trust in it shall suffer sorrow and disappointment" (524). The explanation for such pessimism was everywhere evident. The party entered the Middle East through crowds of beggars, cripples, lepers, and babes with flies clustered at their eyes, their mothers too apathetic to brush them away (464, 473). As the pilgrims moved toward the heart of the Christian mystery, things became progressively more miserable, more concentratedly appalling, and much less inspiring. Palestine was about the size of an American county (502). Jerusalem was but a village of four thousand (556). It was more than just a topographical observation for Twain to remark: "I must begin a system of reduction. . . . I have got everything in Palestine on too large a scale" (486). Everything. So upon reaching Bethlehem, he touched "with reverent finger, the actual spot where the infant Jesus lay, but I think—nothing" (601).

So far as this area of the world was concerned, Mark Twain's disillusionment was complete. He had found Jerusalem "mournful and dreary and lifeless." Everywhere he had been assailed by "lepers, cripples, the blind, and the idiotic" (559). In the context of this depressing reality, he was obliged to visit tomb after tomb: that of Noah, Joseph, Jesus, Adam (443, 553, 560, 567). But everything remained stone dead. Adam generated parodic mourning, and at the grave of Jesus, Twain exploded in disdain. The site was "scandalized by trumpery, gewgaws, and tawdry ornamentation" (560). It was difficult, Twain said, not to get the impression that Christ had been crucified in a Catholic church (572).

This move back through time, first through the aesthetic pretensions and moral cynicism of western Europe, then into the sordid poverty of the Middle East, and finally to the fraudulence and dust of the Holy Land itself, constituted a primary revelation for Mark Twain. The force of the incessantly dreadful poverty quite overwhelmed him. Palestine was "a hopeless, dreary, heart-broken land" (606). All that remained of value was the memory of a good Savior. But he could not really accept the idea that this figure had once walked this ground or any ground accessible to him—"the gods of my understanding have been always hidden in clouds and very far away" (472).

If the first conclusion to the long journey took place at Jaffa when they returned to the ship—"the long pilgrimage was ended"—five more chapters and a "Conclusion" were yet to follow. *The Innocents Abroad* winds down through a series of endings. The tentativeness and variety of the book's gestures at closure suggest Mark Twain's own uncertain commitment. The great search back through time to the heart of Christianity had proved to be a terrible deception. Jaffa offered a farcical footnote to this loss of illusions in the encounter with the remnants of the "Adams Jaffa Colony." These were the humiliated followers of a prophet who, they now recognized, had "shamefully humbugged" them (613). Mark Twain identifies this leader by four roles that in his experience were always at best equivocal: actor, adventurer, Mormon, and missionary. At heart, Adams was a confidence man, no better in kind than those guidebook writers and Christian ministers and guides whom Mark Twain had learned to distrust. The same mocking reality that gave this false leader the name Adams designated a Moses as their savior—Moses Beach of the *New York Sun*, who charitably paid their fares back to Maine.

The second conclusion occurred when the party reached the Egyptian Sphinx. "After years of waiting, it was before me at last" (628). The Sphinx impressed Mark Twain deeply. He reads into its visage feelings that are often discovered in Jesus Christ. "The great face was so sad, so earnest, so longing, so patient. There was a dignity not of the earth in its mien, and in its countenance a benignity such as never any thing human wore" (628–29). There is no jeering here about a nose broken off, such as Twain had indulged in with European statues. Rather, he is impressed by the stoic impassivity of the Sphinx. It has contemplated the ocean of human misery for five thousand years, not judging it, not mocking it, not condemning it—"pathos dwells in these grave eyes"—but merely looking over and past history "at nothing— nothing but distance and vacancy" (629). In the presence of the Sphinx, Twain said that he felt something of what he supposed he would feel when he was at last standing "in the awful presence of God" (629). If so, it was a majestic but not a condemnatory deity. Although Twain could not incorporate the associations that the Sphinx generated in him into any acceptable cosmic system, here was a power he could revere—asexual, all-knowing, sympathetic but reserved, and ultimately above the tumult and confusion, knowing that finally nothing means anything, that at the farthest reach of this preternatural vision there was only "distance and vacancy" (629).[4]

The third ending descends into involvement and contempt again. It occurs with the party's actual arrival back in New York harbor. One can detect Mark Twain's mood in the last phrase of that chapter: "and the long strange cruise was over. Amen" (642). But of course the book was still not complete because the feelings of disappointment and vexation suggested by that "Amen" had to be purged one last time, as they then were by Twain's reprinting the savagely satiric article he had written for the *New York Herald* upon their return. The article offended many of the passengers because of Twain's unconcealed resentment at having spent more than five months in the company of "venerable fossils" (645). But when Twain says that the expedition might better have been called "The Grand Holy Land Funeral Procession," one can see that quite beyond the aged participants, much had died for him on this pilgrimage. Not that he was a committed Christian before he visited the Holy Land. In part he had joined the trip with the expectation that it would afford materials to satirize. On the other hand, Twain had not been altogether a disbeliever either, and the tawdry grimness of the Holy Land had certainly dispelled a number of illusions.

The "Conclusion" proper to the whole narrative was written a year later. In a somewhat mellower mood, Mark Twain first offered a tribute to his fellow passengers, then turned to enumerate his memories of places visited. The names of various important cities are listed with a characterization for each. Milan, Venice, and Rome all receive extended descriptions, and there is "majestic Gibraltar glorified with the rich coloring of a Spanish sunset and swimming in a sea of rainbows" (650). But as he comes to the last paragraph, what had formerly been the climactic focus of the trip was now relegated to one among many places. Jerusalem was only "sacred." Twain ends both his recapitulation of the journey and his book with—one would never guess— Damascus. "Damascus, the 'Pearl of the East,' the pride of Syria, the fabled Garden of Eden, the home of princes and genii of the *Arabian Nights,* the oldest metropolis on earth, the one city in all the world that has kept its name and held its place and looked serenely on while the Kingdoms and Empires of four thousand years have risen to life, enjoyed their little season of pride and pomp, and then vanished and been forgotten!" (651).

This final ending has several revealing features. It is, first of all, a severely idealized version of the Damascus that Mark Twain had described earlier in the book. When he first saw the city from the mountain, he thought it an incredibly beautiful oasis in a rocky hell and noted that tradition claimed that

---

[4]Opinions differ, though. For Everett Emerson, the description of the Sphinx "goes on and on" and is no more than "sentimental rhetoric" composed to please Olivia Langdon and Mrs. Fairbanks (*The Authentic Mark Twain: A Literary Biography of Samuel L. Clemens* [Philadelphia, 1984], 51, 54).

this was where the Garden of Eden had been located. No more, though. Once Damascus was entered, "the paradise is become a very sink of pollution and uncomeliness" (456). The principal chapter on Damascus ends with Twain's reaction to a leper hospital there—"horrible!" (464).

But I think we can determine what drew Mark Twain to the later, sanitized celebration of Damascus. Jerusalem could not serve. It was too deeply discredited in his mind. On the other hand, the association of the Garden of Eden with Damascus placed it imaginatively in that context of the innocent and naturally beautiful beginning of mankind. The fantasies of the *Arabian Nights* also won Twain's heart with all the magic tricks associated with genii and the high dignity of princes. Like the Sphinx, Damascus also had the virtue of unusual endurance, of surviving the vicissitudes of the swarming human insect. And finally—it is the note on which the book closes—men's puniness, vulnerability, and mortality are underlined. The transcendent figure, whether Colonel Sherburn on the roof of his porch in *Huckleberry Finn,* or Satan in *The Mysterious Stranger,* or the Sphinx, is a figure superior to ordinary human pretensions and as such ever central in Mark Twain's imagination. He wanted permanence, solidity, thereness. This book concludes by emphasizing how much of humanity has "vanished and been forgotten."

Works Cited

Twain, Mark. *The Innocents Abroad; or, The New Pilgrim's Progress.* Hartford, CN: American Publishing Co., 1897.

Twain, Mark. *Life on the Mississippi.* New York: Limited Editions Club, 1944.

Twain, Mark. *Notebooks & Journals.* 3 vols. Berkeley: University of California Press, 1975–79.

What's in a Name: Sounding the Depths of *Tom Sawyer*

John Seelye

Tom Sawyer is a name as familiar to us as our own. We grow up with it, perhaps are weaned from lesser literature on the book of that title, so that eventually the name and the story attached to it become part of our collective memory, stored away like a half-remembered experience. If one of the pleasures in rereading *Adventures of Huckleberry Finn* is the discovery of new, sometimes startling dimensions—for Huck, as Lionel Trilling observed in 1948, grows up as we grow, changes as we change—one of the joys of rereading Tom's *Adventures* is rediscovering things just as they were. It is like returning to a homeplace preserved under glass—or in aspic. Contra Thomas Wolfe, you may go home again, to find both time and the river unchanged. But because Tom does remain a boy, we are inclined to shrug him off as a lesser creature, as an instance of arrested development, especially when he is compared to the much beloved Huck Finn. Yet it won't do to turn Tom Sawyer away with a shrug. He bears careful attention. Like Hamlet he deserves studying.

As Louis Rubin, Jr., long ago observed, the reputation of Mark Twain's first boys' book would be far greater had the author never written the sequel. For the problem is not so much that Mark Twain went on to write a continuation in which Tom plays a lesser and even a foolish role, but that the sequel is superior to the original. A marvelous amphibian, *Huckleberry Finn* is a book that can be read and enjoyed by both adults and children, an accomplishment next to which *Tom Sawyer* can only suffer by comparison. To judge the earlier novel with the canons of adult literature is unfair, for Mark Twain himself declared to William Dean Howells that it was "professedly and confessedly a boy's and girl's book"—at least by the time he had cut out all the "dirty" parts; and it should be evaluated on the author's terms. Certainly Mark Twain at times can be caught talking to the reader over the head of his little hero; at times he condescends, as when he describes the process by which the pirates of Jackson's Island become homesick little boys. Yet we need only as adult readers reach the Jackson's Island episode—the literal as well as the symbolic

Reprinted from *Sewanee Review* 90 (Summer 1982), 408–29. Copyright © 1982 John Seelye. By permission of the author. (A revised version of this essay has also appeared as the Introduction to Mark Twain, *The Adventures of Tom Sawyer* [New York: Penguin Books, 1986]).

midpoint in the book—to acknowledge the power of the genius who is arranging the action.

At that point, moreover, Tom Sawyer is literally in charge of the plot, becoming an early example of the *auteur* principle. A prankster from the start, by the middle of the book he has mounted a huge hoax, a scenario which will bring the residents of St. Petersburg to the threshold of tragedy only to yank them back into comic relief and laughter. He is the resident Puck of St. Petersburg, fun-bent with a jug of magic drops that often bring tears— of grief then mirth; and as such he is clearly the agent of the author. A psychoanalyst has pointed out that Tom means twin, and that a sawyer to a river pilot like Mark Twain was a submerged tree trunk and a hazard to navigation. As both a mischief-maker and an author of self-starring dramas Tom Sawyer is a subliminal projection of Sam Clemens, firmly rooted in obscure depths from which the book bearing his name draws considerable power. To dismiss the book as not being great adult literature may be easy, but few readers, of any age, can set *Tom Sawyer* aside once they start to read it.

By contrast *Huckleberry Finn* has a much slower and less intriguing development, in which a suspenseful plot is set aside for a leisurely episodic one. In both novels the influence of Charles Dickens is obvious, but the element of cliff-hanging gothicism is more nearly dominant in *Tom Sawyer*, from the grave-robbing scene ("borrowed" from *A Tale of Two Cities*) to the extended ordeal of Tom and Becky in McDougal's Cave. When Tom catches his glimpse of Injun Joe deep underground, like Oliver Twist awakening to see Fagin peering in through his bedroom window at the Maylies' house, he is frozen in a frame that most of us, having shared the vision as children, will carry with us to the grave. Like Dickens, Mark Twain had an undeniable skill at scaring the daylights out of us, and he was in this regard a man with a golden arm, to which were affixed a hand and fingers of sterling silver.

Mark Twain (again like Dickens) resorted for his effects to sometimes shabby tricks, to what were by 1876 wornout stage properties; and like the creator of *Oliver Twist* Mark Twain in *Tom Sawyer* relies too often on chance and strained coincidence for his turns of plot. And yet, paradoxically, the staginess and the sleights-of-hand are engaging to children, who are willing to take their wonders where they find them; nor can we detach the theatrics from the melodrama which lends both books their special power. As adult readers we may object to these elements, but as children we did not; and in returning to *Tom Sawyer* we can enjoy it most if we regard it as an excursion into a zone created by few works of fiction. *Huckleberry Finn* may be a classic of adult literature, yet it is in that regard but a small room in an enormous house of fiction. But how few are the books of children that have managed to endure beyond the decade in which they were written. *Tom Sawyer* is one of that select company, and the boy would appreciate the honor—no small accomplishment.

If in the marvelously flexible voice of Huck Finn there is abstracted the eternal innocence that was the romantics' notion of childhood, then in the shape of Tom Sawyer there is centered a darker, yet more vital force, the demonic power we associate also with Dickens. He expresses an urge that mingles love and hatred, creativity and destruction, energies identified with poltergeists and juvenile delinquents, an urge expressive of the midpoint between childhood and adolescence—puberty. Tom is in that connection much closer to the Artful Dodger and Master Bates than to pusillanimous Oliver. But where we view Huck Finn's world through Huck's eyes and descend into his troubled soul, we are seldom treated to more than a momentary glimpse of Tom Sawyer's motivation. The deepest we get is into a cliché, the semiparodic portrayal of the miseries of young love, the all-too-familiar world (to adults) of Romeo and Juliet. It is a territory from which we (as adults and children) are happily rescued by a timely discharge of slops from the place where the balcony should stand; and we are returned thereby to the picaresque world once again—as if by the hand of Juliet's nurse. But about the hidden springs motivating Tom's repeated attempts to gain attention by performing stunning feats of showmanship we hear very little, which suggests that we are here very close to the "twin" in Tom Sawyer—and to the "sawyer" also—that is to Sam Clemens himself.

In his old age Clemens as Mark Twain raged against Theodore Roosevelt for his imperialism and political theatricality, but when the old man in the white suit attacked the president for being a "fourteen-year-old" and a "show-off," he was more self-revealing than he knew. Mark Twain's Roosevelt was but Tom Sawyer grown older, and Tom Sawyer old was also Sam Clemens, on both a literal and figurative level. That demonic power of which I have spoken is in literature often expressed through melodrama, a genre dealing in the terrific opposition of emotional forces; and if Tom Sawyer's world is rife with the anxieties of puberty, it is also explosive with melodramatic encounters. Adolescent anxieties and volatile melodrama express the soul of the man who was known by his friends for his fits of rage and was called Youth by his wife. If we learn little directly of the inner workings of Tom Sawyer, we catch glimpses of those of Sam Clemens, who shared with Dickens the capacity to communicate subliminally his private terrors by projecting them upon a melodramatic stage.

In a number of ways much of Samuel Langhorne Clemens's life approximated theater, once the former printer's apprentice from Hannibal, Missouri, became the chief writer-in-residence in Hartford, Connecticut. Having expended his youth and young manhood searching for a career—the most satisfactory period being the years he spent as a riverboat pilot—Clemens had by 1870 seen his newspaper penname gain worldwide recognition. Thenceforth he became a substantial if not always steady citizen. taking to himself a wife who produced several charming daughters, a family customarily on display in a Hartford mansion often compared to a riverboat, which soon came to resemble most the kind of boat called Show. Increasingly Mark Twain became the best-known and most beloved author in America, displacing those venerable Fireside Poets Longfellow and Whittier with something much more in tune with the Gilded Age, a process that was completed when Mark Twain also became white-haired and oracular.

But with old age came something other than good grayness —the fireside manner—for the course of true fame seldom runs smooth, and Sam Clemens's bankruptcy in his middle years seems to have taken away more than his money. He regained his wealth, yet Hamlin Hill in treating the last part of Clemens's life has called him a Lear, once again driving home the essential theatricality of the man's mature life, here tragic. The white suit associated with this last phase was first displayed when Mark Twain appeared before a congressional committee to argue for international copyright, a gesture that convulsed Howells with embarrassment, but that was typical of the man who displaced Phineas T. Barnum as Connecticut's chief showman. Though professing to despise the lecture circuit and to be uncomfortable with his popularity as a humorist, Mark Twain was very good at working an audience into gales of laughter; and his written work often projects real or metaphorical bits of comic or melodramatic theater, whether the burlesque Shakespearean dramatics of the duke and dauphin in *Huckleberry Finn* or Colonel Sherburn's address to the lynch mob in the same book. Among the home amusements enjoyed by the Clemens girls playacting ranked high. Though *The Prince and the Pauper* provided the basis for one such home drama, being a book with a distinctly Dickensian and melodramatic character, it is *Tom Sawyer* which of all Mark Twain's books for children most resembles a play in its shape. This novel is so theatrical in form and mood that an apocryphal tradition exists that it was once framed as an actual drama.

First of all, where so many of Mark Twain's books, fiction or otherwise, are travel books, the adventures of Tom Sawyer take place near town, and all of the hero's excursions, whether to Jackson's Island or McDougal's Cave, eventually end with his return home, Consequently the action of *Tom Sawyer* has the conventional limits of a stage play, even to observing (loosely) the classical unities of time and place. No new characters of any importance are introduced after what amounts to the climax of the first act, the graveyard episode. Thus Mark Twain's celebration of boyhood's free spirit is one of the most carefully controlled (and contrived) of his fictions, in which the picaresque impulse to break and run is checked. As Dixon Wecter and others have shown us, *Tom Sawyer* is rich in autobiographical details—the matter of (and with) Hannibal—most of which are transformed only slightly to meet the exigencies of fiction. That those exigencies are nearly neoclassical in rigidity suggests one good reason why we should give *Tom Sawyer* a closer look.

The theatrical aspect of the novel is introduced in the opening pages, wherein Aunt Polly delivers a dramatic monologue as from a stage. At a critical point, as on the stage, Tom is dragged out of a closet, and by a clever boy's stratagem he escapes punishment. The first scene ends when Tom streaks over the backyard fence with the agility of a small animal, and he will be seen performing this trick several times in succeeding chapters, ending with his flashing vault over Judge Thatcher's fence after he has thrown a rock through the window whence came his shower of slops. The image of Tom scrambling repeatedly over a fence is a lovely bit of theater, identifying him with both mischief and precipitous escape, much as the fence itself—so symbolic of organized society—will serve as a stage prop attesting to his abilities of managing the arena in which he appears.

Much of what follows is likewise the stuff of theater, whether the comedy of grade-school graduation ceremonies or the sentimental set piece of Muff Potter's pathetic praise of his loyal little friends. Most notable, perhaps, is Tom's series of invented dramas, most of which embody the spirit of misrule; as during the Christmas season in medieval times, the summertime world of the book establishes a charmed zone in which children are in charge. As in the loving complaint by Aunt Polly that opens the action, what the children produce by way of entertainment is mostly mischief, a creative turmoil over which Tom Sawyer rules supreme. In a certain sense the Feast of Misrule survives as Halloween, and *Adventures of Tom Sawyer* is an extended series of Halloween pranks, played against a backdrop of childhood and other haunts, as Tom's Sherwood Forest gives way to a graveyard which becomes a haunted house opening into a haunted cave.

The original seed for this aspect of *Tom Sawyer* may be found in Mark Twain's notebook for 1866, a list of childhood superstitions recalled from his youth. The early chapters of the book are a virtual compendium of folklore about popular enchantments, which reaches a high point with the first appearance of Huck Finn, superstition incarnate, lugging a dead cat. There follows the priceless debate between the boys concerning the best way to get rid of warts, facetious fun (on the author's part) that results in the trip to the graveyard, where the boys go to settle the point. This establishes a pattern repeated throughout the book, in which childish games turn into often grim reality. Thus the repetition of superstitious matter leads directly to the first appearance of Injun Joe, whose murder of Dr. Robinson and false testimony against Muff Potter will provide one of the chief threads if not the most important strand of the plot. Thenceforth the matter of childish superstitions is tied to the melodramatic stuff of dime novels—and melodramas, a darkening action providing counterpart to the sentimental love story centered by Becky Thatcher; these apparently disparate directions are finally joined by the climactic episode in McDougal's Cave.

Another strand is provided by Tom's penchant for playacting, beginning with his rendezvous with Joe Harper in the forest on Cardiff Hill, where the two boys play Robin Hood. The most extended episode in this theatrical strand involves the stay on Jackson's Island, where the boys pass the time by playing pirates and Indians, preparing for their dramatic return to society as their own funeral ceremonies are unfolding. Thus the "natural" theater of a funeral is usurped by the drama of a surprise resurrection, which strikes the townspeople as a marvel but which is the careful work of Tom Sawyer, who chooses the most dramatic moment in which to appear. While the boys are still on the island, Joe Harper is the first to threaten defection because of homesickness; and though he is tempted back, he will be dropped from the action thenceforth, to be replaced by Huck Finn as Tom Sawyer's comrade. Joe is last seen distributing Sunday-school literature from a basket. He is not enough of an outlaw for Tom Sawyer's melodramatic purposes.

What follows next is among the least satisfactory (though one off the most memorable) parts of the book, involving the torn frontispiece of Mr. Dobbins's anatomy book and ending with the extended parody of schoolhouse ceremonies. Containing sublimated sexuality that verges on the sadomasochism associated with Victorian pornography, it ends with a burlesque that quotes the turgid romantic prose Mark Twain associated not only with sentimentalism but with the feminine "literary" sensibility of his day. During this sequence Becky Thatcher is at her most unattractive, and the love between the two children is expressed by mean and hurtful tricks. That is, having been returned from the theatrical (and male) world of Tom's imagination to the domestic (female) world of St. Petersburg—from a zone of unrestrained boyhood to an erotic comedy of manners in which lies and deception characterize boy-girl relationships—we are brought very close to psychic depths beyond the sounding of children.

On the superficial (i.e. chivalric) level, Tom does the "right" and gallant thing, and takes Becky's whipping for her. The lovers are reconciled, and the schoolroom sequence closes with the comic ceremonies. But the series of adventures that follow are shared not by Tom and Becky but by Tom and Huck, a darkening melodrama haunted by the specter of Injun Joe much as the village theater is centered by the loving and tearful Aunt Polly. As it was on Jackson's Island, the bond being celebrated is the male one, a union which the drunken derelict Muff Potter blesses by his symbolic laying-on of hands through the bars of his cell window. Potter, as his name suggests, is a vagrant, a pitiful symbol of freedom gone bad, and is an adult counterpart to Huck Finn. Though innocent of the crime for which he is to be tried, he is guilty of robbing graves, and is a real outlaw—not the romantic one Tom is ambitious to become. Reaching out through his bars, he is a symbol of "good" badness in restraint; and it is Tom who, soon after the world of summertime vacation begins, will effect Potter's freedom, thereby starting the second phase of the Injun Joe sequence, that will end with the "imprisonment" and death of the truly guilty malefactor. Operating almost entirely outside the limits of town— with side trips to such out-of-bounds places as the old tannery and the "Temperance" tavern—the action of the last part of the book is a symbolic extension of the world of pirates and Indians which Tom earlier established on Jackson's Island, a world made up entirely of boys and men.

Soon after his recovery from the measles—a well-timed separation from a society in the throes of evangelical salvation—Tom more thoroughly cleanses his own soul (and conscience) by testifying on behalf of Muff Potter, a sudden little drama that repeats the theater of the boys' earlier resurrection. It also launches Tom on his next adventure, a search for hidden treasure following the stage directions of Edgar Allan Poe which nearly drops the two boys into the vengeful clutches of Injun Joe. Thenceforth thoughts of the half-breed will seldom fade (though they have earlier), and as Tom and Huck travel through the world of summer the novel is supposed to celebrate, the action turns out to be something of an Indian summer too. The domestic comedy of the village stage increasingly gives way to melodrama, and the matter of Hannibal that is evoked moves away from cats and pain-killer to much darker memories of village life.

Dixon Wecter tells us that the original Injun Joe was a respectable member of the lower levels of Hannibal society, but Indians hoping for good press may count on little help from Mark Twain. From *Roughing It* onward, the American aborigine is presented as a subspecies of Yahoo, largely because Sam Clemens's own experience with Indians was limited to degenerate tribes in Nevada and California. What he read in books, magazines, and newspapers published during the 1870s, a period during which the Sioux and Apaches were waging bloody warfare in defense of their homeland, certified (even sanctified) his notion that Indians were brutes worthy only to be exterminated. But the Indians for whom he reserved his most savage contempt were the Indians of Fenimore Cooper—Cooper's Indians he called them—who were guilty not so much of inhuman torture of their hapless white victims as of literary offenses beyond the pale of civilized behavior. Injun Joe is little more than an escapee from Cooper's fiction, for like the Mingo named Magua in *The Last of the Mohicans* he has vowed revenge because he has been horsewhipped by whites. In Cooper's novel Magua attempts to avenge himself against Colonel Munro by forcing Cora, his daughter, into unholy wedlock, while Injun Joe plans on tying the widow of the man who whipped him to her bed and mutilating her; and both situations convey considerable sexual implication. Wecter traces the episode to an incident in which actual rape may have been threatened, one scarcely suited, as he notes, to a children's book. Yet to the adult reader the image of a woman tied to a bed is hardly subliminal.

Injun Joe—again like Magua—is much more than a sexual menace: he is evil personified, who does bad things because he likes to. In Cora Munro, who has a touch of negro blood that makes her attractive to other dark people, Cooper created an American counterpart of Scott's Jewish heroine Rebecca, and in the half-breed Injun Joe there is much that evokes Dickens's Fagin. He is an avatar of satanic malevolence, a dark figure haunting the boyhood Eden, the summertime world of green and gold. Curiously enough we never do learn what Injun Joe looks like. In contrast to Huck's description of Pap at the outset of his own adventures (and Pap in many ways is Injun Joe crossed with Muff Potter—or Fagin with Sikes), in which personified evil appears like a corpse bobbing up from the depths of the river, Injun Joe is mostly a psychological presence, not a physical being. This is true of most of the characters in the book, who are known by a few symbolic properties—Aunt Polly's thimble or Becky's golden braids—or, most important, by their costumes.

Here again is the theatrical property, as when Huck first appears in his ragged outsized clothes; and Injun Joe is recalled most vividly in terms of his disguise, as a ridiculously bearded, bewigged, deaf-and-dumb Spaniard, who halfway along changes "green goggles" for "an eyepatch." Where Dickens is a skillful user of disguises, making of Monks a ubiquitous figure of evil who haunts the action, Mark Twain's use of the device is so outrageous as to suggest he is past believing in his own technique. Yet the white-wigged, green-goggled half-breed is the kind of Halloween character which in the hands of the more skillful (but no more powerful) melodramatist Robert Louis Stevenson will become Blind Pue; and as a figure of pure fright Injun Joe certainly anticipates, as he may well have inspired, that subsequent specter.

What is most fascinating about Injun Joe, however, is not what repels but what attracts, for the boys are drawn to him, even as they are tensed to flee, by the outlaw's association with the fabulous treasure he has found. The gold dug up in the haunted house, moreover, links Injun Joe in turn with the legendary river pirate James Murrell, a cutthroat celebrated by Mark Twain in *Life on the Mississippi* as a transcendent villain, who put the vaunted Jesse James of later times in the shade. Murrell's gold has been bought with human lives, yet it becomes the grail which Tom and Huck set out to discover (more however as amateur detectives than as knights of the roundtable—not until Philip Marlow will the two combine), a search that brings Huck to true heroics and that ends in an accidental and unsuspected way. Injun Joe's accidental discovery of the treasure provides a wonderfully comic yet frightening scene, purely theatrical, as our attention is divided between what is going on downstairs in the haunted house and what is occurring above. On one part of the stage, as it were, the outlaws stumble upon the gold, while on another the boys, like frightened angels, witness the event unseen, an audience of two that has no desire to enter the action below, but that entertains a powerful wish to get hold of the gold.

The melodrama will continue as they attempt to solve the meaning of "Number 2," but it is Huck who increasingly dominates this strand of the narrative, as the boy outlaw turned detective trails the Indian outlaw through the darkened village to the rendezvous atop Cardiff Hill. Tom's further association with Injun Joe picks up literally where Huck's leaves off, not on the hill but down in the cave, where melodrama becomes intensified until it takes on the quality of nightmare. In the cave episode, moreover, Mark Twain gives the complex mixture of terror and desire with which Injun Joe is associated yet another and deeper dimension, evoking age-old myths and plunging his young hero into shadows much darker than any summoned up on the stage. In a certain sense McDougal's Care lies under Cardiff Hill, for as the hill earlier provided Tom Sawyer his stage for playing at Robin Hood—a stage that for Huck turns into a real scene of banditry—so what lies below it is a playground suddenly converted into a place of terror, a tunnel of love become a house of horrors. It is a nightmare world focused by the lost children and haunted by the specter of Injun Joe, the pastoral yet tragic tale of the babes in the woods reset in a distinctly American yet universal scene, a limestone cave that evokes primordial caverns, measureless to man but all too familiar to children.

Walter Blair first pointed out that *Adventures of Tom Sawyer* is composed of different stories that take their separate narrative ways, often independent of one another. Like the distinct divisions between the various zones of Tom Sawyer's world, from Aunt Polly's parlor to the hidden chambers of the cave, these narratives may be seen as essentially disjunctive, and in terms of literary craft they are; but in the final episode of the novel Mark Twain manages to bring most of them together in a way that testifies to the unconscious artistry that was his greatest gift. In the cave the story of Tom and Becky merges with the story of Tom, Huck, and Injun Joe, as the schoolroom, graveyard, and haunted house are suddenly telescoped. Tom's greatest joke on Aunt Polly and the village involves his mysterious disappearance with Huck and Joe Harper and the fears that he and his friends have been drowned, and the cave episode repeats the situation, with the villagers once again turning out to search for the missing children. This time it is no joke, and the pair are perilously close to being entombed when Tom finds the back entrance to the cave, an act of real heroism that brings him even more celebrity. Little of what has happened earlier is not repeated thematically in the cave episode, and even Injun Joe's presence there is a direct effect of Huck's otherwise independent adventure on Cardiff Hill. This climactic joining of strands results in a transcendent example of children's literature, which ends with the vastly satisfying discovery of the hidden gold, converting the nightmare of menace into a dream of wish-fulfillment.

Before going on to explore the depths of the cave episode, we must first put *Tom Sawyer* into context, the better to understand the implications of the story's conclusion. If *Tom Sawyer* is put in the shade by the book by Mark Twain that followed it, its shadowy aspect can be all the more appreciated by looking at the novels for boys written by other authors which preceded it, chief among them being Thomas Bailey Aldrich's *The Story of a Bad Boy* (1869). Aldrich's Tom Bailey (as the boy's name suggests) is like Tom Sawyer an autobiographical projection, and like Mark Twain's Tom he is a maker of ornate mischief, having a superabundance of natural energy which is pitted against the conformist rigidity of a New England village. P. T. Barnum in his *Autobiography* (1855) had portrayed his own Yankee youth in much the same light, and there is more than a touch of Barnum in Tom Bailey, who like Tom Sawyer is something of a showman, given (like Barnum) to staging elaborate hoaxes. . . .

Where writers like Aldrich, [Lousia May] Alcott, and [Horatio] Alger all rebelled against society's norms by becoming artists who created children who eventually come under the sway of the laws of work and wage, Mark Twain, who spent much of his adult life trying to convince the world that he was as much a responsible businessman as an artist, created two boys who in quite different ways embody irresponsibility: Huck, the permanent refugee from civilization, and Tom, the everlasting player of games of his own invention. At the story's end the Good Bad Boy has become a Rich Boy also, and may thenceforth become a Playboy, which is indeed what he does. But Huck, soon after his own adventures begin, forswears his wealth and resumes the tattered rags of perpetual flight.

Set against the dominant myth of success as celebrated by Horatio Alger, the story of Tom Sawyer is clearly subversive, having less to do with hard work than with good luck abetted by a quick wit. Ben Franklin, the archetype of Alger's boys, had plenty of luck and wit to use it also, but he had to work long and hard to attain the "competency" that enabled him to retire in his middle age. Tom Sawyer realizes the American dream at the threshold of adolescence. He does so, moreover, by striking it rich California style, imitating in small the gold rush that Mark Twain persistently regarded as the national event which signaled an end to the old American dream of pastoral contentment—Franklin's happy mediocrity—even while, as Sam Clemens, he did everything he could to increase his personal fortune, plowing the profits from his book into ill-fated investments, most of which were aberrant expressions of the technological spirit that Ben Franklin had helped set in motion and that scotched the old Jeffersonian dream of rural bliss. Which turns out after all to be no more than the dull placidness of St. Petersburg on a summer's day, as peaceful and as boring as Eden before the Fall. Henry Nash Smith observed that the Jeffersonian plan was not conducive to the production of exciting literature, and Tom Sawyer is but one in a long line of American heroes whose adventures are, in Anthony Hilfer's phrase, a revolt against the village.

Much as Tom himself can never settle for a humdrum life of work and wage, so his *Adventures* soon runs out of village materials, and both book and boy head for the familiar gothic graveyard and the forest beyond. From Cooper's *The Pioneers* to Howe's *Story of a Country Town* this has been the traditional movement of American fiction with a small-town setting. The romantic and gothic elements are intensified during the episode in the cave, and though Tom's last and "real" adventure ends with the discovery of the gold, the novel ends with Tom's plans to use the cave as yet another theatrical backdrop. This sets the scene for the sequel, in which Tom Sawyer will be converted from a Lord of Misrule into a literary arbiter of "rules" second only to Aristotle. In terms of the unity of *Adventures of Tom Sawyer* the end returns us to an earlier point in the story, the cave being added to Cardiff Hill and Jackson's Island as a playground for the exercise of Tom's imagination. As a place, moreover, it is of a piece with Tom's forest arena, which is located in the "center of the woods" under a huge old oak, a setting which evokes druidical mysteries; and before it becomes just another clubhouse, the cave serves as an important arena of transformation, at a much deeper level than the one on top of Cardiff Hill. The connotations of woods and oak tree suggest that Tom is a pagan whose world is the wildwood beyond the boundaries of town, and the drama enacted deep down below seems part and parcel likewise of ancient adventures acting out even older mysteries.

The original cave in Hannibal was named for a Doctor McDowell, a fantastic eccentric who kept cannon stored in it for a projected invasion of Mexico and likewise placed there the embalmed body of (it was said) his own daughter in a copper cylinder. But life sometimes veers from the accepted decorums of fiction, and Dr. McDowell's fancies play no part in *Tom Sawyer*. What Mark Twain did with the cave in terms of contemporary literature was to scotch it, adapting the real place to the formulaics of Sir Walter Scott and Fenimore Cooper. American writers from Charles Brockden Brown on who wished to stage gothic fictions were forced to make do with the conditions of the American landscape, and lacking the ruins of the old world they resorted to the cliffs and caves of the new. In associating western caves with bandits and stolen gold Mark Twain had the real-life example of Cave-in-Rock, near where the Ohio joins the Mississippi, which was the sanctuary of the Brothers Harpe, notorious river pirates who operated in the early years of the nineteenth century. But most likely he (or at least Tom Sawyer) had in mind the literary cave that shelters one of Scott's greatest outlaw heroes, Rob Roy, the good man turned bad by adversity and therefore a Scottish equivalent to Robin Hood.

Mark Twain is on record about the "literary offenses" of both Scott and Cooper, yet *Tom Sawyer* and its sequel contain episodes clearly derived from the adventures concocted by those masters of the historical romance, never more so than in the depths of McDougal's Cave, even the name of which evokes Scott's hero-villain the Black Douglas. Thus the terrifying glimpse Tom catches of Injun Joe may evoke Oliver Twist's glimpse of Fagin, but it also recalls the horrifying moment in *The Last of the Mohicans* when "the malignant, fierce, and savage features" of Magua appear at the entrance to the cavern at Glen's Falls. Tom, like the heroes of the romances which are his favorite reading, eventually leads Becky to safety, his ordeal providing a three-day rite of passage from which he emerges a true champion. Yet it is a ritual that sets the romances of Scott on their collective ear, for unlike the Waverley heroes, who often end their romantic adventures convinced that a normal middle-class life is best after all, Tom Sawyer is never absorbed into the dominant culture; they mistake the romantic ideal for reality but then discover their errors and mend their ways, but Tom's romantic "illusions" are often verified, as with his recovery of the treasure. For Tom —to refer to the quixotic pattern important to both Scott and Mark Twain—windmills become true giants and barbers' bowls *are* gold helmets. Only in the sequel does Tom become a victim of his illusions—in *his* adventures all dreams come true. Suspended between the worlds of nightmare and wish-fulfillment, *Adventures of Tom Sawyer* is a book of dreams—which is why it is preeminently a book for children.

Once again it is the gold that turns the trick, and of the many ironies that unfold in *Tom Sawyer* none is more complex than when Tom and Becky flee deeper and deeper into the cave, escaping the bats who are no real danger save in the eyes of superstitious children: they are in effect not fleeing but advancing, both toward the "other" (secret) entrance and toward the place where Injun Joe has hidden the gold. Huck, in following Joe through the maze of village streets, is pursuing a parallel quest, but a false one that will erupt as his real adventure, from which he emerges a hero. Tom's flight brings him perilously close to Injun Joe also, with ultimately delightful results for himself and Huck. In the figure of the half-breed all mysteries converge, a coincidence that entails more than a convenience of plot. Up on Cardiff Hill Injun Joe is the conventional villain of melodrama, his evilness enhanced by his mixed blood, the half-breed being a miscegenetic type depicted in much nineteenth-century American literature as being inherently vicious. But down in the cave Injun Joe becomes something much deeper, a nightmare apparition associated with myth and fable.

Tom Sawyer, in using his kite string (a boyhood token of restrained flight as play) as a guide, with one end fastened close to the sleeping Becky, evokes the story of Theseus exploring the labyrinth with the help of Ariadne; and if McDougal's Cave has a resident minotaur, it is Injun Joe. But the Minotaur, the beast with the human head that feasts on maidens, is type and symbol for a legion of mythological monsters, the cannibalistic ogres who populate folk and fairy tales. Like the giant in "Jack and the Beanstalk" Injun Joe is not only a frightening monster (willing to eat bats if not little children): he is also the guardian of a fabulous stolen treasure. As ogre, then, he is the kind that is not slain but outwitted; and though in the story Injun Joe dies from starvation, leaving his treasure to any who may wish to take it, Tom Sawyer alone has the knowledge and the wit to find the gold. In effect he acts out an age-old plot, a "real" adventure in which he steals the treasure from the thief, thereby merging his heroics with the archetypes whose adventures supply the original stuff of the oldest children's stories, fairy tales that are fragments of ancient pagan myths.

Mark Twain makes a subtle point when he shows that Tom Sawyer, who cannot even under duress commit the simplest bit of Scripture to memory, has easily memorized the adventures of Robin Hood so he can play by the book. Playing by the book is Tom Sawyer's greatest game, one that will be reduced to two-dimensionality in *Adventures of Huckleberry Finn*; but in his own *Adventures* it is a guide to his essential character. Inside the village, whether in the schoolroom or parlor, he constantly resists playing by the rules: that is left to such good boys as Sid, Willie Mufferson, and Alfred Temple. But out in the forest, on the island, or eventually in the cave it is Tom who makes up the rules, and everyone must play by them. *His* scripture is the story of Robin Hood and its dime-novel equivalents, much as his religion is associated with the greenwood, his liturgy with superstitions. In this light—the green light—Tom Sawyer can be seen, if only for a flickering moment, as a devotee of Pan. Even though Tom is driven to reducing his reading to rules, as rules they become a version of chivalric code, the kind associated not with knights but with outlaws, whose code is distinctly their own.

This merely reinforces the most important point of the book, which is that Tom Sawyer, unlike the good bad boys who precede him (whether T. B.

Aldrich's Tom Bailey or Horatio Alger's Ragged Dick), remains unregenerate, forever committed to the world of play. Though celebrated as a hero by the town, he refuses to accept the terms of the final act in all hero stories, whether spun by ancient bards or by Sir Walter Scott. Having found the gold he should also get the girl; but Becky, like Joe Harper before her, drops from sight thenceforth, as the courtship ritual is converted to Tom's courting of Huck, male bonding certifying the essential subversiveness of the story. Not only does Tom not marry Becky, but he in effect returns the action of the book to the Jackson's Island theme, the celebration of eternal boyhood: Tom simply will not grow up. As the Puck of St. Petersburg, of course, he cannot, and from the boyish Panjandrum of St. Petersburg to Barrie's Peter Pan is not a very long leap.

It is time therefore that we stop insisting that Tom Sawyer, boy and book, be other than what they are. We must leave them both alone, preserved forever like Dr. McDowell's daughter, whose heart stopped at the age of fourteen. We may, like the callous tourists recalled by Mark Twain in his *Autobiography*, haul the preserved child up out of storage and comment on his failings. But do not expect him ever to change: like him or loathe him, he forever remains Tom Sawyer, rooted deep in waters dangerous to uninformed pilots, whether critics or merely readers who make the mistake of traveling upstream from *Adventures of Huckleberry Finn*. We may dismiss Tom Sawyer as a case of arrested development, but the novel that bears his name is not so easily put down; and where children are concerned, that is the truest test of literature. Not a few of us grownups, like Tom Sawyer (and Mark Twain), are unredeemed children in that regard too.

Life on the Mississippi
Revisited

James M. Cox

I should first explain my title. [When I first] wrote about *Life on the Mississippi*,[1] I . . . sought the formal connections in the book that would betray a coherence beneath the drifting and disparate current of narration. Failing to find enough of them to satisfy my craving for literary unity, I tended to conclude that the book, thought remarkable in parts, could not really stand by itself. And so, in dealing with it in my book on Mark Twain, I treated "Old Times on the Mississippi" as a separate entity precisely because it offered sufficient focus and form to represent a complete moment in Mark Twain's progression toward and away from what I, along with most other critics, determined was his masterpiece: *Adventures of Huckleberry Finn*. My determination determined me to use Mark Twain's long account of his return to the river in *Life on the Mississippi* as little more than a preview of Huck Finn's adventures. This time I want to see the book as a book in the life of Mark Twain.

Given its title, it ought to be a book about life on the Mississippi River, yet anyone who has read it realizes that, though it is about the great river running out of and through the heart of the nation, it is just as much a book about the life of Mark Twain. No, that is not quite right. It is rather a book in which the life of Samuel Clemens is both converted and enlarged into the myth of Mark Twain. But there is more. We cannot read this book—or any of Mark Twain's books—without helplessly participating in and even contributing to this myth, for all his works, rather than being ends in themselves, seem means toward the end of mythologizing their author. Thus I shall begin by suggesting how both we and he have collaborated in creating the myth.

No one would deny that we have mythologized Mark Twain as a native literary genius—and that "we" is not merely the popular audience but the

Reprinted from *The Mythologizing of Mark Twain*, ed. Sara deSaussure Davis and Philip D. Beidler (Tuscaloosa: University of Alabama Press, 1984), pp. 99–115. Copyright © 1984 The University of Alabama Press. Used by permission.

[1]See my *Mark Twain: The Fate of Humor* (Princeton: Princeton University Press, 1966), pp 105–26, 161–67.

academic or literary audience as well. The very fact that two audiences always come to mind in our thinking about Mark Twain indicates how profoundly Mark Twain (as the name implies) divided and still divides his audience. He was, after all, a popular writer and at the same time a great writer. He was recognized as such in his own time and remains so recognized to this day. And as such he represents a division—almost a contradiction—for there is more than a little doubt on both sides of the equation whether the two identities are not mutually exclusive. We on the academic side are even more prone to see the mutual exclusiveness, it seems to me, than those who love Mark Twain as a popular writer.

This initial or "master" division is but an index to a host of divisions Mark Twain has both represented and excited. There are the embattled arguments about whether he is Western or Eastern, vernacular or genteel in identity; whether he is a journalist or an artist, a writer or performer, a confident voice of the people or an embittered misanthrope; and finally whether he is an author or a businessman. Far from being of recent vintage, these arguments, or some of them, took shape in Mark Twain's lifetime; and in the work of Paine, Mencken, Brooks, DeVoto, and Henry Smith they were developed, intensified, and refined. Their persistence until this day reminds us of how deep the divisions have always been.

Equal to the divisions, and even controlling them, is a unity of a very special kind. The reason the persistent divisions have attracted adherents is that Mark Twain always seems to occupy both sides of each division. If there was some underground rift, there was nonetheless the single public personality operating under an exposed pen name—a personality which seemed in his own time, and seems in our time too, to be larger than his writing, or at least seemed and seems not confinable to what we are pleased to call literature. It was just this larger figure that spent itself in lecturing, investing, philosophizing, advertising, and tycooning in the expansive age of finance capitalism in which he had his being. We see, and Mark Twain's contemporary audience saw, the divisions because Mark Twain in both his lecturing and writing railed at his own involvement in such "extra-literary" activity. At the same time, there was a single Mark Twain who never even tried to conceal Samuel Clemens (though Samuel Clemens on occasion recklessly tried to conceal Mark Twain) because the pen name, even as it exposed the divisions, nonetheless contained them. The containment was managed through a humor and a clarity that perpetually disarmed the anger and the contradictory complexity the divisions somehow generated.

To face Samuel Clemens' pen name is not only to see the divisions Mark Twain's audience saw but also to see the figure of the author who projected them. Much as we might wish to see this author in the businessman's or lecturer's role of betraying his "literary" career, making the writer in him subordinate to the businessman or speculator or inventor also in him, there remains a Mark Twain who emerges before us as nothing but writing. To read his notebooks is to see him turning everything at hand into writing. If he is traveling, it is never to take a vacation to get away from his "profession" but to turn every trip and every observation into a book.

Of course it is possible to say that the books aren't literature so much as padded filler to meet the subscription contracts he had entered into, as if writing were a business instead of a profession. There is no gainsaying such an evaluation: not even Mark Twain could gainsay it as he struggled to complete the books on time (and "completion" for him often meant filling out or up a number of pages even as he angrily knew his inspiration tank was dry) for the best market moment. Yet if he could not gainsay the evaluation, he nonetheless had a deeper knowledge that something about the whole realm of what had come to be called literature in the nineteenth century was confining, even suffocating, for the figure he all but helplessly knew himself to be. The literary world was a world that, in its refinements, became filled with grown-up one-horse men, whereas the world toward which he journeyed was to be occupied by boys he would imagine in a mythic form much larger than the race of men that descended from them. Moreover, this author of boyhood knew that he would always be freer and larger than the books he wrote. In other words, the books, rather than effacing him and thereby becoming representations of his authorship, or dramatizing him and thereby reducing him to a character, were made to *enlarge* him precisely because they could not contain him.

By way of touching upon this enlargement, I want to stress just how the East–West division, though it has constituted a continual critical debate about Mark Twain's identity, is actually a very reduced image of the geographical space Mark Twain mythically occupied. Such an axis—accentuated by the criticism and contention of Brooks and DeVoto—fails to take into account the North–South axis that Mark Twain also occupied. For Mark Twain touches all four points of this country's compass. Small wonder that he would finally wish to girdle the world in *Following the Equator* even as he was beginning to imagine fantasies of polar seas.

If we look at Hannibal, Missouri, where Samuel Clemens grew up, we see that it is on the Mississippi River, which was then flowing south into slavery. At the same time, it is just far enough north to be where West was South and East was North—since the Missouri Compromise of 1820 had polarized the country on a North–South axis along the line that surveyors Mason and Dixon had driven west in the eighteenth century. That political axis came to dominate the identity of his home state and village. And if the drift of the river of his youth was directly north to south, dividing east from west (as the Appalachian Mountains, running south–southwest, had previously divided them), the stretch of river he piloted was from St. Louis due south (albeit meanderingly so) to New Orleans.

If we sketched his life out of this historical and geographical configuration, we could say that Samuel Clemens fled (or deserted or escaped) the political North–South axis, once it completely volatilized, to go West where he would find a pseudonym with its origins inescapably in the river world he had left behind him, and then came into an East (which had been North) as a Westerner, there to begin reconstructing, in the age of Reconstruction, a South of Boyhood which had never existed but which he made the most real dream in our literature. That is why the language of *Huckleberry Finn*, predicated on the profound Northern sentiment of freedom, is nonetheless Southern much more than Western in its identity—which is why, by virtue of its one fatal word, it is under threat of ban to this day. . . .

Mark Twain . . . at once designates the four points on the American compass and spans the time in which those four points had been confused by politics, morality, law, and finally war. If the war was the violence which clarified the morality and politics by rewriting the law, it was also the moment when Samuel Clemens found the pseudonym by means of which he reentered the Union, to which he had been a traitor, and evaded the Confederacy from which he had deserted.

He was indeed a Western outlaw in the deepest sense of the term. Of all our major writers, only Ezra Pound is a match for him in this regard. Unlike Pound, who was completing his long revolutionary poetic life when he became a traitor, Mark Twain's treason preceded his long career in prose, and, when the Civil War ended, he needed all of the humor afforded by his pseudonymous identity to disarm the moral sense of the Northeastern society he determined to enter—a society ready to judge, and even to sentence, the historic identity of Samuel Clemens.

When, after fifteen years of humorously reconstructing himself in New England society, he returned to the Mississippi in 1882 for the express purpose of writing the travel book that was to be *Life on the Mississippi*, he was at last returning in the person of Mark Twain to the river where the very term of his pen name had its origin. By the time of his return, he had made what he rightly called his *nom de guerre*, if not a household word, at least sufficiently famous that he met a steamboat of that name on the river of his youth.

He had, as we know, already returned to the river in his writing, having written seven sketches which William Dean Howells had published in the *Atlantic* (from January to August 1875) under the title "Old Times on the Mississippi," and when he came to the actual business of writing his travel book, he inserted those sketches wholesale. They constitute chapters 4 to 18 of *Life on the Mississippi* and are often referred to as the "first half" of the book, though they constitute only one-fourth of its contents. These are inevitably the chapters critics cite as the "strong part" of the book, whereas the remaining three-fourths are often dismissed as one more example of Mark Twain's unfortunate hauling and filling and padding for the subscription trade. Rarely are they incorporated into a critical vision of the book's esthetic; they are instead used by biographers to fill out the life of Samuel Clemens.

It is not my purpose in revisiting this book to show the marvelous unity that is perceptible beneath the discontinuous multiplicity of these chapters. . . . Even so, that earlier writing, "Old Times on the Mississippi," seems to have more so-called unity than the travel portion of the completed book. Being a work of memory rather than a book worked up from travel notes, and being devoted to the more univocal subject of Mark Twain's apprenticeship as a pilot, it has a more continuous narrative line than the discursive chapters that recount the actual return to the river. Yet anyone who truly detaches all seven sketches and looks at them will see that there was much discontinuity in "Old Times," particularly in the last two sketches, in which Mark Twain, departing from the Bixby-Cub vaudeville structure to detail the nature of the pilot's power and independence, thrusts in statistics of racing times and records to accompany a string of anecdotes and historical incidents connected with the great days of steamboating. And anyone who looks at the critical literature on Mark Twain will see that what has been most emphasized about "Old Times" is the humorous vision of Mark Twain learning to be a pilot who could "read" the river.[2] Indeed, the famous passage that invariably is trotted out of that book (as if it might be a "trot" for all future students) is the one in which Mark Twain sees the river as a test the pilot literally has to read in order to see the snags and reefs which, while dimpling the surface and adding beauty to the current, pose the threats and potential disasters that the experienced pilot's eye recognizes on the face of the water.

Such a passage, in addition to standing out as a wonderfully easy landmark for literary readers whose stock in trade is seeing the world in the figure of a text, has the summarizing clarity that is the very trademark of Mark Twain's prose. I certainly don't want to negate it, but it shouldn't be allowed to characterize either the book or the river.

At the same time, if we see why it is such a dominating passage we can by inference begin to see why "Old Times" is equally dominating in the later structure of *Life on the Mississippi*. The passage, in projecting the river as a text, shows the relation of piloting to writing. Similarly, in the career of Mark Twain "Old Times" represented (and here I am seeing it *as* the *Atlantic* sketches, not as part of *Life on the Mississippi*) that moment when Samuel Clemens, reconstructing his life under his pen name, had, in reaching the river of his youth, reached the place in his life where the name "Mark Twain" is sounded. And of course it is sounded in those sketches—once when Bixby runs the Hat Island Crossing, to the applause of an audience of experienced pilots who, having gathered to watch, have stayed to admire the feat. The call "Mark Twain" is in this instance a crisis call, not a safe-water sign. But Bixby, calm and deadpan, guides the boat through with such ease and grace that one of the onlookers says: "It was done beautiful." The second time the term is sounded, the perennially confident and complacent cub is at the wheel. By way of administering a lesson to Pride, Bixby has arranged for the leadsman to

---

[2]The most penetrating and suggestive treatments of this passage that I know are by Henry Nash Smith, *Mark Twain: The Development of a Writer* (Cambridge, Mass.: Harvard University Press, 1962), pp. 77–81, and Larzer Ziff, "Authorship and Craft: The Example of Mark Twain," *Southern Review*, 12 n.s. (1976), 256–60.

make false calls in safe water, and has also arranged for an audience to watch the fun. Hearing "Mark Twain" in what he has hitherto been confident is a bottomless crossing, the cub loses his confidence and desperately shouts to the engine room, "Oh Ben, if you love me, *back* her! . . . back the immortal *soul* out of her," only to be met with a gale of humiliating laughter from the assembled onlookers. Thus, as Samuel Clemens reconstructs his life under his pen name, he sounds the name not once but *twice* (which takes us right back to the divisions with which we began): once as a mark of the crisis so close beneath the deadpan mastery of Bixby's art, and once as a false call arranged by the master to humiliate the cub. And always this sound rings out for an audience's admiration or ridicule.

From these two moments which define the art of the master and the humiliation of the apprentice, who themselves constitute the division contained in the unified humorous reconstruction of the past (written in the waning years of national reconstruction), we can, I think, begin to see the dimensions of the world Samuel Clemens was inventing under the signature of Mark Twain. It was a world where art was a guild of master and apprentice come into the industrial age of steam; it involved both experience and memory (the master artist and pilot, Bixby, had both to know the river and to remember it); and it was art as a performance before an audience—in other words, public art, or at least art performed in public.

The signature of the author, who had once been the humiliated cub and now humorously reconstructs the past, was actually a call—a *sound*—and thus was a *sounding* in the full meaning of the word. In its original meaning it designated shallow water that could be safe or precarious, depending on whether a steamboat was approaching shallows or leaving them. The art of piloting lay precisely in negotiating depths so slight that the dangerous bottom could all but be perceived on the surface. Moreover, the greatest demands of the art were required in going downstream. In such a situation, the pilot had force behind him in the form of the natural, powerful, treacherous, and wandering drift of a mighty current he had to cross and recross as he pursued the unmarked channel forever changing on each trip he made. The art of piloting, though it all but enslaved the pilot to the current on which he rode, paradoxically conferred upon him a privilege and power that made him independent of all social and political pressures. Majestically isolate in the pilothouse, he looked with lordly freedom upon the beauty and danger of the moving river bearing him upon its current.

The pilot and his art were, as every critic of Mark Twain sooner or later comes to realize, not only the embodiment of Mark Twain's experience on the river; they were metaphors for the figure of Mark Twain the writer.[3] The

---

[3]For interesting discussions relating the art of piloting to the art of writing, see Edgar J. Burde, "Mark Twain: The Writer as Pilot," *PMLA* 93 (1978), 878–92; Sherwood Cummings, "Mark Twain's Theory of Realism; or the Science of Piloting," *Studies in American Humor*, 2 (1976), 209–21; and Larzer Ziff, "Authorship and Craft," 246–60.

remembered independence of the pilot was thus an expression of the writer's dream of autonomy and his determination to be free of conventional form. And the pilot's necessarily skeptical eye, surveying the deceptions of current and surface, was but a promise of the very identity of the writer and his pen name. For even in discussing Mark Twain's art we cannot quite tell whether we are discussing the art of Samuel Clemens. What we know, and all we know, is that there is a difference between them, a difference exposed in the text of every title page. Yet, for the life of us, we can't quite tell what the difference is. Neither Mark Twain nor Samuel Clemens could, I think, quite tell the difference—other than that a division was being signified even as a reconstructed unity was being discovered.

We can perhaps tell this much. The past life of Samuel Clemens was being humorously invented by virtue of, and by vice under, the authority of Mark Twain. The virtue was no doubt the art; the vice was no doubt the lie. And in "Old Times" the reconstruction had reached back across the division of the Civil War (which, if it had once divided the country, now divided the history of the country between the Old Republic and the New Union) to the river where Samuel Clemens could remember his youth even as Mark Twain could at last be sounded. To see so much ought to allow us to see that the signified division between Mark Twain and Samuel Clemens comes to us as a doubt—a doubt as deep, we want to say, as that with which Nathaniel Hawthorne invested his creative enterprise. But I want to say that it was and is as shallow as the depth the sounding "Mark Twain" designates. It is not a deep doubt but is right on the surface where we always see it but never know how to read it precisely because it is so easy to see and is humorously and pleasurably and clearly and easily right in front of us.

So much for the "Old Times" of the *Atlantic* sketches; now for *Life on the Mississippi*. Here the first point to see is that it is not Mark Twain reconstructing the life of Samuel Clemens as his own life but the record of Samuel Clemens returning to the Mississippi in the person of Mark Twain whom he cannot hide. In "Old Times" the *I* of the narrative, effacing both Samuel Clemens and Mark Twain in the comic act of apprenticeship played out by Bixby and the Cub, showed Mark Twain approaching the edge of fiction. It is hardly accidental that, at the time of writing the *Atlantic* sketches, he had just finished collaborating with Charles Dudley Warner on the satiric novel *The Gilded Age* (the collaboration itself signifying Mark Twain's entry into fiction, as well as his—and Samuel Clemens'—inability to write a novel by himself/ themselves). But *The Gilded Age* and "Old Times" put him at the threshold of full-length fiction. As a matter of fact, even before he completed the *Atlantic* sketches he was at work on *Tom Sawyer*—the book he was to call a hymn written in prose to give it a worldly air.

In the figure of Tom Sawyer, he had indeed reached the poetic origins of youth lying behind the past of both Mark Twain and Samuel Clemens. More important, through the figure of Tom Sawyer, Mark Twain had discovered

Huck Finn, whom he would release to begin his own narrative. But Huck's voice, released in the first centennial of the Republic (and surely one of the best things invented in that first centennial), couldn't complete its own story in that first surge. Instead, Mark Twain's inspiration tank ran dry.

This early portion of *Huckleberry Finn*, Mark Twain's raft book, stands in relation to the completed novel much as "Old Times" stands in relation to *Life on the Mississippi*, his steamboat book—and I think it of no little consequence that Mark Twain was actually in the process of completing both books as he returned to the Mississippi.[4] He had already begun the latter, publicly, in "Old Times" (though of course he had given no public inkling in the sketches that this was to be the beginning of a travel book, and there is no evidence that he thought of it at the time *as* a beginning). The other he had driven to the point where the raft is run over by a steamboat (a hiatus which shows, both precisely and symbolically, the two books running into each other).[5] To begin to see such a possibility is to see that it would take a trip back to the great river itself to drive the books on their parallel courses.

When he actually came to compose *Life on the Mississippi*, Mark Twain set up a casual but nonetheless definite structure, dividing the history of the river into five stages. Here is the way he asserted his structure on the fourth page of the Author's National Edition:

> Let us drop the Mississippi's physical history, and say a word about its historical history—so to speak. We can glance briefly at its slumbrous first epoch in a couple of short chapters; at its second and wider-awake epoch in a couple more; at its flushest and widest-awake epoch in a good many succeeding chapters; and then talk about its comparatively tranquil present epoch in what shall be left of the book.[6]

Using his declaration of structure as a means of finishing off the three-page first stage, the river's physical history, he proceeded to devote the slight remainder of chapter 1 and all of chapter 2 to the historical history, primarily concentrating on the river's great explorers. To the third stage, the wider-awake epoch, he devoted only one chapter, despite his promise of two, and that chapter is primarily made up of the raftsman passage from *Huck Finn*. "Old Times" is converted from the seven sketches into fourteen chapters that make up the flush-times epoch. And the actual travel book, detailing the "tranquil present epoch," comprises chapters 18 to 60. His casual declaration

---

[4]Anyone interested in the conception, composition, and interpretation of *Life on the Mississippi* will find Horst H. Kruse's *Mark Twain and "Life on the Mississippi"* (Amherst: University of Massachusetts Press, 1981) indispensable. For a briefer account which corrects many prior errors and misconceptions concerning the composition of *Life on the Mississippi*, see Guy A. Cardwell, "Life on the Mississippi: Vulgar Facts and Learned Errors," *Emerson Society Quarterly*, 46 (1973), 283–93.

[5]Walter Blair's "When Was *Huckleberry Finn* Written?" *American Literature*, 30 (1958), 1–20, remains the most succinct and authoritative effort to establish the chronology of composition of *Huckleberry Finn*. For the full account of Mark Twain's composition of *Life on the Mississippi* during the summer of 1882, see Kruse, pp. 43–91.

[6]I use the Author's National Edition because it is the text most readily available in libraries to the general reader.

of structure, accentuated by repeated references to writing as speaking ("say a word about," "so to speak," and "talk about"), points up the fact that the first two stages—the physical history and the historical history—take up all of 16 pages of the total 496 in the Author's National Edition. The other three stages, which Mark Twain inversely calls epochs, convert the history of the river into the life of Mark Twain.

But that is only the beginning. The two epochs that precede the travel-book account of the tranquil present epoch, constituted (as they are) of the manuscript episode of Huck Finn and the wholesale importation of "Old Times," show that even as Mark Twain was doubly capitalizing on his past published writing he was also looting his future masterpiece. Nor is that all. If we did not know that the raftsman episode had been taken out of *Huckleberry Finn*, we would never miss it; moreover, it can be inserted wholesale into that book without disturbing the narrative sequence. Of course, arguments can be and have been made as to whether the episode should be left out or put into *Huckleberry Finn*,[7] but the fact that it can be either in or out tells us more about the nature of *Huckleberry Finn* than a host of critical elucidations about its place in or out of the narrative. And beyond that, if we did not know that the chapters constituting "Old Times" were previously published as a unit, I am not at all sure that we would or could so confidently say that these chapters are the exquisite sections of the book. Knowing so much keeps us, in a real sense, subtracting from the structure and art of the book in order to add to the figural myth of Mark Twain. The only comfort I can see in this nice problem is that if we participate in making Mark Twain somehow larger than his books, we are doing just what Mark Twain himself did.

So much for the declared structure and the enlarged Mark Twain. We are still left with the devalued travel book. By way of showing how we might look at the material of the book, I want to quote its opening paragraph. Unlike the famous river-as-text passage, previously alluded to, or the "When-I-was-a-boy" passage opening "Old Times," or the "You-don't-know-about-me" beginning of *Huckleberry Finn*, this passage has never, to my knowledge, been singled out for attention.

> The Mississippi is well worth reading about. It is not a commonplace river, but on the contrary is in all ways remarkable. Considering the Missouri its main branch, it is the longest river in the world—four thousand three hundred miles. It seems safe to say that it is also the crookedest river in the world, since in one part of its journey it uses up one thousand three hundred miles to cover the same ground that the crow could fly over in six hundred and seventy-five. It discharges three times as much water as the St. Lawrence, twenty-five times as much as the Thames. No other river has so vast a drainage basin; it draws its water-supply from twenty-eight states and territories; from Delaware on the Atlantic seaboard, and from all that country between that and Idaho on the Pacific slope—a spread of forty-five degrees of longitude. The Mississippi receives and carries to the Gulf water from fifty-four

[7]For a thorough account of this issue, see Peter D. Beidler, "The Raft Episode in *Huckleberry Finn*," *Modern Fiction Studies*, 14 (Spring 1968), 11–20.

subordinate rivers that are navigable by steamboats, and from some hundreds that are navigable by flats and keels. The area of its drainage basin is as great as the combined areas of England, Wales, Scotland, Ireland, France, Spain, Portugal, Germany, Austria, Italy, and Turkey; and almost all this wide region is fertile; the Mississippi valley proper, is exceptionally so.

The resonance of the passage—with its array of facts, its grandly marshaled parallelisms, and its imposing quantitative crescendo—obscures what seems a grand joke. For right at the center of this first paragraph, and as a culminating fact about the great river's size, Mark Twain climactically announces that the Mississippi drains Delaware. This "fact," set in the majestic current of an imposing list of seemingly scientific and geographic measurements, is difficult to see precisely because it is in such a *current* of prose. If we take the passage and juxtapose it against the celebrated passage on reading the river, I think we can see how, implicitly, we are challenged to read a text.

That joke in the center of the first paragraph is equivalent to a snag in the river big enough to tear the bottom right out of a steamboat. If we have missed the snag on our first or second or third reading, seeing it instantaneously exposes what has been mere absence of vision as humiliating stupidity, and at the same time converts the feeling of humiliation into an enormous gain of pleasure as we recognize ourselves in the act of becoming master pilots. The sudden glory of our pleasure in this new-found identity shouldn't blind us to the fact that we both have and need the ignorant and complacent cub in us.

But I want to make more of this initial joke in *Life on the Mississippi* in the return visit to the book. It shows that if the Mississippi is a mighty current, so is language. The reason we miss the joke or "stretcher" is that the effect of the parallel clauses extending the size of the Mississippi carries us right by the snag. To see this force of language working is to be at the heart of narrative deception; it is also to see the function of the snag, which is nothing less than Mark Twain's deliberate deviation from a sequence of "truths" to which we have too complacently become adjusted. Those who miss the snag won't be killed, as they might be if they were pilots on the other current. They will just be comfortable jackasses, of which the world of readers is already full. Those who "get it," while they won't be sold, had better remember that they didn't always get it, and so will have a humiliatingly complacent past they have to convert into the pleasure of looking at others miss what they have lately come to see. Then there will be those who always got it—some of whom will of course be lying, whereas others will too much lie in wait, always on the lookout for every lie and every joke. And of course there will be those who insist that it wasn't much of a joke anyway, some of whom never had, and never will have, a sense of humor, and others who will be inwardly miffed that they had to have it shown them. Finally, there will be those adamant few who contend there is no joke. After all, they could say, the passage *means* to say that the Mississippi draws its water from the twenty-eight states and territories *between* Delaware and Idaho.

Read with that determination, "from Delaware on the Atlantic seaboard" is what we might call Mark Twain's redundant stutter in preparing himself to assert the area of the river's drainage basin. Against such resistance, I can't claim with arrogant assurance that this isn't Mark Twain's intention; I merely want to retain a skeptical eye on the passage, keeping the possibility that it might be—just might be—a joke.[8] It would not be a big joke, since Delaware is after all a small state; and, considering the geographical centrality I have claimed for Mark Twain, there is a rich conclusiveness in seeing him have the Mississippi "suck in" an Eastern Seaboard state. But the more important point is to see all these enumerated responses to the passage, including this last contention, as constituting an expansive humorous consciousness in Mark Twain's audience.

Seen from such a perspective of expansion, the book becomes what it is: an accumulating of every kind of narrative—Mark Twain's past, masquerading as present narrative; his importation of what he calls the emotions of European travelers as they confront the Mississippi; the broadly humorous tall tales the pilots tell him in order not so much to deceive him as to draw him out of the incognito with which he futilely tries to conceal his identity; the bogus letter of a supposedly reformed criminal preying upon the charity of gullible do-gooders wishing to believe lies (the letter, actually written by a Harvard confidence man, dressed out in the form of sentimentally appealing illiteracy); the fake narratives of spiritualists claiming to have conversations with the dead; the self-advertising lies of salesmen hawking oleomargarine and cotton-seed oil as manufactured replacements for traditional substances; the intruded yarns of gamblers conning other gamblers; the romantic guide-book legends of Indian maidens (and on and on). Yet all along the way there is penetrating information, exquisite criticism of other books on the Mississippi, pungent observations of the culture of the great valley, acute commentary on the society, literature, and art of both pre– and post–Civil War America.[9] Information and history are so interlaced with tall tales, intruded jokes, and seemingly irrelevant "loitering and gab" that truth and exaggeration scarcely can be told apart. Finally there are the episodes that Mark Twain recounts of his boyhood as he reaches Hannibal—narratives which biographers have all too often taken as the traumatic, true experience of Mark Twain's childhood, although they have about them the aspect of indulgent (as well as invented) guilt fantasies.

[8]But contenders for a serious reading will have to contend with the fact that Mark Twain repeats the claim that the Mississippi drains Delaware: "A few more days swept swiftly by, and La Salle stood in the shadow of his confiscating cross, at a meeting of the waters from Delaware, and from Itasca, and from the mountain ranges close upon the Pacific, with the waters of the Gulf of Mexico, his task finished, his prodigy achieved (Life on the Mississippi, Author's National Edition, p. 16)". I suppose it would be possible to argue that Mark Twain was so stupid that he didn't know that the Mississippi doesn't drain Delaware!

[9]Stanley Brodwin's "The Useful and Useless River: Life on the Mississippi Revisited," Studies in American Humor, 2 (1976), 196–208, is a splendid interpretation of the structure and meaning of the continuity, as well as the discontinuity, of these episodes.

A way of seeing it all, in a bit of nubbed down compression, would be to remember that the pilot whom Mark Twain meets on the *Gold Dust* is called Rob Styles (the actual name was Lem Gray, and he was killed in a steamboat explosion while Mark Twain was writing the book). How right a name to be waiting for Mark Twain as he hopelessly tries to hide his own identity! For Mark Twain does indeed *rob styles*, showing us, by implication, our outlaw writer operating as a literary highwayman, ready to raid even his own work to flesh out his book. How much of the King and the Duke he has in him! No wonder he comes back to that name of his in this part of the book, showing that it had first been used by Isaiah Sellers (and here what is presumably the true name is nonetheless perfect), a veritable Methuselah among riverboat pilots.

Samuel Clemens had thoughtlessly yet irreverently parodied the old man's river notes and the lampoon had, according to Mark Twain, silenced the old captain, leaving him to sit up nights to hate the impudent young parodist. And so Mark Twain says that when, on the Pacific Coast, he had set up as a writer, he *confiscated* the ancient captain's pen name. He concludes his account by saying that he has done his best to make the name a "sign and symbol and warrant that whatever is found in its company may be gambled on as being the petrified truth."[10]

Never mind that Samuel Clemens didn't first use his *nom de guerre* on the Pacific Coast (we experts see *that* joke).[11] The point is that, if in "Old Times" Mark Twain had shown the memory, skill, anxiety, courage, humiliation, and the joke attending the leadsman's call, he now shows the aggression, theft, parody, and comic guilt attending the act of *displacing* the ancient mariner of the river. Having confiscated the old man's pen name, he makes his own life and writing identical with the *epochs* of the river's emergence from the sleep of history.

The "petrified truth," which the name Mark Twain is said to signify, is itself the broadest of jokes. The actual truth is as elusive as the shape of the river that Horace Bixby had said the pilot must know with such absolute certainty that it lives in his head. Through all the shifts of perspective in this book, through all the changes of direction, the abrupt compression of space, and wayward digressions to kill time, there is yet a single writer whose shape seems somehow in *our* head, rather than in the shifting book before us. That figure is of course the myth of Mark Twain, growing out of and beyond the book that cannot contain him. We might devalue, and have devalued, this book, but in devaluing it we are already preparing to use it as a foil for *Huckleberry Finn*, the book that was waiting to be finished even as Mark Twain brought this one to an abrupt conclusion.

[10]Because of Mark Twain's notorious penchant for unreliability, the scholarship devoted to his account of acquiring his pen name is necessarily extensive. The most authoritative treatment of this episode, at once summarizing and correcting prior scholarship, is in Kruse, pp. 82–90.

[11]Samuel Clemens' first known use of "Mark Twain" occurred on 3 February 1863 in the Virginia City *Territorial Enterprise*, well before he left Nevada for California.

And this mythic figure, always materializing above his books, whose shape is in our heads, seems in his way as real as the great river—seems, indeed, to be that river's tutelary deity. He is the figure who, more than any of our writers, knows the great truth that Swift exposed in the fourth book of *Gulliver's Travels*: that if man cannot tell the truth, neither can language. Language can only lie.

In this connection, it is well to remember those Watergate days when Richard Nixon said that he would make every effort to find out "where the truth lies." Apparently, Nixon never saw the joke in his assertion, but Mark Twain would certainly have seen it since he knew that the truth lies everywhere, and nothing can really lie like it. Being our greatest liar, he knew how much he believed in and needed the beautiful and powerful and deceptive river at the center of his country. It was a muddy river—the river he knew—so that you couldn't see the bottom, which was always so near, and it ran south into slavery just as man's life runs down into the slavery of adulthood. It rolled from side to side, wallowing in its valley as it shifted landmarks and state boundaries. It could hardly be bridged, and to this day has few bridges on it between New Orleans and St. Louis. It was, and still is, a lonely river for anyone upon its current. Lonely as it is, and monotonous too, it remains a truly wild river. Even now it may burst its banks and head through the Atchafalaya Bayou, leaving New Orleans high and dry. For it is a living river, always changing, always giving the lie to anyone who counts on its stability.

If Mark Twain grows out of the lie that language can't help telling, the great river grows out of some force that language cannot name. To begin to study the current of Mark Twain's prose in this book is to begin to sense the power of that other current that his discontinuous narrative displaces more than it represents. How good it is that Mark Twain does not spend all his time—he actually spends quite little—in describing, analyzing, or celebrating the river. If his book is not a great book, as great books go, it is well worth revisiting.

Revisiting it makes me know that it is time for the present generation of critics to take up Mark Twain. With their problematics, their presences-become-absences, and their aporias, they will be able to see the river as the genius loci of Mark Twain's imagination. I very much believe that this newer criticism, dealing as it can and does with discontinuity and open-ended forms, should be able to give a better account of Mark Twain's structure and language than the generation of New Critics who relied on the closed structures of lyric, drama, and novel. In the gap—I had almost said aporia—between Samuel Clemens and Mark Twain, these critics may see, as if for the first time, the writer's two I's which yet make one in sight.

A "Raft of Trouble":
Word and Deed in *Huckleberry Finn*

Laurence B. Holland

Criticism of *Huckleberry Finn* has defined a consensus that the book's closing section is seriously flawed, for even those who find the last twelve chapters to be coherent in conception agree that the incidents relating Tom's "evasion" scheme for rescuing Jim are indulgently overwritten and in execution are as embarrassing as Hemingway claimed they were in *The Green Hills of Africa*. After chapter 31, he declared, "the rest is just cheating," and he advised people to stop reading the book at this point, apparently at the end of chapter 31, where "Jim is stolen from the boys" and sold by the fraudulent King.[1] The chapters are nevertheless well enough executed to bear rereading, and the scenes that terminate Tom's evasion scheme are so well done and so vivid that they demand more attention than Hemingway's injunction tempts us to give. In themselves they provide a significant context for the disclosure that Miss Watson has freed Jim in her will, and they illuminate the connections between the final section and earlier parts of the book and the profound folly on which Twain's novel rests. Moreover, the incidents help reveal how Twain's idiom and narrative form create the moving if somberly comic and ironic vision that lies at the heart of Twain's masterpiece.

What *Huckleberry Finn* is about is the process, with its attendant absurdities, of setting a free man free. This is the issue from the moment Huck, born free but staging and feigning his own death, seeks refuge on Jackson's Island, though the book seldom speaks explicitly about this matter in terms such as "freedom" and "liberation." It speaks more often instead of "rescuing" and "saving" important characters. The theme is figured chiefly, however, in the central case of Jim, without being confined exclusively to him, and it is first

Reprinted from *Glyph 5: Johns Hopkins Textual Studies* (Baltimore: Johns Hopkins University Press, 1979), pp. 66–80. Copyright © 1979 The Johns Hopkins University Press. Used by permission.

[1]Hemingway's memory was somewhat blurred; the two "boys" were not together when Jim was sold in chapter 31, nor when Jim was recaptured as recounted in chapter 42. Hemingway's linking of Huck and Tom, however, the implication that they owned the Negro "stolen" from them, and his incorporation of the term *nigger* in Jim's name ("Nigger Jim") displays ways in which readers are implicated in the actions of *Huckleberry Finn*. See *The Green Hills of Africa* (1935; reprint ed., New York: Charles Scribner's Sons, 1963), p. 22.

phrased definitively in the closing section (in chapter 42), when Jim's legal emancipation is divulged: "Tom Sawyer had gone to all that trouble and bother to set a free nigger free!" The process of setting a free man free is left unfinished at the end, but the closing section does not wrench the book from its course; it reveals in sharper light the profound irony that governs the book and that we should avoid simplifying. The central importance of this irony to the coherence of the book is obscured, I think, by a genetic approach to Twain's narrative even in such incisive analyses as those of Henry Nash Smith and Leo Marx, which emphasize Huck's vernacular speech, Huck's role as narrator, and Twain's difficulties in finishing his manuscript, to the comparative neglect of Jim's role and the scapegoating that is entailed by Twain's comic strategies.[2] The irony is shaped by Twain's desperately felt need for liberation and by a mixture of scorn for, and acquiescence in, the impulses, habits, and institutions that leave the quest for freedom still unsatisfied and all but paralyzed. The irony is deepened by Twain's tacit acknowledgment of his own, Huck's, and Jim's involvement with Tom Sawyer's world, and by Twain's recognition of the moral implications of his stance toward his subject and of the fictive form that generates his vision

At the risk of reading the book backward, let us begin with the incidents in chapter 40, which tell of Huck's and Jim's decision to risk Jim's exposure in order to seek a doctor for Tom. Tom's fantastic escape plans (inspired by the tales and historical accounts he takes for models) have called for enemies, and his insane "nonnamous letter," warning the Phelpses of the impending escape, has brought to the cabin a posse of fifteen farmers equipped with dogs and armed with guns. They shoot at the fleeing threesome and wound Tom in the leg before the three can make it to safety on the raft. Before the fact of Tom's wound is divulged, Jim is allowed to lavish praise on the beauty of the plan and its execution, and Huck is allowed a sigh of relief at precisely the moment when he steps onto the raft and proclaims his joy at Jim's liberation. But in view of the frequency with which Jim has had to be rescued before (to say nothing of what is shortly forthcoming), Huck's exclamation is as comic as it is genuine: "Now, old Jim, you're free *again*, and I bet you won't ever be a slave no more." It is somberly comic not only because it is overconfident but also because the recurring necessity of freeing Jim, underscored by Twain's italics of "*now*" and "*again*," has become by this time at once a moral imperative and an ineffectual routine. Both that moral pressure and that sense of futility lie deep within *Huckleberry Finn*.

The incident continues as Tom's excitement mounts, doubled by his discovery that he has been shot and leading him to disregard his wound in

---

[2]See Henry Nash Smith, *Mark Twain: The Development of a Writer* (Cambridge: Harvard University Press, 1962), pp. 113–37, and his recent *Democracy and the Novel: Popular Resistance to Classical American Writers* (New York: Oxford University Press, 1978), pp. 104–27; and Leo Marx, "The Pilot and the Passenger: Landscape Conventions and Style of *Huckleberry Finn*," *American Literature* 28 (1956): 129–46, and his *The Machine in the Garden: Technology and the Pastoral Ideal in America* (New York: Oxford University Press, 1964), pp. 319–41.

surrender to his fancies. With the cockiness of a young executive and the lunacy of Tom-foolishness he is still superintending the affair at the end of the chapter. His comparison of Jim's rescue to that of King Louis XVI, however, embedded though it is in Tom's indulgent fantasies, has ominous implications. It is disturbing because Jim's royal French counterpart was not saved from the guillotine and also because Tom's first aid—he is bandaging himself with a shirt left behind by the Duke—recalls the fraudulent King and Duke, who in chapter 19 called out from shore, begged Huck to "save their lives," and instantly were rescued from the "trouble" on shore and admitted to the raft.

The insecurity of the raft as a refuge for Huck and Jim, and the inseparable mixture of comic antics (foolish in both word and deed) with desperately urgent matters,. are of central importance throughout *Huckleberry Finn.* In this late incident Tom's foolishness is significantly related to the matching folly of Huck and Jim, who decide, despite Tom's strenuous objections and attempts to block their efforts, that Huck should venture to shore to bring a doctor to Tom. Saving Tom, freeing him from danger, is taking precedence over setting Jim free. This decision—the deed that results in Jim's capture and shortly threatens him first with hanging and then with being sold at auction—is one of the most important events in the book and it is made by Huck and Jim in a moment of deliberation that Twain renders in telling details. These details underscore the fact that the decision is mutual and that Jim is given the crucial task of putting it into words.

After "consulting—and thinking" together for a solemn moment in silence, Huck is certain what Jim will say but insists: "Say it, Jim." And Jim, revealing to Huck that he is admirably "white inside," reveals their mutual folly, speaking without a trace of pretense or hollowness in the dialect that Twain renders so painstakingly. Taking Tom as a model of unselfish conduct, Jim asks whether Tom, were he the runaway slave, would urge friends to "save me" instead of helping a wounded comrade. Jim concludes that role-model Tom would not say that and then concludes: "Well, den, is *Jim* gwyne to say it? No, sah—I doan' budge a step out'n dis place, 'dout a *doctor*; not if it's forty year!"

Even before the reader learns (or remembers) that their decision has dire consequences for Jim, their folly is transparent in taking Tom as a model of selflessness, since Tom's antics consistently assign to himself the role of heroic superintendent of his adventures. Yet his wound is a fact and in the days before penicillin it is serious; the Doctor later wants medical assistance but does not dare abandon Tom to get it. What makes Tom ludicrous in this scene—his willingness to disregard his own danger—also lends some support to Jim's feeling that Tom would not put his own safety ahead of a friend's, but does not justify the full measure of heroism that Jim and Huck credit to him. Both the folly of Huck's and Jim's decision and its moral rightness are sanctioned by the episode, which nowhere suggests that Huck and Jim should follow Tom's fantasy-ridden advice by neglecting his wound and continuing their flight. And in reaching this decision Huck and Jim are as close in rapport as they have ever been. The bond between them has been close before—

when promising not to disclose each other's whereabouts, when relaxing on the raft, when Huck humbles himself before Jim or listens to that black King Lear's penitent confession of cruelty to a daughter whose mute silence he misunderstood. The bond between them is close again when Jim hugs Huck in joy after their separation, and when they decide finally to cut loose from the King and Duke. But now they actually make a deliberate decision in utter reciprocity and do so in words that Huck asks Jim to speak.

The serious consequences of their decision come to light in chapter 42 when the Doctor returns with Tom feverish on a stretcher and with Jim tied and guarded by the posse of men who recaptured him on the raft. Twain's denouement, the disclosure that Miss Watson legally freed Jim two months earlier, casts the entire narrative in a sharper light, and certain details in which he describes the capture of Jim serve as echoes both of Tom's evasion and of the trip down the river—an earlier "evasion" as it is now made to appear—on the raft.

Before divulging the fact that Jim is already legally free, Twain does nothing to relax the danger that Jim faces. Though in peril frequently before, Jim is now threatened with hanging by some of the posse who wish to make him an object lesson to other Negroes. Moreover, they blame Jim alone for the "raft of trouble," as Huck calls it, which has overwhelmed the Phelpses and the neighborhood, in their ignorance making Jim the scapegoat for the project that Tom, with Huck's grudging assistance, has launched. Jim is saved only by the reasoning that Twain was to treat in its full nightmarish absurdity at the end of *Pudd'nhead Wilson:* Jim's legal owners would demand payment if their property were destroyed by hanging; therefore Jim must be spared and held for a proper period of time before being sold, if unclaimed, at auction. Huck is at once pained and helpless in recounting Jim's reimprisonment. The cruelty is condemned implicitly, and challenged by Huck's intention to tell Aunt Sally about Jim's service to Tom, but it is not challenged in act. One of Huck's longest sentences in the book renders at once the cruelties inflicted on Jim (the cursing and cuffing) and also Huck's anguished paralysis at witnessing Jim's confinement, which seems ominously unbreachable and final. And his account persistently recalls Jim's treatment earlier in the cabin by the Phelpses and by Tom and Huck, making clear that Jim's treatment now, though far worse, is precisely similar to what it was then. This time he is tied with heavier chains to the cabin itself instead of to the bedstead, he is now given only bread and water to eat, the escape hole is filled up, and now a bulldog and armed white guards, instead of approachable Negroes, are posted. But he is put in the "same" cabin; he is chained "again."

What Huck's long and apprehensive sentence prepares for is the Doctor's recollection of his discovery of Jim aboard the raft—a "yarn," as Huck calls it, that is intended to arouse admiration and kinder treatment for Jim, but whose effect on the posse is minimal; it persuades them merely to stop cussing Jim. Huck's highest hope is merely that they would add meat and greens to Jim's diet, and lighten the load of chains, and even this proves sanguine. Huck thinks it best not to "mix in," though he hopes that when he tells the Doctor's "yarn" to Aunt Sally it will move her to make Jim more comfortable.

One reason why the Doctor's account is significant is that it is one of the most moving and genuine tributes to Jim in the book, and one of the most vivid glimpses of Jim's service to a friend while "resking his freedom to do it." Rendered in colloquial speech as authentic as Huck's, it functions to strengthen the reader's admiration of Jim's heroism. A second reason, however, is that the Doctor's sympathy is wholly contained within the confines of loyalty to the slavery system. His statement returns at the end to the reductive and negative statement with which he opens his recollection: "He ain't no bad nigger, gentlemen; that's what I think about him." Yet it includes a strangely tender, nakedly simple description of Jim's betrayal. The glimpse of Jim's betrayal that the Doctor gives serves more vividly than the news of his sale by the King to reveal and condemn implicitly the earlier betrayals that have occurred in the course of the book. When some men unexpectedly row by the raft at dawn, Jim "as good luck would have it" is sitting beside Tom in a familiar posture "with his head propped on his knees, sound asleep," and the Doctor recalls that "I motioned them in, quiet, and they slipped up on him and tied him before he knew what he was about, and we never had no trouble."

The facts that the Doctor's tribute to Jim is notably ex post facto, and that the events of the summer have culminated in Jim's recapture, reinforce the irony of Twain's masterpiece. The raft that is now vulnerable to incursions by the Doctor and the posse has before been vulnerable to the King and the Duke, who along with Jim and Huck turn the raft into an image of the civilization with its discontents on shore. Efforts to protect Jim have had to be repeated repeatedly before. Indeed Huck's dream of freedom—escape from civilization, liberation from the burdensome six thousand dollars that was the reward he had won in *Tom Sawyer,* and escape from Pap and surrogate or adoptive parents—is countered by another dream of freedom projected in Jim: his longing to escape from slavery and enter *into* the civilization that chafes Huck; Jim's clinging to the sacred five-cent piece he wears around his neck and his desire *for* the money, the eight hundred dollars, that would buy freedom for his family; Jim's longing to be reunited with his wife and daughter and to *assume* the role of husband and father. These antithetical dreams of freedom are sustained in an uneasy ambiance through to the end of the novel.

In this context, Tom's evasion scheme, in its very extremes of indulgent excess, is appropriate indeed. Tom's antics confer the burden of heroism on Jim but make a cruel and diseased mockery of it. Jim's is the burden of Orpheus to charm (with a "jews-harp") the rats and serpents that flock around him, but in Tom's fantasies Jim winds up with the head of a rattlesnake in his mouth. Tom's antics are in effect the rehearsal for the ominous enslavement that ensues when Jim is enchained "again" in the "same" cabin. Jim's enslavement, and the process of liberation offered in the book—Jim in chains in the cabin, Jim disguised as King Lear or a sick Arab aboard the raft, Jim chained on the raft pretending to be a recaptured runaway—both make a scapegoat of Jim and are virtual mirror images of each other. Liberation dissolves into enslavement and they come close, without actually doing so, to cancelling each other out. Jim stands at the end, legally free but without the substance of freedom envisioned for him by William Blake in "America: A Prophecy": "Let the enchained soul, shut up in darkness and in sighing. . ./Rise and look out; his chains are loose, his dungeon doors are open;/And let his wife and children return from the oppressor's scourge." Jim stands free but severed from his wife and daughter, all but forgotten by Huck, with nothing like Lear's one hundred knights or Orpheus's lyre, with little but the forty bucks given him by Tom to insure the promise of William Blake and others who have helped invent the American dream. The tortured irony that defines Jim's predicament encompasses also Huck, who at the end stands immobile, the possessor still as Jim informs him of his six grand, fantasizing about an escape to the Territory which seems increasingly impossible of attainment. Huck would go to "the territory ahead of the rest." But that Territory is not a green continent accessible in space but a fleeting moment receding into a past now "Forty or Fifty Years Ago." By the time Huck got there, "the rest"—the Kings and Dukes, the Tom Sawyers, probably the Aunt Sallies—would soon be there in numbers to hail him and seek accommodation on the raft.

In such a world of balked hopes and tortured expectations, Miss Watson's deathbed decision to free Jim is singularly fitting. Even the suddenness, indeed the sportiveness, of its introduction in the text is appropriate to the pre–Civil War era when such emancipations were often afterthoughts, so to speak, all too infrequent, always tardy, and no doubt, like the Emanicipation of 1862, prompted in part by mixed motives. There is nothing careless, nor self-indulgent, about Twain's treatment of the incident in chapter 42. Good-natured Tom, returning to consciousness and (all hope) sanity, divulges the information instantly when he hears that Jim is in danger of being sold: Miss Watson was "ashamed" of her intent to sell Jim and "said so"; just before she died she "set him free in her will." However questionable her motives (they are usually questioned, though there is little evidence about them), these details are telling in a narration where declaring things in spoken speech, willed intentions, and the activity of writing are crucial matters, as they have become long before "yours truly," Huck Finn, stops the story that has become his epistle to the world for the simple reason that "there is nothing more to write about." The reality Huck summons up in the book includes the prose styles and other styles to which Huck, and "The Author" of the opening notice about dialects used in the book, so often draw attention: Pap's way of speaking; Tom's style of behavior, which Huck usually admires; fashions in poetry and painting at the Grangerfords' house, the "ignorantest kind of words and pictures"; charcoal graffiti, in the room where Pap's corpse is recognized by Jim in chapter 9. It includes the Doctor's "yarn," as Huck calls it, and the countless tales Huck tells during his trip down the river, to say nothing of the crucial incident to which I have already attached importance when Jim's saying, and the silent decision jointly made with Huck that it articulates, define at once Jim's moral heroism and his folly. The *virtu* if not the virtue of Tom's evasion scheme is, as Huck grudgingly says in chapter 34, that it will "make. . . talk," and making *talk*, or the illusion of it as Professor Richard Bridgman cautions us to say,[3] is important to Huck's and Twain's colloquial idiom.

More importantly the narrative proper opens with a bibliographical ploy that locates Huck as the figure in a book named *Tom Sawyer,* and in chapter 31 Huck's dramatic decisions—to turn Jim over to the authorities, then to tear up the letter in which he had articulated that first decision and to give over reforming—these decisions are made in a counterpoint of written and spoken speech. Whether genuine and durable or not, Huck's moral commitments are made not in severance from his civilization but in an entanglement, more properly an engagement, with its very foundation, namely language. He makes his first decision in an experiment with written language, then undoes it in an action that redeems, for brief moments, the Widow Douglas's injunction in chapter 3 to "help other people, and do every thing I could for other people, and look out for them all the time, and never think about myself." His famous declaration about going to hell, presumably spoken but like everything in the book inscribed in the print that issued from type fonts and presses, is made in the only moral vocabulary Huck has, which folds both the Sunday School or Revival Sermon vocabulary, and Huck's colloquial idiom, into the phrase "go to hell."

This conjunction of spoken speech, decision-making, and writing relates to Miss Watson's will in ways I shall return to presently. But another strikingly controlled notation about Miss Watson's deed—namely, that she did this "two months ago"—illuminates a peculiar resiliency in the prose style of *Huckleberry Finn* and intricacies in the temporal dimension of the narration that I should dwell on briefly. As for the matter of style, what I wish to insist on is that the ostensible "now" of the present tense in the book, and the ostensible "then" of the past tenses, enforce each other insofar as they can be distinguished in the prose, but that they virtually dissolve into each other without actually doing so, and that what Huck presents to us, perhaps obviously, is an act of memory that is sometimes identified explicitly as such in the phrasing.

The stance of *Huckleberry Finn* is that of direct address, careful and conscious, to both the subject and the reader. It places Huck in a continuous present, as we usually call it, before the reader. He talks to us at the opening, telling us in the "here and now" to look him up in the index to *Tom Sawyer,* and addresses us at the end, talking to us about what Tom is doing now and what he plans to do now, signing off as "yours truly" (his narration impulsively becomes epistolary) even after noting "the end." But Huck at times tells us that he is remembering things in a style that sustains the illusion of the "there

[3]Richard Bridgman, *The Colloquial Style in America* (New York: Oxford University Press, 1966), pp. 11, 20.

and then": "I can't ever get it out of my memory, the sight of them poor miserable girls and niggers" (chapter 27). The very illusion of remembering is rendered by the style, even when nothing is said explicitly about remembering. The rightfully famous description of Huck's father, Pap, in chapter 5 is not a sudden response, not the "first jolt" or shock in the so-called immediate present of Pap's ominous return, but a deliberate recapitulation, mounting in intensity, of Pap's appearance, composed on the basis of frequent confrontations and thoroughly digested, considered details: "He was most fifty, and he looked it. His hair was long and tangled and greasy, and hung down, and you could see his eyes shining through like he was behind vines. It was all black, no gray; so was his long, mixed-up whiskers. There warn't no color in his face, where his face showed; it was white; not like another man's white, but a white to make a body sick, a white to make a body's flesh crawl—a tree-toad white, a fish-belly white."

Huck's remembering includes repressed memories of things he refuses to enlarge upon and anticipations of the future: "It made me so sick I nearly fell out of the tree. I ain't agoing to tell all that happened—it would make me sick again, if I was to do that. I wished I hadn't ever come ashore that night to see such things. I ain't ever going to get shut of them—lots of times I dream about them" (chapter 18). Often the vividness of the present inheres in the act of telling or talking to us whereas the incidents spoken of take place in the past: "The way I lit out and shinned for the road in the dark there ain't nobody can tell"—there ain't nobody can tell "now" about the way he lit out back "then." To combine the effect of the vivid present and the remembered past Twain often uses one of the easiest displacements known in colloquial speech: "Well, when they was all gone the King he asks. . . ." (chapter 26) in which past and present tenses are interchangeable. In the famous and beautiful passage at the opening of chapter 19, where Huck in orderly fashion describes the combination of pleasure and apprehensiveness in life aboard the raft, what Huck "could" hypothetically see, what he "would" recurringly see each day, what he "maybe" detected in the sign-language of the river's surfaces, and what he does sense apprehensively as threats to his safety on this far from idyllic raft—these modes and tenses dissolve into each other: "We would watch the lonesomeness of the river, and kind of lazy along, and by-and-by lazy off to sleep. Wake up, by-and-by, and look to see what done it, and maybe see a steamboat, coughing along upstream. . . ." A few paragraphs later, just after invoking a sky "speckled with stars" and the darkness brightened by a "world of sparks" from a steamboat's chimneys: "Just as I was passing a place where a kind of cow-path crossed the crick, here comes a couple of men tearing up the path as tight as they could foot it." The King and Duke are about to ask for and be offered instant refuge on the raft.

The resilience of this style, which makes possible a vivid presentness in narration fueling a process of remembering, and which translates imperceptibly the counterpoint of telling and listening in a fictive present into shared recognition and reenactment of Huck's remembered past, heightens the significance of a feature we too often neglect in considering Twain's master-piece, namely that it is a historical novel that early draws attention to that fact. Huck's insistence that we refer for his provenance to the earlier book *Tom Sawyer* is in keeping with the cast back into the past that is launched on the title page: "Scene: The Mississippi Valley. Time: Forty to Fifty Years Ago." The future imperatives in the "Notice" to the reader posted by Twain's delegate the "Chief of Ordinance" ("persons attempting to find a plot in it will be shot"), and the note "Explanatory" about its dialects in the present tense signed by "The Author," are already governed by this extension of temporal perspective to encompass the movement back from 1885 to the decade straddling 1840. Whether or not Twain was indulging in the nostalgia that the novelist Wright Morris has found a threat to all American fiction,[4] in *Huckleberry Finn* the past of, say, 1840 stands in a troubled, strained relation with the writing of the book or its publication in 1885. "Forty to Fifty Years Ago" in effect defines a dilemma that is dramatized, in the narration, by the quite exact, seemingly gratuitous specification that Miss Watson's declaration of repentance and her liberation of Jim in her will took place "two months" ago. This fact does not belatedly skew the written structure of the book but buttresses the principles that constitute it. It brings 1885, in its relation to 1840, to the verge of discontinuity but sustains a perilous continuum in which "now" and "then," "now" and "again," both challenge and engage each other.[5]

Once Twain can be presumed to have stumbled or decided upon this feature of his denouement, he did not arrange a recent demise for Miss Watson, though her dying as recently as four or five weeks before the concluding episode would have provided Tom with the safety of legality he enjoys when perpetrating his evasion scheme, while making her death virtu-ally simultaneous with Huck's tearing up his letter to her, his decision not to inform on Jim. Instead, Twain's timing of her death assigns a priority in time to her words and deeds, her spoken declaration and her written will, which haunt the resolution of the novel, stir and agitate its rhythms. The priority of Miss Watson's will underscores the fact that Huck's bold and solemn decision was not to free Jim, in any tangible and full sense, but vaguely to protect him, that it was not as crucial as Huck had thought at the time or not crucial in ways he thought, that his decision was not as dangerous and courageous as it has seemed. Miss Watson's will gives the status of a ritual gesture to Huck's momentous decision, places at a distance the drama and urgency of Jim's legal fate, relegates to the past any opportunity to give Jim the freedom he deserves. Insofar as Miss Watson's written will is moved further back from the

---

[4]Morris argues the dangers of nostalgia in *The Territory Ahead* (New York: Harcourt, Brace, 1958), passim, but finds that what Huck lost "in the wilderness of his nostalgia" was recaptured by Twain "in this lucid moment of reminiscence and craft," p. 88.

[5]"Forty or Fifty Years Ago," the notation on the title page, places the action between 1835, the year of Twain's birth, and 1845. In chapter 40, Jim's determination to wait out a doctor for Tom even if it takes forty years would project the action ahead into the decade of 1875–1885, when Twain was writing the book.

closing episodes of Twain's denouement, it is removed too from the years in the 1870s and 1880s when Twain, who never freed a slave in his life, was ensconced in Hartford writing *Huckleberry Finn*. By seeming sportive and unexpected, and distant, Miss Watson's act enforces the sense of futility that deepens toward the end of *Huckleberry Finn*. The option to write out or inscribe Jim's legal freedom was Miss Watson's in 1840. Moreover the chance of setting a freed Negro free seems dim in chapters 42 and 43, with Jim in chains again, then freed suddenly to stand jobless and alone, with nothing but a meal, Tom's forty-dollar payment, and the prospect of a camping trip in the Territory with the boys to satisfy his dream of freedom in a promised land. Yet the task of redeeming Jim's legal freedom, fulfilling the promise that legal freedom makes possible, that unfinished business haunts and troubles the denouement of Twain's novel. The sequence of incidents that have come so near to nought in 1840 and stand so far back in time from 1885 in the temporal perspective of the book bring this historical fiction to the brink of irrelevance for the post–Civil War world. Yet precisely because it verges on irrelevance it speaks with all the more pointed relevance across the span of forty or fifty years in 1885 to define the task and impose the charge of setting a nation of freedmen free. The flukish fact of Jim's legal freedom, and the failure of his world to flesh it out with the family, the opportunities, and the community that would give it meaning, define with haunting and painful relevance, and with absurd precision, the problem of setting a free Negro free, which is the pressing problem, in all its extensions, in post–Civil War America and more recent decades.

In forging this timeliness from the receding past, accommodating the tensions between Tom's sportive fantasies and the somber realities they mirror in American society, or accommodating the tensions between the diverging dreams of freedom that are suspended in the comradeship of Jim and Huck, *Huckleberry Finn* becomes not so much a novel as a romance. In saying that I resort to a binary terminology I do not like, and particularly I would not want to imply that the book is any less novelistic in its textures and strategies for being a romance. What I have in mind are basic features of imaginative fiction that Henry James insisted were possible in either the so-called novel or the so-called romance but that are usually denominated by the latter term: the evocation of the "possible" and visionary rather than the "actual"; fiction's status as fiction, its daring, as Hawthorne defined the task of the romancer, to locate itself "on the utmost verge of a precipitous absurdity."[6] *Huckleberry Finn* generates and yields a vision, a possibility made real in language though not yet actualized in the behavior of Huck and Tom or Mark

    [6]James insisted that the best fiction, as in Zola, Scott, and Balzac, functions as both novel and romance, which are "different sorts and degrees" of the same fictive undertaking, in the New York Edition's preface to *The American* (New York: Charles Scribner's Sons, 1909). See *The Art of the Novel*, ed. Richard P. Blackmur (New York: Charles Scribner's Sons, 1934), p. 31. Hawthorne's statement appears in a letter of November 1850, quoted in James T. Fields, *Yesterdays with Authors* (1871; reprint ed., Boston: Houghton Mifflin, 1900), p. 56.

Twain on Asylum Hill in Hartford, nor in the relations generally of white, black, or brown people since. It creates a vision that would redeem the promise of Jim's legal freedom, would redeem the failed and failing effort to set a Negro free, and it sanctions the promise of that vision, makes it the moral imperative, the willed inscription, that governs this fiction. It does this by pushing all the fictive conventions it uses, including what we usually recognize as novelistic ones, to the limit, where they become a fully imaginative act. The very plausibility of its illusionistic representation—the fullness with which this plausibility is achieved in the river landscapes, the spruced-up domestic interiors or the dingy rooms aboard floating abandoned houses, the untidy yards of marginal farms, and above all the colloquial idiom of Huck and the other characters as well—the fully representational illusion that this book prints to us is a kind of fictive magic, a lie, which yields the *Adventures of Huckleberry Finn* and the vision burgeoning within it. It is all the more magical for seeming not to be, for seeming to concede priority to a reality independent of the imagination. And the text is haunted by the recognition of its status as fiction and of the moral hazards entailed in the enterprise of fiction. Indeed it is haunted by the implications of the particular narrative structure that Twain devised for his masterpiece.

Twain begins to play with the matter of lying fantasy on the first page when Huck wryly alludes to the intrusion of lies, or more cautiously "stretchers," in *The Adventures of Tom Sawyer.* Even earlier, faking it in the guise of a deputy "Chief of Ordinance," Twain has taken the preposterous stance of one who will banish and shoot misguided readers, the stance taken in chapter 2 by fancy-ridden Tom Sawyer, who declares that intruders on his gang "must be sued" and second offenders "must be killed." One paradigm for Twain's narration in the book is the episode where Huck and Jim make a decision in silence while Huck delegates to Jim the task of speaking it in words, and then Jim for them both engages in a flight of fancy that is an act at once of folly and of heroism, imagining for Tom a freedom from self that exceeds the facts. Twain, like Huck in this instance, remains ostensibly and actually silent throughout the narration—"Say it, Huck"—creating the lie that Huck speaks or writes the book that unfolds, word by printed word, in the silence of fiction before us.

Twain's narration, and the complicity in the world he projects that is revealed in his narrative form, are illuminated by a hilarious and profoundly revealing essay he wrote in 1882, "The Decay in the Art of Lying." There, addressing Hartford historians whom he said were masters of the art, he defined the lie as a "Virtue . . . , the fourth Grace, the Tenth Muse," and, declaring with guilty abandon that lying is an unavoidable "necessity of our circumstances," he called on all to "train ourselves to lie thoughtfully . . . , to lie for others' advantage, and not our own; to lie gracefully and graciously, not . . . clumsily . . . ," to lie not "with pusillanimous mien" but "firmly" without "being ashamed of our high calling." He defined one particular category of lie that has a particular bearing on *Huckleberry Finn:* the "silent lie," the "deception which one conveys by keeping still and concealing the truth," or what he called in another essay ("My First Lie and How I Got Out of It") the "lie of silent assertion."[7]

On such a "lie of silent assertion" depends the closing section of Twain's book which so disturbs us, when Tom Sawyer starts to blurt out the fact of Jim's emancipation but then smothers it in silence.[8] By his "lie of silent assertion" Tom is able to stage the rescue of Jim, which is so cruel and intended to be so entertaining: the "evasion" with its pretentions to righteousness, its tawdry melodrama, which produces the "raft of trouble" at the end; the fakery, and sport that debase Jim and then endanger Jim and Tom both; the "fun" that "makes talk" and that Huck, disguised as Tom, helps perpetrate; the folly that Twain exposes to the shame of our condemnation, Tomfoolishness indeed. Aunt Sally as well as Huck detects the absurdity of "setting a free nigger free." Twain could hardly have overlooked the fact that his own *Adventures* and their suspense are founded on the same silent lie. However much his art depended on improvisation, his improvisations were those of an expert performer who by the 1880s could anticipate the dubieties of fiction and the risks of his own methods. When revising his narrative and giving it the endorsement of his pseudonym, he knew the final shape it had taken. Miss Watson, around 1840, had legally freed Jim but neither Tom nor Twain had told readers so until the last minute.

Moreover it was Twain who stopped Tom in midsentence—"Say it, Tom"— and Twain it was, though with more complex motives than Tom's, who thought up the crude sport that is condemned in Tom, the "adventure" as Tom calls it to which Twain devoted so much of the *Adventures of Huckleberry Finn*. Twain's conscience is therefore stirred not only by the guilt he feels as a Tom Sawyerish, fish-belly white citizen who never freed a slave in his life, but by the lie he perpetrated in the very act of forming his fiction, holding to the logic of its suspense, founding its entertainment and its moral drama on Tom's crude sport and his "lie of silent assertion." As it approaches its completion, the fiction becomes fully confessional. *Mea culpa* (1840): Miss Watson's writing, not Tom Sawyer, not Mark Twain, freed the Negro Jim.

Huck Finn likewise, when he looks back and remembers the incident on the raft when he tore up the letter to Miss Watson, now knows that Jim has been freed. But to reenact the drama that constitutes his heroism, to re-create it in its vividness and moral urgency, Huck must in memory keep to the lie of silence. The very elemental form of the narration inescapably involves its

---

[7]Quotations are from *The Writings of Mark Twain*, Author's National Edition, 25 vols. (Hartford, Conn.: American, 1899–1907), 20:364–70, and 23:161.

[8]Comparable instances occur earlier but have no relation to the narrative structure of the book. In chapter 31 the Duke cuts off in midsentence his disclosure of Jim's whereabouts, but Huck already knows it. In chapter 27, during the Wilks affair, Huck keeps quiet about the King's fraudulent sale of the Wilks' slaves on the probably sanguine grounds that the fraud will be exposed and that "the niggers would be back home in a week or two."

narrator and its author in a fraud or lie and can be made a worthy or redeeming act only if the lie generates in language a vision, with its moral pressure, which extends beyond the facts of incident and warm companionship which the language presents. And the lie can be made to have that effect because the silence is not only a deception but an expressive form that yields concerns, recognitions, and aspirations beyond anything made explicit. The same willed silence that enables Tom and Twain to hide facts is an enabling form. The result is that chapter 31, rendering Huck's crucial decisions, burgeons with a pressure of moral urgency and commitment which most of us have felt but which exceeds anything actually true of Huck's behavior before or since. The actuality of Huck's feelings and behavior since leaving the river, as occasionally on it, have fallen short of the vision presented in this chapter. Indeed the very chapter dramatizes also Huck's lapse into passivity, vague protestations and improvisations, and neglect of Jim that are so conspicuous later. All Huck literally does is to perform an essentially negative act, deciding not to disclose Jim's whereabouts. One of the most terrifying moments in the book, coming directly after Huck tears up his letter to Miss Watson, occurs when Huck's grief-stricken tribute to Jim takes the form of claiming that he, rather than the King or Duke, *owns* Jim. Buried in the lie of silent assertion, hidden or muted but expressed in the silence, is the recognition that Huck has not the power to free Jim, that his act at best postpones the question of how to help Jim gain his dream of freedom. Yet when Huck recalls the incident of writing and tearing up his letter and the experience of making his decision, the deeds become something more, owing to the pressure of Twain's silent guilt, which is all the stronger for remaining tacit, repressed or compressed within the lie of silence. That pressure enforces the pressure of commitment afterward in memory, which commemorates the decision made earlier on the river and strains to make Huck's tribute to Jim the governing vision of Huck's adventure. It becomes the willed commitment to a liberation never made explicit, a fulfillment enacted only in the voiced cadences of Huck's spoken, Twain's written, speech. Created in the lie is the will to make the action convincingly seem, and in the language to be, a commitment of the moral imagination beyond what Twain knows it was then in fact. *Mea culpa* (1885): Jim and all fellow creatures should be, but are not yet, free. Huck's lie like Tom's will be a lie but it must be a better lie than his. Huck's lie must not only hide a fact but generate a vision. The lie must be suspenseful and dramatic like Tom's, and, just as Tom's will dramatize his petty ingenuity and show of valor, Huck's must dramatize his own flawed heroism. But Huck's drama must survive, in the durable rhythm of human speech, Huck's own later betrayals of Jim on the Phelps farm. Huck's lying words must be better prose than Tom's. In sum, Huck's idiom and drama must have better style. And they do, notably in chapter 31, where Huck makes his famous decision. The section opens with words whose recurring "I" sounds identify the protagonist of the drama and the high pitch of intensity to which his colloquial instrument is tuned:

So I was full of trouble, full as I could be; and didn't know what to do. At last I had
an idea; and I says, I'll go and write the letter—and *then* see if I can pray. Why, it
was astonishing, the way I felt as light as a feather, right straight off, and my
troubles all gone. So I got a piece of paper and a pencil, all glad and excited, and
set down and wrote:

That paragraph is followed by one of the most efficient letters in English.
Huck says that he tore it up, but it appears, usually without so much as a
crease or a hyphen, in every copy of the book, defining now and again, then
and still, the imminence of Jim's betrayals:

> Miss Watson your runaway nigger Jim is down here two mile below Pikesville and
> Mr. Phelps has got him and he will give him up for the reward if you send.—Huck
> Finn.

The letter is followed by a long paragraph in which the conjunction "and," the
word "time," and the floating "ing's" of present participles recapture what
Huck has before betrayed and will betray again but commemorates in the
"now" of memory:

> I felt good and all washed clean of sin for the first time I had ever felt so in my
> life, and I knowed I could pray now. But I didn't do it straight off, but laid the
> paper down and set there thinking—thinking how good it was all this happened so,
> and how near I came to being lost and going to hell. And went on thinking. And got
> to thinking over our trip down the river; and I see Jim before me, all the time, in
> the day, and in the nighttime, sometimes moonlight, sometimes storms, and we a
> floating along, talking, and singing, and laughing. But somehow I couldn't seem to
> strike no places to harden me against him, but only the other kind. I'd see him
> standing my watch on top of his'n, instead of calling me, so I could go on sleeping;
> and see him how glad he was when I come back out of the fog; and when I come to
> him again in the swamp, up there where the feud was; and such like times; and
> would always call me honey, and pet me, and do everything he could think of for
> me, and how good he always was; and at last I struck the time I saved him by
> telling the men we had small-pox aboard, and he was so grateful, and said I was the
> best friend old Jim ever had in the world, and the *only* one he's got now; and then I
> happened to look around, and see that paper.

Taut, brief sentences, with clipped "t" sounds and "x's," then define the final
crisis:

> It was a close place. I took it up and held it in my hand. I was a trembling, because
> I'd got to decide, forever, betwixt two things, and I knowed it. I studied a minute,
> sort of holding my breath, and then says to myself:
> "All right, then, I'll *go* to hell"—and tore it up.
> It was awful thoughts, and awful words, but they was said. And I let them stay
> said; and never thought no more about reforming.

And so *Huckleberry Finn* got banned by fish-belly whites in Concord,
Massachusetts, where there are or were people skinned in white who do not
want their children to know about young Huck Finn, his forged integrity, his
charged language and grammatical errors, and the vision burgeoning in his

ripe adolescence. And the book more recently has been forced off the required reading lists in New York City, at the University of Massachusetts, and in Deland, Florida, at the insistence of collegians skinned in black who do not see, created in the antics of the Negro Jim, the aspirations of a people and the stature of a man. And we, with our fool imaginations, carry the burden of this lying fiction still as we translate it in our rereadings of it, moved in imaginings if not in undoubted deeds, to set these freedoms free.

Huck, Jim, and American
Racial Discourse

David L. Smith

They [blacks] are at least as brave, and more adventuresome [compared with whites]. But this may perhaps proceed from a want of forethought, which prevents their seeing a danger till it be present. . . . They are more ardent after their female: but love seems with them to be more an eager desire, than a tender delicate mixture of sentiment and sensation. Their griefs are transient. Those numberless afflictions, which render it doubtful whether heaven has given life to us in mercy or in wrath, are less felt, and sooner forgotten with them. In general, their existence appears to participate more of sensation than reflection. To this must be ascribed their disposition to sleep when abstracted from their diversions, and unemployed in labor.

—Thomas Jefferson, *Notes on the State of Virginia*

Almost any Euro-American intellectual of the nineteenth century could have written the preceding words. The notion of Negro inferiority was so deeply pervasive among those heirs of "The Enlightenment" that the categories and even the vocabulary of Negro inferiority were formalized into a tedious, unmodulated litany. This uniformity increased rather than diminished during the course of the century. As Leon Litwack and others have shown, even the abolitionists, who actively opposed slavery, frequently regarded blacks as inherently inferior. This helps to explain the widespread popularity of colonization schemes among abolitionists and other liberals.[1] As for Jefferson, it is not surprising that he held such ideas, but it is impressive

Reprinted from *Mark Twain Journal* 22:2 (1984), 4–12. (This essay has also appeared in *Satire and Evasion?: Black Perspectives on Huckleberry Finn*, ed. James S. Leonard, Thomas A. Tenney, and Thadious M. Davis [Durham, NC: Duke University Press, 1992], pp. 103–20.) By permission of *Mark Twain Journal*.

[1]The literature on the abolition movement and on antebellum debates regarding the Negro is, of course, voluminous. George M. Fredrickson's excellent *The Black Image in the White Mind* (New York: Harper Torchbooks, 1971) is perhaps the best general work of its kind. Fredrickson's *The Inner Civil War* (New York: Harper Torchbooks, 1971) is also valuable, especially pp. 53–64. Leon Litwack, in *North of Slavery* (Chicago: U of Chicago P, 1961) 214–46, closely examines the ambivalence of abolitionists regarding racial intermingling. Benjamin Quarles presents the most detailed examination of black abolitionists in *Black Abolitionists* (New York: Oxford UP, 1969), although Vincent Harding offers a more vivid (and overtly polemical) account of their relationships to white abolitionists; see *There Is a River* (New York: Harcourt, Brace, Jovanovich, 1981).

that he formulated so clearly at the end of the eighteenth century what would become the dominant view of the Negro in the nineteenth century. In many ways this father of American democracy—and quite possibly of five mulatto children—was a man of his time and ahead of his time.

In July 1876, exactly one century after the American Declaration of Independence, Mark Twain began writing *Adventures of Huckleberry Finn*, a novel that illustrates trenchantly the social limitations that American "civilization" imposes on individual freedom.[2] The book takes special note of ways in which racism impinges upon the lives of Afro-Americans, even when they are legally "free." It is therefore ironic that *Huckleberry Finn* has often been attacked and even censored as a racist work. I would argue, on the contrary, that except for Melville's work, *Huckleberry Finn* is without peer among major Euro-American novels for its explicitly antiracist stance. Those who brand the book racist generally do so without having considered the specific form of racial discourse to which the novel responds. Furthermore, *Huckleberry Finn* offers much more than the typical liberal defenses of "human dignity" and protests against cruelty. Though it contains some such elements, it is more fundamentally a critique of those socially constituted fictions—most notably romanticism, religion, and the concept of "the Negro"—which serve to justify and disguise selfish, cruel, and exploitative behavior.

When I speak of "racial discourse," I mean more than simply attitudes about race or conventions of talking about race. Most importantly, I mean that race itself is a discursive formation which delimits social relations on the basis of alleged physical differences.[3] "Race" is a strategy for relegating a segment of the population to a permanent inferior status. It functions by insisting that each "race" has specific, definitive, inherent behavioral tendencies and capacities which distinguish it from other races. Though scientifically specious, race has been powerfully effective as an ideology and as a form of social definition that serves the interests of Euro-American hegemony. In America, race has been deployed against numerous groups, including Native Americans, Jews, Asians, and even—for brief periods—an assortment of European immigrants.

For obvious reasons, however, the primary emphasis historically has been on defining "the Negro" as a deviant from Euro-American norms. "Race" in

---

[2]For dates of composition, see Walter Blair, "When Was *Huckleberry Finn* Written?" *American Literature* 30 (Mar. 1958): 1–25.

[3]My use of "racial discourse" has some affinities to Foucault's conception of "discourse." This is not, however, a strictly Foucaultian reading. I prefer an account of power which allows for a consideration of interest and hegemony. Theorists such as Marshall Berman, *All That Is Solid Melts into Air* (New York: Simon & Schuster, 1982) 34–35, and Catherine A. MacKinnon, "Feminism, Marxism, Method, and the State: An Agenda for Theory," *Signs* 7.3 (1982): 526, have indicated similar reservations. However, Frank Lentricchia ("Reading Foucault [Punishment, Labor, Resistance]," *Raritan* 1.4 [1981]: 5–32; 2.1 [1982]: 41–70) has made a provocative effort to modify Foucaultian analysis, drawing upon Antonio Gramsci's analysis of hegemony in *Selections from the Prison Notebooks* (New York: International Publishers, 1971). See Foucault, *The Archaeology of Knowledge*, *Power/Knowledge*, ed. Colin Gordon (New York: Pantheon, 1980) esp. 92–108; and *The History of Sexuality*, vol. 1 (New York: Vintage, 1980) esp. 92–102.

America means white supremacy and black inferiority,[4] and "the Negro," a socially constituted fiction, is a generalized, one-dimensional surrogate for the historical reality of Afro-American people. It is this reified fiction that Twain attacks in *Huckleberry Finn*.

Twain adopts a strategy of subversion in his attack on race. That is, he focuses on a number of commonplaces associated with "the Negro" and then systematically dramatizes their inadequacy. He uses the term "nigger," and he shows Jim engaging in superstitious behavior. Yet he portrays Jim as a compassionate, shrewd, thoughtful, self-sacrificing, and even wise man. Indeed, his portrayal of Jim contradicts every claim presented in Jefferson's description of "the Negro." Jim is cautious, he gives excellent advice, he suffers persistent anguish over separation from his wife and children, and he even sacrifices his own sleep so that Huck may rest. Jim, in short, exhibits all the qualities that "the Negro" supposedly lacks. Twain's conclusions do more than merely subvert the justifications of slavery, which was already long since abolished. Twain began his book during the final disintegration of Reconstruction, and his satire on antebellum southern bigotry is also an implicit response to the Negrophobic climate of the post-Reconstruction era.[5] It is troubling, therefore, that so many readers have completely misunderstood Twain's subtle attack on racism.

Twain's use of the term "nigger" has provoked some readers to reject the novel.[6] As one of the most offensive words in our vocabulary, "nigger" remains heavily shrouded in taboo. A careful assessment of this term within the context of American racial discourse, however, will allow us to understand the particular way in which the author uses it. If we attend closely to Twain's use of the word, we may find in it not just a trigger to outrage but, more important, a means of understanding the precise nature of American racism and Mark Twain's attack on it.

Most obviously, Twain uses "nigger" throughout the book as a synonym for "slave." There is ample evidence from other sources that this corresponds to one usage common during the antebellum period. We first encounter it in

[4]This is not to discount the sufferings of other groups. But historically, the philosophical basis of Western racial discourse—which existed even before the European "discovery" of America—has been the equation of "good" and "evil" with light and darkness (or white and black). See Jacques Derrida, "White Mythology," *New Literary History* 6 (1974): 5–74; Winthrop Jordan, *White over Black* (New York: Norton, 1968) 1–40; and Cornel West, *Prophesy Deliverance* (Philadelphia: Westminster P, 1982) 47–65. Economically, the slave trade, chattel slavery, agricultural peonage, and color-coded wage differentials have made the exploitation of African Americans the most profitable form of racism.

[5]See Lawrence I. Berkove, "The Free Man of Color in *The Gradissimes* and Works by Harris and Mark Twain," *Southern Quarterly* 18.4 (1981): 60–73; Richard Gollin and Rita Gollin, "*Huckleberry Finn* and the Time of Evasion," *Modern Language Studies* 9 (Spring 1979): 5–15; Michael Egan, *Mark Twain's Huckleberry Finn: Race, Class and Society* (Atlantic Highlands, N.J.: Humanities P, 1977) esp. 66–102.

[6]See Nat Hentoff's series of four columns in the *Village Voice* 27 (1982): "Huck Finn Better Get out of Town by Sundown" (May 4); "Is Any Book Worth the Humiliation of Our Kids?" (May 11); "Huck Finn and the Shortchanging of Black Kids" (May 18); and "These Are Little Battles Fought in Remote Places" (May 25).

reference to "Miss Watson's big nigger, named Jim" (chap. 2). This usage, like the term "nigger stealer," clearly designates the "nigger" as an item of property: a commodity, a slave. This passage also provides the only apparent textual justification for the common critical practice of labeling Jim "Nigger Jim," as if "nigger" were a part of his proper name. This loathsome habit goes back at least as far as Albert Bigelow Paine's biography of Twain (1912).[7] In any case, "nigger" in this sense connotes an inferior, even subhuman, creature who is properly owned by and subservient to Euro-Americans.

Both Huck and Jim use the word in this sense. For example, when Huck fabricates his tale about the riverboat accident, the following exchange occurs between him and Aunt Sally:

> "Good gracious! anybody hurt?"
> "No'm. Killed a nigger."
> "Well, it's lucky; because sometimes people do get hurt." (Chap. 32)

Huck has never met Aunt Sally prior to this scene, and in spinning a lie which this stranger will find unobjectionable, he correctly assumes that the common notion of Negro subhumanity will be appropriate. Huck's offhand remark is intended to exploit Aunt Sally's attitudes, not to express Huck's own. A nigger, Aunt Sally confirms, is not a person. Yet this exchange is hilarious precisely because we know that Huck is playing on her glib and conventional bigotry. We know that Huck's relationship to Jim has already invalidated for him such obtuse racial notions. The conception of the "nigger" is a socially constituted and sanctioned fiction, and it is just as false and absurd as Huck's explicit fabrication, which Aunt Sally also swallows whole.

In fact, the exchange between Huck and Aunt Sally reveals a great deal about how racial discourse operates. Its function is to promulgate a conception of "the Negro" as a subhuman and expendable creature who is by definition feeble-minded, immoral, lazy, and superstitious. One crucial purpose of this social fiction is to justify the abuse and exploitation of Afro-American people by substituting the essentialist fiction of "Negroism" for the actual character of individual Afro-Americans. Hence, in racial discourse every Afro-American becomes just another instance of "the Negro"—just another "nigger." Twain recognizes this invidious tendency of race thinking, however, and he takes every opportunity to expose the mismatch between racial abstractions and real human beings.

For example, when Pap drunkenly inveighs against the free mulatto from Ohio, he is outraged by what appears to him to be a crime against natural laws (chap. 6). In the first place, a "free nigger" is, for Pap, a contradiction in terms. Indeed, the man's clothes, his demeanor, his education, his profession, and even his silver-headed cane bespeak a social status normally achieved by only a small elite of white men. He is, in other words, a "nigger" who refuses to behave like one. Pap's ludicrous protestations discredit both himself and

[7]*Mark Twain: A Biography* (New York: Harper, 1912).

other believers in "the Negro," as many critics have noted. But it has not been sufficiently stressed that Pap's racial views correspond very closely to those of most of his white southern contemporaries, in substance if not in manner of expression. Such views were held not only by poor whites but by all "right-thinking" southerners, regardless of their social class. Indeed, not even the traumas of the Civil War could cure southerners of this folly. Furthermore, Pap's indignation at the Negro's right to vote is precisely analogous to the southern backlash against the enfranchisement of Afro-Americans during Reconstruction. Finally, Pap's comments are rather mild compared with the anti-Negro diatribes that were beginning to emerge among politicians even as Twain was writing *Huckleberry Finn*. He began writing this novel during the final days of Reconstruction, and it seems more than reasonable to assume that the shameful white supremacist bluster of that epoch—exemplified by Pap's tirade—informed Twain's critique of racism in *Huckleberry Finn*.[8]

Pap's final description of this Ohio gentleman as "a prowling, thieving, infernal, white-shirted free nigger" (chap. 6) almost totally contradicts his previous description of the man as a proud, elegant, dignified figure. Yet this contradiction is perfectly consistent with Pap's need to reassert "the Negro" in lieu of social reality. Despite the vulgarity of Pap's personal character, his thinking about race is highly conventional, and therefore respectable. But most of us cannot respect Pap's views, and when we reject them, we reject the standard racial discourse of both 1840 and 1880.

A reader who objects to the word "nigger" might still insist that Twain could have avoided using it. But it is difficult to imagine how Twain could have debunked a discourse without using the specific terms of that discourse. Even when Twain was writing his book, "nigger" was universally recognized as an insulting, demeaning word. According to Stuart Berg Flexner, "Negro" was generally pronounced "nigger" until about 1825, at which time abolitionists began objecting to that term.[9] They preferred "colored person" or "person of color." Hence, W. E. B. Du Bois reports that some black abolitionists of the early 1830s declared themselves united "as men, . . . not as slaves; as 'people of color,' not as 'Negroes.'"[10] Writing a generation later in *Army Life in a Black Regiment* (1869), Thomas Wentworth Higginson deplored the common use of "nigger" among freedmen, which he regarded as evidence of low self-esteem.[11] The objections to "nigger," then, are not a consequence of the modern sensibility but had been common for a half century before *Huckleberry Finn* was published. The specific function of this term in the book, however, is neither to offend nor merely to provide linguistic authenticity. Much more importantly, it establishes a context against which Jim's specific virtues may emerge as explicit refutations of racist presuppositions.

8See Arthur G. Pettit, *Mark Twain and the South* (Lexington: U of Kentucky P, 1974).

9*I Hear America Talking* (New York: Van Nostrand Reinhold, 1976) 57.

10*The Souls of Black Folk*, in *Three Negro Classics*, ed. John Hope Franklin (New York: Avon, 1965) 245.

11(Boston: Beacon, 1962) 28.

Of course, the concept of "nigger" entails far more than just the deployment of certain vocabulary. Most of the attacks on the book focus on its alleged perpetuation of racial stereotypes. Twain does indeed use racial stereotypes here. That practice could be excused as characteristic of the genre of humor within which Twain works. Frontier humor relies upon the use of stock types, and consequently racial stereotypes are just one of many types present in *Huckleberry Finn*. Yet while valid, such an appeal to generic convention would be unsatisfactory because it would deny Twain the credit he deserves for the sophistication of his perceptions.[12]

As a serious critic of American society, Twain recognized that racial discourse depends upon the deployment of a system of stereotypes which constitute "the Negro" as fundamentally different from and inferior to Euro-Americans. As with his handling of "nigger," Twain's strategy with racial stereotypes is to elaborate them in order to undermine them. To be sure, those critics are correct who have argued that Twain uses this narrative to reveal Jim's humanity. Jim, however, is just one individual. Twain uses the narrative to expose the cruelty and hollowness of that racial discourse which exists only to obscure the humanity of *all* Afro-American people.

One aspect of *Huckleberry Finn* that has elicited copious critical commentary is Twain's use of superstition.[13] In nineteenth-century racial discourse, "the Negro" was always defined as inherently superstitious.[14] Many critics, therefore, have cited Jim's superstitious behavior as an instance of negative stereotyping. One cannot deny that in this respect Jim closely resembles the entire tradition of comic darkies,[15] but in some instances apparent similarities conceal fundamental differences. The issue is: does Twain merely reiterate clichés, or does he use these conventional patterns to make an unconventional point? A close examination will show that, in virtually every instance, Twain uses Jim's superstition to make points that undermine rather than revalidate the dominant racial discourse.

The first incident of this superstitious behavior occurs in chapter 2, as a result of one of Tom Sawyer's pranks. When Jim falls asleep under a tree, Tom hangs Jim's hat on a branch. Subsequently Jim concocts an elaborate tale about having been hexed and ridden by witches. The tale grows more

---

[12]See Ralph Ellison, "Changing the Jock and Slip the Yoke," in *Shadow and Act* (New York: Random House, 1964) 45–59; Chadwick Hansen, "The Character of Jim and the Ending of *Huckleberry Finn*," *Massachusetts Review* 5 (Autumn 1963): 45–66; Kenneth S. Lynn, *Mark Twain and Southwestern Humor* (Boston: Little, Brown, 1959).

[13]See especially Daniel Hoffman, "Jim's Magic: Black or White?" *American Literature* 32 (Mar. 1960): 47–54.

[14]Even the allegedly scientific works on the Negro focused on superstition as a definitive trait. See, for example, W. D. Weatherford, *Negro Life in the South* (New York: Young Men's Christian Association P, 1910); and Jerome Dowd, *Negro Races* (New York: Macmillan, 1907). No one has commented more scathingly on Negro superstitions than William Hannibal Thomas in *The American Negro* (1901; New York: Negro Universities P, 1969); by American definitions he was himself a Negro.

[15]See Fredrick Woodard and Donnarae MacCann, "*Huckleberry Finn* and the Traditions of Blackface Minstrelsy," *Interracial Books for Children Bulletin* 15.1–2 (1984): 4–13.

grandiose with each repetition, and eventually Jim becomes a local celebrity, sporting a five-cent piece on a string around his neck as a talisman. "Niggers would come miles to hear Jim tell about it, and he was more looked up to than any nigger in that country," the narrator reports. Jim's celebrity finally reaches the point that "Jim was most ruined, for a servant, because he got so stuck up on account of having seen the devil and been rode by witches." That is, no doubt, amusing. Yet whether Jim believes his own tale or not—and the "superstitious Negro" thesis requires us to assume that he does—the fact remains that Jim clearly benefits from becoming more a celebrity and less a "servant." It is his owner, not Jim, who suffers when Jim reduces the amount of his uncompensated labor.[16]

This incident has often been interpreted as an example of risible Negro gullibility and ignorance as exemplified by blackface minstrelsy. Such a reading has more than a little validity, but it can only partially account for the implications of this scene. If not for the final sentence, such an account might seem wholly satisfactory, but the information that Jim becomes, through his own story telling, unsuited for life as a slave introduces unexpected complications. Is it likely that Jim has been deceived by his own creative prevarications—especially given what we learn about his character subsequently? Or has he cleverly exploited the conventions of "Negro superstition" in order to turn a silly boy's prank to his own advantage?

Regardless of whether we credit Jim with forethought in this matter, it is undeniable that he turns Tom's attempt to humiliate him into a major personal triumph. In other words, Tom gives him an inch, and he takes an ell. It is also obvious that he does so by exercising remarkable skills as a rhetorician. By constructing a fictitious narrative of his own experience, Jim elevates himself above his prescribed station in life. By becoming, in effect, an author, Jim writes himself a new destiny. Jim's triumph may appear to be dependent upon the gullibility of other "superstitious" Negroes, but since we have no direct encounter with them, we cannot know whether they are unwitting victims of Jim's ruse or not. A willing audience need not be a totally credulous one. In any case, it is intelligence, not stupidity, that facilitates Jim's triumph. Tom may have had his chuckle, but the last laugh clearly belongs to Jim. . . .

In another instance of explicitly superstitious behavior, Jim uses a hair ball to tell Huck's fortune. One may regard this scene as a comical example of Negro ignorance and credulity, acting in concert with the ignorance and credulity of a fourteen-year-old white boy. That reading would allow one an unambiguous laugh at Jim's expense. If one examines the scene carefully, however, the inadequacy of such a reductive reading becomes apparent. Even if Jim does believe in the supernatural powers of this hair ball, the fact remains that most of the transaction depends upon Jim's quick wits. The

---

[16]Daniel Hoffman, in *Form and Fable in American Fiction* (New York: Oxford UP, 1961), reveals an implicit understanding of Jim's creativity, but he does not pursue the point in detail (331).

soothsaying aside, much of the exchange between Huck and Jim is an exercise in wily and understated economic bartering. In essence, Jim wants to be paid for his services, while Huck wants free advice. Jim insists that the hair ball will not speak without being paid. Huck, who has a dollar, will only admit to having a counterfeit quarter. Jim responds by pretending to be in collusion with Huck. He explains how to doctor the quarter so that "anybody in town would take it in a minute, let alone a hair-ball" (chap. 4). But obviously it is not the hair ball that will benefit from acquiring and spending this counterfeit coin.[17]

In this transaction, Jim serves his own interest while appearing to serve Huck's interest. He takes a slug which is worthless to Huck, and through the alchemy of his own cleverness contrives to make it worth twenty-five cents to himself. That, in antebellum America, is not a bad price for telling a fortune. But more important, Twain shows Jim self-consciously subverting the pre-scribed definition of "the Negro," even as he performs within the limitations of that role. He remains the conventional "Negro" by giving the white boy what he wants, at no real cost, and by consistently appearing to be passive and subservient to the desires of Huck and the hair ball. But in fact, he serves his own interests all along. Such resourcefulness is hardly consistent with the familiar one-dimensional concept of "the superstitious Negro."

And while Jim's reading is formulaic, it is hardly simpleminded. He sees the world as a kind of Manichean universe, in which forces of light and darkness—white and black—vie for dominance. Pap, he says, is uncertain what to do, torn between his white and black angels. Jim's advice, "to res' easy en let de ole man take his own way" (chap. 4), turns out to be good advice, because Huck enjoys life in the cabin, despite Pap's fits of drunken excess. This mixture of pleasure and pain is precisely what Jim predicts. Admittedly, Jim's conceptual framework is not original. Nonetheless, his reading carries considerable force because it corresponds so neatly to the dominant thematic patterns in this book, and, more broadly, to the sort of dualistic thinking that informs much of Twain's work. (To take an obvious example, consider the role reversals and character contrasts in *Pudd'nhead Wilson* or *The Prince and the Pauper*.) And most immediately, Jim's comments here reflect tellingly upon his situation as a black slave in racist America. The slave's fate is always torn between his master's will and his own.

In this reading and other incidents, Jim emerges as an astute and sensitive observer of human behavior, both in his comments regarding Pap and in his subtle remarks to Huck. Jim clearly possesses a subtlety and intelligence which "the Negro" allegedly lacks. Twain makes this point more clearly in the debate scene in chapter 14. True enough, most of this debate is, as several critics have noted, conventional minstrel-show banter. Nevertheless, Jim demonstrates impressive reasoning abilities, despite his factual ignorance. For

---

[17]See Thomas Weaver and Merline Williams, "Mark Twain's Jim: Identity as an Index to Cultural Attitudes," *American Literary Realism* 13 (Spring 1980): 19–30.

instance, in their argument over "Poly-voo-franzy," Huck makes a category error by implying that the difference between languages is analogous to the difference between human language and cat language. While Jim's response— that a man should talk like a man—betrays his ignorance of cultural diversity, his argument is otherwise perceptive and structurally sound. The humor in Huck's conclusion, "you can't learn a nigger to argue," arises precisely from our recognition that Jim's argument is better than Huck's.

Throughout the novel Twain presents Jim in ways which render ludicrous the conventional wisdom about "Negro character." As an intelligent, sensitive, wily, and considerate individual, Jim demonstrates that race provides no useful index of character. While that point may seem obvious to contemporary readers, it is a point rarely made by nineteenth-century Euro-American novelists. Indeed, except for Melville, J. W. DeForest, Albion Tourgée, and George Washington Cable, white novelists virtually always portrayed Afro-American characters as exemplifications of "Negroness." In this regard the twentieth century has been little better. By presenting us with a series of glimpses which penetrate the "Negro" exterior and reveal the person beneath it, Twain debunks American racial discourse. For racial discourse maintains that the "Negro" exterior is all that a Negro really has.

This insight in itself is a notable accomplishment. Twain, however, did not view racism as an isolated phenomenon, and his effort to place racism within the context of other cultural traditions produced the most problematic aspect of his novel. For it is in the final chapters—the Tom Sawyer section—which most critics consider the weakest part of the book, that Twain links his criticisms of slavery and southern romanticism, condemning the cruelties that both of these traditions entail.[18] Critics have objected to these chapters on various grounds. Some of the most common are that Jim becomes reduced to a comic darky,[19] that Tom's antics undermine the seriousness of the novel, and that these burlesque narrative developments destroy the structural integrity of the novel. Most critics see this conclusion as an evasion of the difficult issues the novel has raised. There is no space here for a discussion of the structural issues, but it seems to me that as a critique of American racial discourse, these concluding chapters offer a harsh, coherent, and uncompromising indictment.

Tom Sawyer's absurd scheme to "rescue" Jim offends because the section has begun with Huck's justly celebrated crisis of conscience culminating in his resolve to free Jim, even if doing so condemns him to hell. The passage that leads to Huck's decision, familiar as it is, merits reexamination:

> I'd see him standing my watch on top of his'n—stead of calling me, so I could go on
> sleeping; and see him how glad he was when I come back out of the fog; and when

18See Lynn Altenbernd, "Huck Finn, Emancipator," *Criticism* 1 (1959): 298–307.

19See, for example, Leo Marx, "Mr. Eliot, Mr. Trilling, and *Huckleberry Finn*," *American Scholar* 22 (Autumn 1953): 423–40; and Neil Schmitz, "Twain, *Huckleberry Finn*, and the Reconstruction," *American Studies* 12 (Spring 1971): 59–67.

I come to him again in the swamp, up there where the feud was; and such-like times; and would always call me honey, and pet me, and do everything he could think of for me, and how good he always was; and at last I struck the time I saved him by telling the men we had small-pox aboard, and he was so grateful, and said I was the best friend old Jim ever had in the world, and the *only* one he's got now; and then I happened to look around, and see that paper. . . . I studied a minute, sort of holding my breath, and then says to myself: "All right, then, I'll *go* to hell"—and tore it up. (Chap. 31)

The issue here is not just whether or not Huck should return a fugitive slave to its lawful owner. More fundamentally, Huck must decide whether to accept the conventional wisdom, which defines "Negroes" as subhuman commodities, or the evidence of his own experience, which has shown Jim to be a good and kind man and a true friend.

Huck makes what is obviously the morally correct decision, but his doing so represents more than simply a liberal choice of conscience over social convention. Twain explicitly makes Huck's choice a sharp attack on the southern church. Huck scolds himself: "There was the Sunday school, you could a gone to it; and if you'd a done it they'd a learnt you, there, that people that acts as I'd been acting about that nigger goes to everlasting fire" (chap. 31). Yet despite Huck's anxiety, he transcends the moral limitations of his time and place. By the time Twain wrote these words, more than twenty years of national strife, including the Civil War and Reconstruction, had established Huck's conclusion regarding slavery as a dominant national consensus; not even reactionary southerners advocated a reinstitution of slavery. But since the pre–Civil War southern church taught that slavery was God's will, Huck's decision flatly repudiates the church's teachings regarding slavery. And implicitly, it also repudiates the church as an institution by suggesting that the church functions to undermine, not to encourage, a reliance on one's conscience. To define "Negroes" as subhuman removes them from moral consideration and therefore justifies their callous exploitation. This view of religion is consistent with the cynical iconoclasm that Twain expressed in *Letters from the Earth* and other "dark" works.[20]

In this context, Tom Sawyer appears to us as a superficially charming but fundamentally distasteful interloper. His actions are governed not by conscience but rather by romantic conventions and literary "authorities." Indeed, while Tom may appear to be a kind of renegade, he is in essence thoroughly conventional in his values and proclivities. Despite all his boyish pranks, Tom represents a kind of solid respectability—a younger version of the southern gentleman as exemplified by the Grangerfords and Shepherdsons.[21] Hence, when Tom proposes to help Huck steal Jim, Huck laments that "Tom Sawyer

---

[20]A number of critical works comment on Twain's religious views and the relation between his critiques of religion and racism. See Allison Ensor, *Mark Twain and the Bible* (Lexington: U of Kentucky P, 1969); Arthur G. Pettit, "Mark Twain and the Negro, 1867–1869," *Journal of Negro History* 56 (Apr. 1971): 88–96; and Gollin and Gollin 5–15.

[21]See Hoffman, *Form and Fable* 327–28.

fell, considerable, in my estimation. Only I couldn't believe it. Tom Sawyer a *nigger stealer!*" (chap. 33). Such liberating activity is proper for Huck, who is not respectable, but not for Tom, who is. As with the previous example, however, this one implies a deep criticism of the status quo. Huck's act of conscience, which most of us now (and in Twain's own time) would endorse, is possible only for an outsider. This hardly speaks well for the moral integrity of southern (or American) "civilization."

To examine Tom's role in the novel, let us begin at the end. Upon learning of the failed escape attempt and Jim's recapture, Tom cries out, self-righteously: "Turn him loose! he ain't no slave; he's as free as any cretur that walks this earth!" (chap. 42). Tom has known all along that his cruel and ludicrous scheme to rescue the captured "prisoner" was being enacted upon a free man; and indeed, only his silence regarding Jim's status allowed the scheme to proceed with Jim's cooperation. Certainly, neither Huck nor Jim would otherwise have indulged Tom's foolishness. Tom's gratuitous cruelty here in the pursuit of his own amusement corresponds to his less vicious prank against Jim in chapter 2. And just as before, Twain converts Tom's callous mischief into a personal triumph for Jim.

Not only has Jim suffered patiently, which would, in truth, represent a doubtful virtue (Jim is not Uncle Tom); he demonstrates his moral superiority by surrendering himself in order to assist the doctor in treating his wounded tormentor. This is hardly the behavior one would expect from a commodity, and it is *precisely* Jim's status—man or chattel—that has been fundamentally at issue throughout the novel. It may be true that the lengthy account of Tom's juvenile antics subverts the tone of the novel, but they also provide the necessary backdrop for Jim's noble act. Up to this point we have been able to admire Jim's good sense and to respond sentimentally to his good character. This, however, is the first time that we see him making a significant (and wholly admirable) moral decision. His act sets him apart from everyone else in the novel except Huck. And modestly (if not disingenuously), he claims to be behaving just as Tom Sawyer would. Always conscious of his role as a "Negro," Jim knows better than to claim personal credit for his good deed. Yet the contrast between Jim's behavior and Tom's is unmistakable. Huck declares that Jim is "white inside" (chap. 40). He apparently intends this as a compliment, but Tom is fortunate that Jim does not behave like most of the whites in the novel.

Twain also contrasts Jim's self-sacrificing compassion with the cruel and mean-spirited behavior of his captors, emphasizing that white skin does not justify claims of superior virtue. They abuse Jim, verbally and physically, and some want to lynch him as an example to other slaves. The moderates among them resist, however, pointing out that they could be made to pay for the destruction of private property. As Huck observes, "the people that's always the most anxious for to hang a nigger that hain't done just right, is always the very ones that ain't the most anxious to pay for him when they've got their satisfaction out of him" (chap. 42). As if these enforcers of white supremacy did not appear contemptible enough already, Twain then has the doctor describe Jim as the best and most faithful nurse he has ever seen, despite Jim's "resking his freedom" and his obvious fatigue. These vigilantes do admit that Jim deserves to be rewarded, but their idea of a reward is to cease punching and cursing him. They are not even generous enough to remove Jim's heavy shackles.

Ultimately, *Huckleberry Finn* renders a harsh judgment on American society. Freedom from slavery, the novel implies, is not freedom from gratuitous cruelty; and racism, like romanticism, is finally just an elaborate justification which the adult counterparts of Tom Sawyer use to facilitate their exploitation and abuse of other human beings. Tom feels guilty, with good reason, for having exploited Jim, but his final gesture of paying Jim off is less an insult to Jim than it is Twain's commentary on Tom himself. Just as slaveholders believe that economic relations (ownership) can justify their privilege of mistreating other human beings, Tom apparently believes that an economic exchange can suffice as atonement for his misdeeds. Perhaps he finds a forty-dollar token more affordable than an apology. But then, just as Tom could only "set a free nigger free," considering, as Huck says, "his bringing-up" (chap. 42), he similarly could hardly be expected to apologize for his pranks. Huck, by contrast, is equally rich, but he *has* apologized to Jim earlier in the novel. And this is the point of Huck's final remark rejecting the prospect of civilization. To become civilized is not just to become like Aunt Sally. More immediately, it is to become like Tom Sawyer.

Jim is indeed "as free as any cretur that walks this earth." In other words, he is a man, like all men, at the mercy of other men's arbitrary cruelties. In a sense, given Twain's view of freedom, to allow Jim to escape to the North or to have Tom announce Jim's manumission earlier would have been an evasion of the novel's ethical insights. While one may escape from legal bondage, there is no escape from the cruelties of this "civilization." There is no promised land where one may enjoy absolute personal freedom. An individual's freedom is always constrained by social relations to other people. Being legally free does not spare Jim from gratuitous humiliation and physical suffering in the final chapters, precisely because Jim is still regarded as a "nigger." Even if he were as accomplished as the mulatto from Ohio, he would not be exempt from mistreatment. Furthermore, since Tom represents the hegemonic values of his society, Jim's "freedom" amounts to little more than an obligation to live by his wits and make the best of a bad situation, just as he has always done.

Given the subtlety of Mark Twain's approach, it is not surprising that most of his contemporaries misunderstood or simply ignored the novel's demystification of race. Despite their patriotic rhetoric, they, like Pap, were unprepared to take seriously the implications of "freedom, justice, and equality." They, after all, espoused an ideology and an explicit language of race that was virtually identical to Thomas Jefferson's. Yet racial discourse flatly contradicts and ultimately renders hypocritical the egalitarian claims of liberal democracy.

The heart of Twain's message to us is that an honest person must reject one or the other. But hypocrisy not honesty, is our norm. Many of us continue to assert both racial distinction and liberal values simultaneously. If we, a century later, continue to be confused about *Adventures of Huckleberry Finn*, perhaps it is because we remain more deeply committed to both racial discourse and a self-deluding optimism than we care to admit.

Adventures of Huckleberry Finn
and Afro-American Literature

Arnold Rampersad

Whenever *Adventures of Huckleberry Finn* is the topic of discussion, we are likely to hear and read a great deal about Ernest Hemingway's remark on the primary place of the book in the history of modern American literature. Hemingway's observations can be found, of course, in *Green Hills of Africa*: "All modern American literature comes from one book by Mark Twain called *Huckleberry Finn*. If you read it you must stop where the nigger Jim is stolen from the boys. This is the real end. The rest is just cheating. But it's the best book we've had. All American writing comes from that. There was nothing before. There has been nothing as good since."

Although the exact meaning of the remark is not altogether clear (at least to me), we can assume that Hemingway saw Mark Twain's novel not merely as a great work in itself—a milestone in American fiction—but also as a great influence on the writers who came after it, even if these writers were unable to surpass *Huckleberry Finn* in the quality of their fiction. (I take Hemingway to mean "fiction" when he wrote "literature.") As much as he also admired Stephen Crane and Henry James, Hemingway obviously thought of *Huckleberry Finn* as the fountainhead of inspiration for American fiction—or the fiction up to October 1935, when the remark was first published. Certainly, Hemingway's biographer Carlos Baker, in his critical study *Hemingway: The Writer as Artist,* proceeded from a careful noting of this remark to a discussion of some of the similarities and differences between Mark Twain's prose style and that of Hemingway.

Whatever Hemingway meant precisely, the wisdom of his placing *Huckleberry Finn* in the most honored position in the history of the national literature has seldom been questioned. Nor do I want to question it here. But does Hemingway's remark also hold true for the relationship between *Adventures of Huckleberry Finn* and black American fiction? In what way or ways is Afro-American fiction descended from, or indebted to, Mark Twain's highly

Reprinted from *Mark Twain Journal* 22:2 (1984), 47–52. (This essay has also appeared in *Satire and Evasion?: Black Perspectives on Huckleberry Finn*, eds. James S. Leonard, Thomas A. Tenney, and Thadius M. Davis [Durham, NC: Duke University Press, 1992, pp. 216–27].) By permission of *Mark Twain Journal*.

influential novel? In what way or ways are this novel and black fiction importantly different? Any attempt to find answers to these questions probably should proceed in as casual a manner as that of Hemingway's observation, in spite of its surface dogmatism. Casually or formally, however, such an attempt might help us to understand a little more about both *Adventures of Huckleberry Finn* and the fictional works of black Americans. And, although it is not my concern here at all, the attempt might also cast some light on the ongoing controversy about the suitability of the book for use by young black readers. (In this respect, it might be useful to point out once again that the term "Nigger Jim," as used by Hemingway and many other American writers, is not to be found anywhere in Mark Twain's writing; it was apparently a figment of Albert Bigelow Paine's imagination—one that struck a responsive chord in Hemingway and many other white Americans.)

Adventures of Huckleberry Finn differs from the bulk of black American fiction, it seems to me, in certain quite specific ways. In the first place (though by no means the most important one), Twain's use of a first-person narrator—a device popular in white American fictions as distinctly different as *Moby Dick, The Blithedale Romance, The Great Gatsby*, and *The Sun Also Rises*—has few counterparts in black American fiction. Until very recent times, only three black American novels of consequence stood out as using the autobiographical mode: James Weldon Johnson's *The Autobiography of an Ex-Colored Man* (1912), Chester Himes's *If He Hollers Let Him Go* (1946), and Ralph Ellison's *Invisible Man* (1952). Why should this be so? If the black American writer has resisted an autobiographical approach to fiction, perhaps the reason may be found, ironically, in the fact that, from the first slave narratives through Washington's *Up from Slavery* (1901), Du Bois's *Dusk of Dawn* (1940), Langston Hughes's *The Big Sea* (1940), and *The Autobiography of Malcolm X* (1964), autobiography has been the single most important literary genre for black Americans. Moreover, the black definition of autobiography has almost always stressed either its moral and confessional tradition or its quasi-moral function in recording the search of the individual and his race for freedom. Surrounding black autobiography, then, has been a respect for its orthodox definition that has probably discouraged experimentation with the form, especially of the notoriously irreverent sort that served Mark Twain so well in *Huckleberry Finn*. The link between black autobiography and the quest for freedom probably has tended to forbid cavalier approaches to the notions of authorial truth and authenticity—notions that Twain mocked in the second sentence of his narrative with Huck's jaunty remark about Mr. Mark Twain telling "the truth, mainly."

A second, related difference lies in the unbroken relationship in *Huckleberry Finn* between autobiography and dialect, linked by Mark Twain to comprise almost certainly the most remarkable single structural element of his book. In so doing, he endowed dialect with a degree of prestige unheard of in black fiction until recent times. Examples in recent black fiction of the combining of autobiography and dialect in Twain's manner are Alice

Childress's *A Hero Ain't Nothin' but a Sandwich* (1973), whose thirteen-year-old narrator is Huck's age and even of his temperament; Al Young's *Sitting Pretty* (1976), whose hero has more than once been compared with Huck by reviewers; and Alice Walker's best-seller *The Color Purple*, whose heroine, Celie, whether or not Walker herself would like the notion, is definitely a black country cousin of Huck Finn. The autobiographical approach in black fiction, interestingly, has coincided with the rise to prominence of women's fiction, where the device seems particularly comfortable; as, for example, in Louise Meriwether's *Daddy Was a Number Runner* (1970).

In his ambition to elevate the prestige of dialect, as announced in the famous note preceding the novel about the "shadings" of dialect (they had "not been done in a hap-hazard fashion, or by guess work; but pains-takingly, and with the trustworthy guidance and support of personal familiarity with these several forms of speech"), Mark Twain has had very few serious followers in black fiction. For all the celebrated daring of the writers of the Harlem Renaissance in the 1920s, black dialect remained so much seasoning in the speech of characters developed by such writers as Rudolph Fisher, Wallace Thurman, Langston Hughes, and Claude McKay, and was virtually shunned in the work of other writers such as W. E. B. Du Bois, Jesse Fauset, and Nella Larsen. This fact is particularly noteworthy because entire poems were written in honest black dialect by such fine poets as Langston Hughes and Sterling Brown, and, earlier, Paul Laurence Dunbar, who published four novels in addition to his poetry. Moreover, Hughes and Zora Neale Hurston collaborated between 1929 and 1930 on a play entirely in dialect, *Mule Bone*. Only writers of fiction stood back from making that complete commitment to dialect without which the epochal success of *Huckleberry Finn* would have been impossible. In the 1930s Richard Wright employed dialect, but again in spare and, according to Hurston in her review of *Uncle Tom's Children* (1938), inept fashion. Hurston herself, the undisputed master of black dialect by virtue of her southern upbringing and her Barnard training as a folklorist, came closest in the 1930s to rendering full tribute to the language of American blacks in *Their Eyes Were Watching God* (1937). But while her characters speak something else, her narrator in the novel speaks standard English, or slips occasionally into a folk-influenced form of educated English. Almost fifty years later, Alice Walker, conscious of an indebtedness to Hurston, perhaps also consciously would take the final step with Celie in *The Color Purple*. In 1943, however, Langston Hughes began building perhaps the best achievement in the fictional use of dialect by a black author when he created in the *Chicago Defender* his extremely popular character Jesse B. Semple, or "Simple," who would converse comically there for over twenty years, in thick dialect, with Hughes's educated and very dull narrator. The books that resulted between 1950 and 1965 (*Simple Speaks His Mind, Simple Takes a Wife, Simple Stakes a Claim, Simple's U.S.A.,* and *The Best of Simple*) were all very well received by critics, who persisted in pointing out, to the Missouri-born Hughes's great satisfaction, the similarities between his work and that of Mark Twain. Ironically, in 1962, at the request of Cyril Clemens, Hughes wrote a brief tribute to the late Ernest Hemingway for the *Mark Twain Journal*.

Daring to entrust his tale to a young, essentially illiterate boy, Mark Twain was confident that countrified speech, far from being a millstone dragging down his fiction, would serve to free his young hero's unvarnished poetic sensibility and rich folk utterance. In contrast, few black writers historically have dared to entrust their tales to members of the black folk or the black masses. Their approach has been one to which Henry James would have granted approval—and writers as different as Wright and Baldwin have admitted the crucial influence of James. Few have dared to entrust their tales to anyone other than a narrator as intellectually and linguistically refined as themselves, someone capable of mediating between the presumably "soiled" black subject, on the one hand, and the ideal, highly bourgeois, and almost entirely white readership expected, on the other. One reads a document such as Richard Wright's "Blueprint for Negro Writing," in which he stresses the importance of folk expression as part of the culture of the black masses, but one looks in vain through his several novels and stories for a release of folk expression comparable to that of Mark Twain in his greatest work.

In another related area of difference, no significant black writer has dared to completely entrust his or her story to a child, as Mark Twain did in *Huckleberry Finn*. In general, the black writer has been reluctant until recently even to approach serious fiction from a child's point of view. Alice Childress comes to mind again, and Tony Cade Bambara in parts of *Gorilla, My Love* (1972). Of older writers, only Langston Hughes with *Not without Laughter* (1930) emerges as an important black novelist who hazarded (certainly the approach is risky) a major statement about Afro-American reality by filtering it through the consciousness of a black child. Richard Wright effectively attempts something similar in his short stories "Big Boy Leaves Home" and "Almos' A Man," but on a far smaller scale, and one that emphasizes violence and fear. Among more recent works, James Baldwin's *Go Tell It on the Mountain* (1953) also exemplifies this interest in the young, though John Grimes's consciousness is but one mediating aspect of Baldwin's novel; moreover, it is difficult to conceive of John Grimes as a child. In black American fiction in general, however, children are seldom seen and even less frequently heard. Or to put it another way—black fictionalists seem to believe that the social reality they describe, and in which their people historically have lived, has never given them leave to depict young lives relatively free from pain, an exemption on which the depiction of the beauty and dignity of childhood probably depends. A paradox remains: scenes of childhood have always been very important in black autobiography; but nineteenth-century black fiction, for example, is virtually devoid of images of black children.

Similarly, the phenomenon of adult fiction readily accessible to young readers, of which *Huckleberry Finn* remains perhaps the best example, also belongs to the white, but not the black, world of fiction. The intelligent, well-prepared young American grows up on adult fiction that is also in part palatable to the young—*Huck Finn, The Red Badge of Courage, Moby Dick* (in some abridged version), *Two Years before the Mast,* the Leatherstocking stories, and so on. The black child has no alternative canon drawn from his or her own writers. The main reason, of course, is that most of these books were written several generations ago, when blacks were recent ex-slaves or only a generation removed from slavery, and when standards of fiction were different; notably, they were written in a time when escapist fiction enjoyed perhaps its greatest prestige. For blacks, escape from slavery was always appealing; but the aim then and later almost always was to escape *into* the whole society, not away from it. The chains that traditionally have bound the black individual in white America before and after slavery have also circumscribed black fiction, forbidding almost all venturing, or adventuring, that does not lead seriously to black freedom. In Chesnutt's *House behind the Cedars* (1900), reading escapist or adventurist fiction leads only to trouble for the black dreamer. Wright's first story, the escapist "Voodoo of Hell's Half Acre," enraged his domineering grandmother (as he mentions in *Black Boy* [1945]). The black writer disciplined himself or herself to write about the search for freedom.

But a fiction about bondage and freedom (in particular, one about slavery, itself) might be precisely the kind of story from which one is inclined to shelter black children. One does so to protect them, in their more susceptible periods of growth, from even the knowledge of extreme human cruelty; in some respects, the controversy over the word "nigger" in *Huck Finn* is an excellent example of such protectionism. The treatment of slavery within the context of adventure has been successfully realized, from the general point of view, in certain works by white writers, but precisely because the slaves were not white. Two works stand out here: *Huck Finn* itself, and Harriet Beecher Stowe's *Uncle Tom's Cabin.* It is surely instructive that neither has achieved unqualified success, to say the least, among black readers. The slave Jim, noble for a while, becomes an object of burlesque before Twain's fiction is complete; in the case of *Uncle Tom's Cabin,* the name of its black hero quickly became a byword among blacks for unmanly compromise.

Much adventuring is written by men for the little boys supposedly resident in grown men, and to cater to their chauvinism. In this respect *Huck Finn* is an extremely American narrative, and also akin to the bulk of black fiction, which until recently was written mostly by men. The importance of the bond between males in *Huck Finn* is reflected in most male black fiction but negatively so, mostly as antifeminine behavior and values. Genuine male bonding is not correspondingly prominent; perhaps the truth is that black fiction, as compared to white, is in general relatively loveless.

Another important area of difference between *Huck Finn* and black fiction concerns the propriety of comedy in a fiction about race. Zora Neale Hurston possessed a rich comic talent, probably the richest in black fiction, and one very much in the Mark Twain tradition. But unlike Mark Twain, in writing comically about blacks Hurston notably avoided the topic of race. Just as the black story has been perceived as too grim to accommodate easily either children or modes of adventure pleasing to the young, so too has it resisted treatment by way of comedy, which is one of the principal glories of *Huckleberry Finn*. Slavery, many blacks would say, is no laughing matter. And yet comedy and slavery have a limited but definite coexistence in the history of black writing. One sees comic depictions of slave life in the dialect verse of black poets such as Daniel Webster Davis and James Carrothers, who were prepared to assist in propagating the myth of a golden age of slavery fostered by white writers as different as Thomas Nelson Page and Joel Chandler Harris. But if black poets were at one point content to serve such a point of view, black fictionalists were almost always opposed to doing so. Charles Chesnutt is perhaps the only black writer of fiction to approach the depiction of slavery with a marked degree of humor and irony. In fact, he writes not of slavery but of neoslavery, the historical aftermath of slavery; moreover, his Uncle Julius laughs, but he also connives and wins. Bent on a degree of real subversion, Mark Twain understood the subversive power of comedy; but it is an aspect of his book that few black writers have paralleled before the current generation. Not the last reason for the primacy of *Invisible Man* among black fictions is its rich comic detail, an aspect that links it to some of the writing of Chester Himes and to the most innovative recent black fiction—that of Ishmael Reed in particular, as in *Mumbo Jumbo* (1972), and of William Melvin Kelley, as in *dem* (1967). Of *Huck Finn*, however, one should remember one thing here; much of the humor is at Jim's expense. Huck and Tom are the tricksters; Jim is largely one of the tricked.

Another, perhaps more decisively important, way in which *Huck Finn* goes against the grain of black fiction is in its typically American "twinning" of white and dark-skinned characters to suggest an ideal American hero who combines the best qualities of the white and some darker race in a merger of complementary abilities and values. This device, analyzed most famously by Leslie Fiedler a generation ago, and present in varying degrees in the works of Cooper, Melville, Twain, and Stephen Crane, is even more dominant in the iconography of popular culture, as seen in figures such as the Lone Ranger and Tonto, Mandrake and Lothar, Tarzan and his apes, Han Solo and Chewbacca, and even in the "twinning" of various white and black performers, invariably male, in television and motion pictures. In rare instances the device has been used to find a vehicle for a gifted black "star" (probably paralyzed in his career because of racism); in general, however, the motivation remains largely the same as that behind Cooper, Melville, and Mark Twain—a sense of a black or Native American familiarity with Nature, noble in essence and finally inaccessible to the white man.

Black writers of fiction have had little time for this oblique approach to characterization and to the problem of race, just as black readers and audiences have probably reacted to such "twinnings" mostly with distrust and annoyance. The black or Indian character, whatever the degree of his "nobility" and his other gifts, is almost inevitably secondary in importance to the white hero. He is only an acolyte in the ritual of American absolution from sin—when he isn't the sacrificial victim. The device allows little flexibility in this aspect of its essence. In *Huck Finn*, Mark Twain exalts Jim—just beyond the level of a white boy—but finally cannot allow him to remain exalted. Jim then becomes little more than a plaything, like a great stuffed bear, for the white boys over whom he once stood morally.

Finally, very few black writers, if any, have been teased by the great question of Nature and its relationship to humanity, which I take to be at the heart of Mark Twain's depiction of the river in *Adventures of Huckleberry Finn*. Whether one sees the river, according to the debate now some forty years old, as a god or as a morally neutral agency, certainly the Mississippi rolls through Mark Twain's novel as a constant reminder of an ultimate force beyond human beings, a force identifiable not merely with the God of Christianity but with Nature itself. The presence of the river and the boy's response to it form the main element by which Mark Twain's fiction deepens philosophically, or perhaps thickens atmospherically. Huck's moral questionings sound and resound in the presence of the river, which represents in this novel the elevating form of the absolute. By contrast, however, black fiction has been notably practical, skeptical, human-centered, and secular. Nature is invoked not as ultimate cause but largely for dramatic effect. Appearing to have ultimate, magical properties in, say, the opening of Hughes's *Not without Laughter*, where a tornado sweeps us into a boy's world (see also Gordon Parks's *The Learning Tree* [1963]), Nature soon loses its shamanlike authority and becomes ultimately subservient to social action. Richard Wright dusts off effects borrowed from the stockroom of literary naturalism for use in *Lawd Today, Uncle Tom's Children, Native Son,* and *Black Boy,* but Nature is finally overridden and reduced, put in its place by the questions of power and politics, history and civil liberties, that have of necessity dominated black thinking.

We have seen that in certain of the areas discussed above, such as the use of folk material, dialect, comedy, and the autobiographical mode, *Adventures of Huckleberry Finn* clearly anticipated eventual trends in black fiction—even if, for much of black literary history, its example went largely ignored. But in what respects was the primacy of Mark Twain's novel relatively immediate, and how was Mark Twain himself very close to the general intentions of the black writer?

The first area concerns the placing of the issue of black character and culture squarely in the context of the search for freedom. Obviously the strategy, or the vision, did not originate with Mark Twain, but with other black writers, on the one hand, and with literary abolitionism, epitomized by Harriet Beecher Stowe, on the other. But Mark Twain wrote as a southerner in a period of intense reaction against blacks; he clearly conceived of his book as, in part, a blow against white reactionary attitudes, against the rising walls of segregation, against lynching, and against the slanderous imputation that blacks were less than human and therefore should be treated with prejudice. Whatever the limitations in his depiction of Jim (and they are considerable), Mark Twain made it clear that Jim was good, deeply human, loving, and anxious for freedom. It is a reflection on American culture that such an approach should be historic.

A related aspect of the novel is its exposure of the South, and to some extent American culture as a whole, as gullible, irrational, violence-prone, mob-threatened, and profoundly hypocritical in touting its possession of superior values. This is a world from which Mark Twain's alienated young, white narrator recoils finally in something like horror, and in comparison to which black Jim, in his patience and love, appears to be positively noble. The acts of exposing the falseness of white and, in particular, southern claims to "civilization" and of resisting the allegation of intrinsic black inferiority have been among the principal concerns of black writers of fiction almost from the beginning of the literature. Except perhaps for Martin R. Delany in his *Blake; or, The Huts of America* (1861–62), Mark Twain went further than any black writer of the nineteenth century, further even than Sutton Griggs in *Imperium in Imperio* (1899), in that he not only repudiated white claims to superiority by virtue of possessing a genuine civilization but depicted those claims as ludicrous.

But the most important way in which *Adventures of Huckleberry Finn* predicts later black fiction is in Mark Twain's depiction of a moral dilemma, or moral inversion, as being at the heart of southern, and by inference American, society. The consequence of slavery and racism is an apparently permanent inversion of moral order, so that right becomes wrong and wrong becomes right; and the individual of consequence, like Huckleberry Finn, follows the instincts of his heart at peril not only to his place in society but also to his own sanity. The man—and it is almost always a man, except in dramas of "passing"—who allows himself to become caught in this dilemma rather than accept the moral disorder masquerading as moral law marks himself as a candidate for existential loneliness or alienation, and probably a violent fate. He or she easily becomes an outsider, like Richard Wright's incoherent, brutish Bigger Thomas, or his more urbane Cross Damon in *The Outsider*; or the embittered and suicidal Richard and Rufus of Baldwin's *Go Tell It on the Mountain* and *Another Country*; or Ralph Ellison's far more charming but nonetheless wildly disoriented hero in *Invisible Man*. In some key respects Huck is one of those white Biggers whom Wright, to his amazement, discovered in the world outside the South, as he revealed in his essay "How Bigger Was Born"; these were persons cut off somehow from their cultures and potentially lethal in their attitudes toward society. Only Huck Finn's white skin and his youth have saved him so far from a bloody fate, although Twain surrounds him with a frightening, signifying level of violence, including Huck's gruesome "murder" of his own self. Bigger could have learned from Huck: "I took the axe and smashed in the door—I beat it and hacked it considerable, a-doing it. I fetched the pig in and took him back nearly to the table and hacked into his throat with the axe, and laid him down on the ground to bleed—I say ground, because it *was* ground—hard packed and no boards" (chap.7). Cross Damon, Wright's hero in *The Outsider*, "kills" himself as Huck did, and watches his own funeral.

But an important difference must be noted. Mark Twain depicted white Huck, but not black Jim, as being torn and alienated; he left it to black writers, or to a more polemical, if less gifted, white writer such as George Washington Cable in *The Grandissimes*, to show what happens when a member of Jim's race acquires Huck's disruptive alienation. This is a crucial point in evaluating the political and racial force of the book: Mark Twain does not suggest that Jim can catch Huck's dangerous virus. More important than the ending, about which everyone writes, this may be the major compromise in *Huck Finn*. Assuredly Twain knew that Huck's attitude could be contagious, and that blacks had more reason than whites to be alienated and angry.

The historic black statement of the condition ascribed in embryo to Huck—but in its black mutation—would come from *The Souls of Black Folk* (1903), in which W. E. B. Du Bois identifies the core of the black American psychology as comprising "two souls, two thoughts, two unreconciled strivings . . . in one dark body, whose dogged strength alone keeps it from being torn asunder." Du Bois's book included, among the essays, a short story in which the conflict is dramatized; the result is a blow struck by a black man against a white—one of the earliest of such acts in black fiction—and the resulting death of the white man and the black hero. Du Bois's book has long been recognized as the most influential single volume in black literature, at least until the appearance of Wright's *Native Son* in 1940. If all Afro-American literature comes from any one source, that fountainhead is most likely *The Souls of Black Folk*, which the authoritative James Weldon Johnson declared in *Along This Way* (1933), published two years before Hemingway's *Green Hills of Africa*, to have had "a greater effect upon and within the Negro race in America than any other single book published in this country since *Uncle Tom's Cabin.*"

In spite of the crucial differences between *Souls* and *Huck Finn*, however, I would venture to say that very near to the fountainhead (nearer than any other work of fiction, including *Uncle Tom's Cabin*) must be *Adventures of Huckleberry Finn*. Although many of the writers of fiction acknowledged the intellectual supremacy of Du Bois, and had little or nothing to say about Mark Twain, it is difficult to miss the affinity between them and the author of *Huckleberry Finn*—especially if one compares Twain with other American masters of fiction such as the much-admired James, or Howells, or Melville, or Sinclair Lewis, or Hemingway himself. In his stress on folk culture, on dialect, and on American humor, Mark Twain anticipated Dunbar, Hughes (who lauded Twain in an introduction to *Pudd'nhead Wilson*), Hurston, Fisher, Thurman, Ellison, Gaines, Childress, Reed, and Alice Walker; in his depiction of alienation in an American context, prominently including race, Twain anticipates other aspects of most of these writers' work and also that of Richard Wright, Chester Himes, Ann Petry, James Baldwin, and Toni Morrison.

In *Adventures of Huckleberry Finn,* Mark Twain flinched before the potentially dangerous confrontation of these two major aspects of his work— its democratic folk and racial features, and its depiction of the alienation and moral disorder endemic to southern and even American culture. Such a confrontation, which in effect (certainly from a black point of view) is akin to a synthesis of Twain and Du Bois, or of *Huckleberry Finn* and *The Souls of Black Folk,* had begun to take place when Hemingway made his celebrated comment in 1935. One sees the meeting in the works of the maturing William Faulkner, who had published *Light in August* three years before and would publish *Absalom, Absalom!* a year later; and, importantly, in the fledgling efforts of the young Richard Wright, still struggling in 1935 to find his own fictive voice.

Mark Twain's Frontier,
Hank Morgan's Last Stand

Richard Slotkin

[Mark] Twain's relation to the Frontier, and to its myth, was central to his development as man and as writer. He was born in the "backwash" of the frontier, of a family that had been part of the pattern of westward emigration until his father's generation, moving from Virginia to East Tennessee to Missouri. The Frontier of myth, received by way of Fenimore Cooper and the "penny dreadful" newspapers, was basic to his imaginative education. His hometown of Hannibal was a terminal for an abortive transcontinental railroad enterprise, and the deluded optimism of the western railroad business was part of the town's civic life. Faced with the loss of his profession as river pilot and with the danger of conscription as results of the Civil War, Twain followed the traditional path of refuge that led beyond the western borders to the mining regions of Nevada and California.

As he looked back on this experience from the perspective of the successful writer, he adopted toward it an ambivalent attitude of celebration and debunking. This ambivalence is reflected in *Roughing It* (1872), his first extensive treatment of his early life. Twain represents his experience as one of demystification. He presents himself as an "innocent," whose ideas and expectations about the West have been gained entirely from the romances of Cooper and his imitators. He expects to meet noble savages and behold Edenic landscape, to befriend Frontier hunters of the Leatherstocking kind. This literary romance is augmented by the more materialistic elements of the Frontier Myth, specifically the expectation of magical access to incredible wealth—the "gold rush" myth.

By juxtaposing the literary and the economic versions of the Frontier Myth, Twain debunks and demystifies both. On the journey his expectation of gorgeous scenery is disappointed by the monotonous landscape over which the stagecoach journeys like a dust-devouring beetle. His expectation of meeting the Noble Red Man is undone by meeting the "Goshoot" Indians of the Great Basin:

Reprinted with the permission of Atheneum Publishers, an imprint of Macmillan Publishing Company from *The Fatal Environment: The Myth of the Frontier Age of Industrialization, 1800–1890* by Richard Slotkin, 1985, pp. 516–32. Copyright © 1985 Richard Slotkin.

The disgust which the Goshoots gave me, a disciple of Cooper and a worshipper of the Red Man—even of the scholarly savages in the *Last of the Mohicans* who are fittingly associated with backwoodsmen who divide each sentence into two equal parts: one part . . . refined and choice of language, and the other part just such an attempt to talk like a hunter or a mountaineer, as a Broadway clerk might make after eating a collection of Emerson Bennett's works and studying frontier life at the Bowery Theater a couple of weeks—I say that nausea . . . set me to examining authorities, to see if perchance I had been overestimating the Red Man while viewing him through the mellow moonshine of romance. The revelations that came were disenchanting. It was curious to see how quickly the paint and tinsel fell away from him and left him treacherous, filthy and repulsive—and how quickly the evidences accumulated that whenever one finds an Indian tribe he has only found Goshoots more or less modified by circumstances and surroundings—but Goshoots, after all. They deserve pity, poor creatures; and they can have mine—at this distance.[1]

Twain's disillusionment takes exactly the form suggested by the newspaper and magazine treatments of the Indian question in the 1869–75 period, and he employs the same formulas that Custer borrowed for his anti-Indian essays of 1867–69—particularly the use of Cooper as the archspokesman for the "romantic" and "sentimental" view and the analogy between the sordid comedy of reservation life and that of the Broadway stage. Twain expands on these attitudes in other sketches published in the sixties and seventies. In an essay on his visit to Niagara Falls, he makes the urban savage association: a naive tourist who uses Cooperian terms to address the pseudo-Indians who manufacture souvenirs is beaten up for his pains, and discovers that these noble red men are all Irish immigrants from Limerick.[2]

Such literary "undoing" was essential to the creative task of *Roughing It* in which Twain was not merely retailing his past life but looking for a literary language appropriate to his vision. The language of traditional romance was not merely inaccurate in depicting reality; its highfalutin manner and presumption of moral omniscience were a persuasive falsification of reality which could distort human behavior in the real world. Whereas the Southwest humorists, whose works Twain read and whose techniques he imitated, had seized instead upon the vernacular, they generally did so with the purpose of emphasizing the quaintness and impropriety of Frontier speech. Twain reverses the ideological charge of the contrast, locating truth and virtue in the vernacular. It is the linguistic equivalent of his handling of landscape description: the "realistic" scene is always one that does not glitter, that deliberately invokes a romantic convention in order to undermine or contradict it.

The "gold fever" with its get-rich-quick ideology is another order of romance or illusion. Twain's first attempts to find gold are motivated by the

---

[1]Twain, *Roughing It* (Berkeley, 1972), p. 146.

[2]Twain, "A Visit to Niagara," in *Sketches New and Old* (1875). The association of wild Indians and wild Irish goes back to the seventeenth century. See Richard Slotkin, *Regeneration Through Violence: The Mythology of the American Frontier 1600–1860* (Middletown, Conn., 1973), pp. 42, 472.

expectation of obtaining a vast fortune for very little expenditure of labor. He learns quite early to suspect the illusory promise of wealth in rocks that are merely gorgeous, and he offers an antiromantic moral: Not only is it true that not all that glitters is gold, but it can be asserted that nothing that glitters is gold. The truth will never be pretty. But this kind of disillusionment does not touch the essential myth of the gold rush, and Twain and his friends persist in thinking they can strike it rich merely by showing up and staking a claim. They stake out a "lumber ranch" on the primeval shores of Tahoe, and through carelessness with fire, burn their forest to ashes. They discover a "blind lead" which will make them millionaires if they will only validate their claim by doing a day's work—and between dreams of future leisure and pursuit of still more glorious illusions of wealth, they somehow fail to do the work. As his adventures proceed, Twain's persona perceives that the essential nature of the illusion offered by the Frontier Myth is its substitution of easy wealth for the necessity of labor. His is a "post-Frontier" sensibility, which insists that "real life" is no longer constituted (if it ever was) to provide farms, ranches, and gold mines to the first comers for no cost. Once Twain discovers his own vocation as reporter and lecturer, he sees the gold rush from a new perspective. It is a "beggar's revel" in which the expectation of wealth produces an economy based entirely on paper values—mining stock whose only value is the expected wealth it symbolizes.

> It was the strangest phase of life one can imagine. It was a beggar's revel. There was nothing doing in the district—no mining—no milling—no productive effort— no income . . . and yet a stranger would have supposed he was walking among bloated millionaires . . . Few people took *work* into their calculations—or outlay of money either; except the work and expenditures of other people. . . . Every one of these wild cat mines—not mines, but holes in the ground over imaginary mines— was incorporated and had handsomely engraved "stock" and the stock was salable, too. It was bought and sold with a feverish avidity on the boards every day . . .[3]

The Frontier beggar's revel is a crude reflection of the larger economic scene which Twain attacks in his first novel, *The Gilded Age* (1873) written with Charles Dudley Warner. Here the dichotomy between the imperatives of labor and the illusions of an easy way to wealth and status is more elaborately worked out. But his larger theme is that of the corruption of both business and politics by the new profit opportunities offered by Reconstruction and the government sponsorship of railroads. At the heart of the novel is the effort of the ebullient Colonel Sellers to finance his own transcontinental railroad. The passages dealing with the promotion of that enterprise are a deliberate parody of the publicity of Jay Cooke's Northern Pacific and the effusions of [William] Gilpin. The scheme is financed by federal money, obtained through bribery under the cover of a philanthropic project: building a college for Negroes in East Tennessee—an area noted for its lack of black population. Again, the Frontier Myth is exposed as a doctrine which makes its believers liable to

[3]Twain, *Roughing It*, pp. 201, 204, 277–78.

fraud and failure. Those characters who build their expectations on the speculative possibilities of Sellers's enterprise are ruined; only those characters who find their work and buckle to it prosper.

But it would be a mistake to reduce Twain's attitude to the ideology of hard work and self-denial he seems to advocate in *Gilded Age*: the pretty illusions of romance and the expectation of a sudden bonanza remained dear to his heart. This ambivalence finds its best reflection in the Tom Sawyer / Huck Finn books which he wrote between 1876 and 1887. Here he reveals his dual allegiance to myth and to realism. Twain's nostalgia for a world in which lost illusions are rediscovered and made good is fully indulged in *Tom Sawyer*. The famous whitewashing episode, and the Bible-ticket "corner" (modeled on Jay Gould's stock market scams) which succeeds it, are celebrations of the boy's cleverness in using the illusions of others—the paper values of his society—for his own real gain. Yet remember that the novel is a parody of Horatio Alger, in which success is achieved precisely by avoiding hard work and good manners, and doing everything just as the bad little boy would do it. Here the contradictions of Twain's viewpoint appear. In *The Gilded Age* he speaks as a respectable adult of the mid–Victorian Age, and he warns the romantic boys that the Frontier is gone, and bread must be earned by the sweat of one's brow. In *Tom Sawyer*, Twain is a boy himself who believes in illusions and prospers nonetheless, who has returned to a world where magic works; where bread is not earned with the sweat of your brow—but rather is loaded with quicksilver (like the processed ore in *Roughing It*), so that it can magically seek you out where you lie hidden across the river. When Tom asserts that robbers are the "most respectable" people in society, the atmosphere of play-fantasy reduces to a mere suggestion one of the bitterest ironies of *The Gilded Age*: that power and prestige were in fact in the hands of Robber Barons and their political lackeys.[4]

The Adventures of Huckleberry Finn brings these contradictions to a head. Huck is faced with a series of crises that compel him to choose between the world of romantic illusion or myth, and reality. He is already disenchanted with Tom Sawyer's robber game when the book begins. When his father forcibly seizes him, imprisons him on the island, and threatens his life, evasion of reality becomes impossible. To survive, Huck has to see through the fictions both of the town (whose religion of legalism and piety is impotent to save Huck) and of Pap—whose claims to the legitimate power of the paternal role are also fictions imposed on reality. Once committed to the real task of escaping from Pap, Huck is required continually to increase his mastery of the borderland between myth and reality: to use the power of lies and fictions effectively against those who would ensnare him, he must himself be quite clear about what is real and what is not. His primary teacher in this process is the slave Jim, who plays Chingachgook to Huck's Leather-

---

[4]Twain, *Tom Sawyer*, chs. 2,4. Compare Judge Thatcher's Sunday school experience in ch. 4 with that of the crooked Senator Dilworthy in *The Gilded Age*, ch. 20. The "quicksilver" gold mill is in *Roughing It*, ch. 36.

stocking—aiding and sustaining Huck, teaching him the lore of the real world, representing the life of authentic feeling which social conventions repress or distort. The mutuality of dependence that unites Huck and Jim in their common quest for escape and survival compels Huck to deal directly with the primary mythology or false religion of his society: the system of chattel slavery, and the ideology of race, social class, and moral authority that sustains the system.

Huck and Jim's adventures on the river provide a series of unavoidable choices that compel Huck to choose between the "illusory" or false values of society—in which, nonetheless, he continues to believe—and the human and material reality of Jim and their friendship. The world of the river is a "magic" and romantic one, described in the romantic terms common to Frontier romances. But in *Huckleberry Finn*, the magic world is a limited one; it cannot spread its power to the world of the shore, in which evil, violence, and greed shape values and behavior. On the contrary, the river itself is invaded, and the raft taken over by the emissaries of the shore.[5]

The contrast of river and shore in *Huckleberry Finn* is an abstraction of the relationship of Frontier to Metropolis. In *Roughing It* this contrast is reflected in the opposition between the "real West" and the illusions of Twain's naive narrator. In *Gilded Age*, the real West is the place of poverty and hard scrabble labor, into which the illusion makers and corrupt speculators of the Metropolis project the false glamour of their mythology and their greed. In *Tom Sawyer*, there is a gentler contrast between the town and the pastoral refuge the boys find on Jackson's Island—described by Twain in the conventional language of Frontier landscape description. But in *Huckleberry Finn*, these variant readings of the symbolic opposition are combined and coordinated into a single symbolism of great complexity and resonance. Huck's successive refuges are Frontiers that fail to live up to the promise, which is to be at once magical in providing happiness and "real"—that is, unprettified, unpretentious, vernacular. Pap's cabin fails as refuge, because Pap is not an alternative to the respectable virtues of the "Metropolis"—merely their perverse inversion. Jackson's Island fails—it is too close to home, and it begins to be assimilated by the Metropolis because slaves and slave catchers can now find the place out. The raft is another kind of refuge, a floating island on which happiness and true speech are possible—but it too is doomed by the flow of river and time which carry it deeper into the slave region. At the Phelps plantation, Tom Sawyer returns and transforms the Underground Railroad (and by analogy, the hope of abolition) into a game whose rules are determined by the conventions of the Metropolis's literary mythology. *Uncle Tom* may have made a war against slavery possible, but as a guide to black liberation it was useless: the vernacular fails, and Jim's liberation becomes a mockery.

Yet at the end, Twain's hero has still not abandoned the hope of finding his way to the mythic Frontier, the place beyond the Metropolis: he is going to

[5]Twain, *Adventures of Huckleberry Finn* (1883).

"light out for the Territory," for the Indian country. This was a notion which Twain meant to pursue, in a projected sequel whose manuscript version is titled "Tom and Huck Among the Indians." The projected story would have extended the mythology-debunking motif that characterizes much of *Huckleberry Finn*. Tom would approach the Indian territory equipped with ideas out of Fenimore Cooper, like the narrator of *Roughing It*; and he would have found that the savage was far more horrid than even that dime-novel Indian villain Injun Joe. This experience of disillusion is not inconsistent with the logic of *Huckleberry Finn*. Given the rhythmic persistence of the experience of disillusion, of the discovery of Frontiers that fail, it is not difficult to see that Huck's "lighting out for the Territory" will disappoint him. But within the framework of *Huckleberry Finn* that sense derives from evidence that the values of the Metropolis are everywhere and continually encroach on the terrain of freedom. "Among the Indians" has a different basis for hopelessness—it is not the corruption of the Metropolis that spoils the West, but the cruel savagery of the natives.

In the novel, Tom, Huck, and Jim were to join a single-family wagon party, including a beautiful young girl betrothed to a wandering hunter. The family is lulled into a false sense of security, in part because they heed Tom Sawyer's Cooperian "wisdom" about the noble red man more than the warnings of the rough plainsman. In the boys' absence, the wagon party is massacred and the girl taken captive. The boys are met by the hunter, who will guide them and lead the rescue attempt; and he is their man of true speech and vision, who unmasks the myth to show the reality. But "realism" in this case requires an honest treatment of the captivity theme. As the Goshoots passage reveals, Twain's ideas about Indians were those of his "tough-minded" contemporaries. These ideas, reflected in his writings for the *Galaxy* and other New York journals in 1869–74, were reinforced by the research he did for "Among the Indians," which took him back to Custer's account of "Hancock's War" of 1866–69. He was convinced that the necessary and inevitable fate of the young girl in the hands of the Indians would have been gang rape; and his young hunter discovers signs that this has indeed been her fate. At this point, Twain abandoned the project. Perhaps, as some Twain scholars have suggested, it was his squeamishness about the theme of rape and his belief that without at least the invocation of rape as a possibility, he would be betraying his commitment to realism and honesty.[6]

Be that as it may, "Among the Indians" reveals Twain's persistence in employing the vocabulary of the Frontier Myth—or his own version of it—as a way of interpreting the social and moral alternatives available to himself and his fictional surrogates. *Huckleberry Finn* presents the closing of the Frontier from the Frontiersman's perspective, as the loss of freedom to an expanding Metropolis; and it suggests that in primitive character—in the personalities of young women, children, and childlike nonwhite races—lies the only alterna-

---

[6]Twain, "Tom and Huck Among the Indians," *Hannibal, Huck, and Tom*, ed. Walter Blair (Berkeley, 1960), pp. 84–88. Blair discusses Twain's use of Western sources, especially Custer, Mrs. Custer, and Colonel R. I. Dodge.

tive to the dangerous values of the white, adult, male order of society. "Among the Indians" is dialectically opposite to *Huckleberry Finn*—what it challenges is the myth of a primitive nobility, of an alternative in man's wilderness condition. The world then becomes a battleground between the Dukes and Dauphins above and the various kinds of crackers and Comanches below.

Such a reading appears in suppressed passages from his earlier books, most notably in "The French and the Comanches" (1879) which he deleted from *A Tramp Abroad*. The essay begins by invoking "cruelty, savagery, and the spirit of massacre," and asserting that this spirit is not unique to savage races like the Comanches. "It is hard to draw a line here, with any degree of exactness, between the French [and] the Comanches," the only differences being that the Comanches do not massacre one another, and that the French are "more ingenious" in their cruelty. What the Comanche does only to people of alien race and culture, the French do to fellow citizens and Christians. Twain then recounts the massacres perpetrated in the course of French history, between different religious, political, and class entities struggling for power, and cites the torture and legalized rape (*droit de seigneur*) of the ancien régime as evidence of their Comanche-like behavior. On the literal level, Twain appears to find the Comanches on the whole less savage than the French, although the point of the essay is of course to discredit both. Nonetheless, the grounds of the distinction are worth noting. Twain offers it as a norm of racial warfare that the "spirit of massacre" should prevail. Where the French reveal their depravity is in treating competition between classes, parties, or interest groups as if it were racial warfare. What is still more horrible is the persistence of this racialization of class warfare down into the enlightened nineteenth century—a persistence revealed by the massacres of Communards in 1871 directed against the proletariat of Paris.[7]

The symbolic language of Twain's works is the product of reading, experience, introspection, and creative effort, and therefore is a personal and peculiar system. But in its major tropes, symbolism, and structuring principles it is clearly cognate with the myth / ideological system that took shape around the Indian wars and labor struggles of the Last Stand period. The linkage of Indian and class warfare, the expectation of massacre as its result, was basic to both systems. What is different is the greater complexity and ambivalence of Twain's own system—a result of his divided identification, both for and against society, for and against the wilderness.

A Connecticut Yankee in King Arthur's Court is Twain's attempt to work all of this into a coherent fictional scheme. A number of coincident factors shaped his changing intentions about the work and his final treatment of the theme. The warfare of capital and labor was of serious concern to him. He shared [William Dean] Howells's concern about the apparent spread of anarchism

---

[7]Twain, "The French and the Comanches," *Letters from the Earth* (New York, 1974), pp. 146–49.

among the laboring classes and a spirit of oppression among the masters of capital. Both men read [Edward Bellamy's] *Looking Backward* and agreed that it might be "a New Bible," pointing the way to resolution of the present difficulties; yet such views were no sooner stated than Twain seems to have begun to doubt them. The "spirit of massacre," he had written, is not a racial trait but "grow[s] naturally out of the social system." The values that Bellamy invoked were, perhaps, unrealistic at best, tyrannous at worst, and in the interim liable to exploitation by cruel and vicious frauds like the scalawags of *The Gilded Age*, Pap or the Duke and Dauphin in *Huckleberry Finn*.

The recently completed cycle of works drawing on the "matter of Hannibal" had sharpened Twain's sense of the ethical consequences of his society's ideology, and had developed to a point of high sophistication his battery of literary tropes—particularly the contrast of "true vernacular" and "false genteel" speech, and the symbolism of race. The cycle had also drawn him back, physically and in memory, to the South and its history: the false "Walter Scott" romanticism of the slave-owning "chivalry," the false promise of Reconstruction, the persistence of racism, greed, and oppression as facts of southern life. His reading provided him with the literary targets for satire which were closely linked with the symbolism in which he perceived these social themes. His rejection of the shallow romanticism of Walter Scott sent him on to read Alfred Lord Tennyson's *Idylls of the King*, whose profounder burden was the struggle between Arthurian order and the disorder of primal savagery. Arthur's continual lament—"All my realm reels back into the Beast"—was a thinly veiled echo of the Victorian fear of the specter of anarchy and social dissolution that awaited a society incapable of resolving peacefully the warfare of labor and capital.

Twain's recent work on "Among the Indians" had also reacquainted him with the language of "savage warfare"—the specifically American version of the conflict between order's "realm" and the anarchy of "the Beast." Among the sources he drew on most heavily was General Custer's *My Life on the Plains*, which gave him a number of natural descriptions and confirmed his ideas about the manner and motive of Indian cruelty. The chapters of that book were being serialized in the *Galaxy* at the same time that Twain's humorous sketches were appearing. The two men may or may not have met each other, but can hardly have missed acquaintance with each other's writing. Twain's continuing interest is also attested by his offering to publish Mrs. Custer's reminiscences of her days with the general on the southern plains. *Tenting on the Plains* appeared in 1887, two years before *Connecticut Yankee*. This Indian war material contributed to the symbolism of class in Twain's story; and the Last Stand may well have been the model for the concluding massacre.[8]

[8]Twain and W. D. Howells, *The Mark Twain–Howells Letters: The Correspondence of Samuel L. Clemens and William D. Howells, 1872–1910*, eds. Henry Nash Smith and William M. Gibson, 2 vols. (Cambridge, Mass., 1960), 2: 579–81, 607–15, 621–28, 631; Justin Kaplan, *Mr. Clemens and Mark Twain* (New York, 1966), pp. 339–40.

The initial intentions of Twain are reflected in the satiric form of the first half of the novel. Twain apparently meant to contrast the progressive spirit of nineteenth-century American values with the regressive ideologies of traditional aristocracy, political monarchism, and established religion or superstition. The literary voice of the hero narrator, Hank Morgan, would be that of the truth-seeing and -speaking vernacular; and vernacular speech, metaphors, and jokes would continually deflate the pretensions of both the language and the ideology of chivalric romance. The point of the joke is crystallized when the Yankee—who has become Arthur's grand vizier—compels the knights to change their heraldic devices for nineteenth-century billboard advertisements—"USE PETERSON'S PROPHYLACTIC TOOTHBRUSH—IT'S ALL THE GO." As the Yankee himself suggests, the point of the joke—and hence its ideological charge—will be lost on an audience that cannot read and has no notion of either advertising or toothbrushes.

Such satiric ironies, however, are generally buried beneath the strong contrasts Twain offers between Yankee progress and Arthurian "benightedness." The Yankee speaks for science against magic, for egalitarian values against the aristocracy of birth, for a merit system of promotion against one based on connections, for an equitable code of laws against law of might, for a sharing of power against the monopolization of force by a privileged class. He is for religious toleration and against cruel and unusual punishments. He founds a patent office to support technological innovation. He is for free trade in commodities and against monopolies of all kinds. He offers England a chance to avoid its medievalism and to leap into the light of modern Americanism without the pain of intervening stages.

The contrast between medieval and American values is heightened by his invocation of the Indian savage as a metaphor for the mental condition of his Arthurian aristocrats. They have the manners and the morals of "white Indians" or "Comanches." This suggests a kind of innocence in them; and in the case of Arthur, it suggests a degree of truth in the idea of the noble savage. In representing the cruelty and ignorance of his aristocrats, Twain is true to the vision of "The French and the Comanches," which associates the aristocracy and the savage to "the spirit of massacre," violence unchecked by reason or conscience. But in Arthur, he suggests a lingering affinity for the notion of innate nobility as an inherited, racial trait: Arthur's royalty of nature is revealed in his reaction to the smallpox victims, and it is even more admirable than the Yankee's calculated and self-protective response.[9]

The relationship of aristocrats to a semienslaved lower class, coupled with the satire of chivalric myths, suggests the analogy between Arthurian Britain and the South of Mark Twain's past. The analogy is made explicit in the section of the narrative which sees the disguised Yankee and the king taken and sold as slaves—a plot device that was a basic formula of abolitionist fiction

---

[9]Twain, *A Connecticut Yankee in King Arthur's Court* (1889), Norton Critical Edition (New York, 1982), pp. 19, 73–74, ch. 29.

in the 1850s. Here the racial analogy with class involves an opposition that complements the white-Indian conflict If the Arthurian knights are the southern chivalry, then the lower classes are an amalgamation of both the actual slave class—the blacks—and of the poor whites, who were dependent economically on the planters and who gave their suffrage to the system that enslaved the blacks and pauperized themselves. If in the Indian-war analogy the Yankee appears as a civilizer among savages, in the southern analogy he appears as a carpetbag philanthropist who aims at abolishing slavery and substituting in its place the political and economic system of the free North. He is an invader from another culture (or time) who can project a tyrannous reconstruction of society only because he has been able to conquer a position at the top of society.[10]

The slavery-Reconstruction metaphor, buttressed by the "savage" metaphor, suggests a racial model for interpreting the difficulties the Yankee faces. Although his ideology is democratic, he wonders if the population itself is "up to revolution grade." As a nineteenth-century chauvinist, he is convinced that the centuries of experience between Arthur and George Washington have brought the Anglo-Saxon, at least, up to that standard. Yet the terms of the analogy that links Arthurian Britain with nineteenth-century America suggest that we should be doubtful of the Yankee's confidence. If the "hinds" of sixth-century Britain share the consciousness of nineteenth-century crackers, perhaps there is something wrong in the germ plasm of the race—just as there is something right in Arthur's nature. It is a corrosive and corrupting doubt for an exponent of democratic revolution. It weakens Hank Morgan, and it weakened Twain himself.[11]

Hank confronts early on the problem of democratic revolution. He justifies the French Revolution and the Reign of Terror as the only possible response to the longer, crueler Reign of Terror imposed on the peasantry by the aristocracy. He asserts that revolutions must be baptized in blood if they are to succeed, for only by engaging and giving power to the rage of the people does a revolution engage them in the work of making society according to their own will and intention. Revolution imposed from the top may give them the forms of freedom; but only an active seizure of freedom for themselves will make them free in truth. (This had been the John Brown / Theodore Parker thesis about the moral necessity of a slave rebellion.)

But Hank has two reasons for shrinking from fully endorsing Red Revolution. The first is that he does not trust the character of the people in whose

[10]Ibid., pp. 51–52, chs. 34–36, p. 228. The episode uses the conventions of the abolitionist romance, as in *Uncle Tom's Cabin, The Octoroon*, etc. See Slotkin, *Regeneration Through Violence*, pp. 442–43. To see the Reconstructionist connection compare Albion W. Tourgée, *A Fool's Errand* (1879), for his treatment of the "Chivalry" as barbarians. Tourgée was a not uncritical supporter of Reconstruction who believed that northern capital and know-how could modernize and liberalize the South. His novel shows those liberal hopes defeated by the racialist superstition, and consequent savagery, of white Southerners; and his anti-Yankee party (like that in Twain's novel) is an alliance of "the Chivalry" with the ignorant poor whites. See also Daniel Aaron, *The Unwritten War: American Writers and the Civil War* (New York, 1975), ch. 13.
[11]Twain, *A Connecticut Yankee*, pp. 171–72.

name he acts. He persistently finds in them evidence of "slavishness"—they are superstitious, they worship wealth and status instead of merit, they toady to power in hope of preferment, they are vicious to those weaker than themselves. Hank Morgan is an elitist whose sense of worth derives from his triumph in the competitive life of the nineteenth century, and from his easy victory over competing authorities in the sixth. His own pride of place, his enjoyment of power and the position of moral superiority, his preference for his own kind—boys and men whose character is that of nineteenth-century "go-getters" in sixth-century dress—incline him to be protective of the social order he means to replace. By borrowing the authority of the old order, he can begin to construct a conspiracy that will "build the new world amid the ruins of the old." He creates a revolutionary vanguard of sorts in the corps of boys whom he organizes and trains in the secret knowledge of the higher technology—a cadre chosen from among the elite previously selected for his "civilization factories" or colleges. But although his notion of aristocracy has a different basis, the social order he creates is still divided between elite rulers and slavish commoners; and although he calls for democracy, his mistrust of the slavish and savage commons persists.

This mistrust underlies his second reason for refusing to foster revolution: his desire to protect the institutional and economic forms of his "new deal" once he has successfully put it in place under royal sponsorship. Thus his revolution—like that of Reconstruction—does not convert the masses to its cause, nor undermine traditional ideas and authorities. Isolated as much as aggrandized by the privileged position it hopes to protect, Morgan's regime— like that of Reconstruction—is finally and fatally environed by an opposition uniting the old aristocracy with the slavish masses whom they oppress and control.[12]

The ambiguity of Hank's position is fundamental to his character; and as the novel proceeds, the contradictions of his values become more and more crucial. His identification as a "Connecticut Yankee" carries positive connotations of inventiveness, cleverness, a capacity for hard and productive work. Yet it also invokes associations of the carpetbagger—especially in Twain's southern drawl—and of the confidence man. He is "the Boss"—a name that suggests both the owner or manager of a factory and the corrupt patron (and presumed tyrant) of an urban immigrant constituency (à la Boss Tweed). His name links him to the famous pirate Henry Morgan—the real-life plunderer of the Spanish Main. "Morgan" is also the name of the great financier and Robber Baron J. P. Morgan—certainly a "respectable" robber, a real-life version of the thing Tom Sawyer plays at being at the conclusion of his *Adventures*. The new order that Hank Morgan substitutes for that of chivalry is precisely the order of J. P. Morgan. The knights cease to ride on errantry and become, instead, speculators in the stock market that has arisen along with Hank's other nineteenth-century improvements—the telegraph, the railroad, and the free press. Hank flatters himself that by following the design of

[12]Ibid., pp. 65–68, 247.

nineteenth-century American progress, he had made possible a society that is both fundamentally stable and yet progressive in just the way that industrial America was progressive: a society in which the holdings and powers of the propertied classes are respected, but which nonetheless is peacefully evolving toward a more perfect democracy.

But Morgan's belief is founded on the literal acceptance of what is only a literary convention. In Twain's earlier books, this type of illusion took the form of belief in literary romance; and it was usually deflated and undone by its parodic confrontation with practical experience and vernacular discourse, of the kind used by Huck Finn. Hank Morgan speaks like Huck Finn, and so we are disposed to accept him as a "realist": yet his romantic illusions also distract him from an attack on the hard realities that still underlie social relations. Hank's illusions take the following form: he believes that since he has parodied and undone the myth of chivalry, altered the basis of privilege from birth to wealth, and changed romantic motives to self-interested ones, he has made impossible the outbreak of disorder that (according to Tennyson) destroyed the Arthurian utopia. Since chivalry is no more, it is impossible that Modred should force a breach between Arthur and Lancelot over Guinevere—romance is less important in these hardheaded days. Hence there will be no war in France, no rebellion by Modred, no last battle, and no reeling of Arthur's realm back into the beast. Such a flattering self-image was very much a part of the Victorian world, which came to believe that the course of progress and economic interdependence had made a world war impossible. But, as Twain shows, the new commercial values merely provide different occasions for strife. Modred and Lancelot fall out over a "killing" made in the stock market, and good nineteenth-century motives destroy Arthur's regime at least as thoroughly as the old chivalric motives in Tennyson.

In its latter portions, Twain's book departs emphatically from the progressive model of Bellamy's *Looking Backward*. Hank has failed as a revolutionary in part because of his Bellamistic faith in rational progress, the organization of society under a managerial elite, and acceptance of the economic tendencies of the trust-building era. The necessity of violence is argued by Hank himself in his meditation on the Reign of Terror, but Hank fails to heed the logic of this meditation. Worse, he fails to understand the nature of the society that has sent him forth. Bellamy's hero fell asleep and awoke to find the revolution accomplished as easily and bloodlessly as in a dream. But Hank Morgan is a "supervisor" at the Colt armaments works, and is thus engaged in expanding society's capacity for administering violence. If Hank is the nineteenth century's man, then Colt's Firearms is the representative of modern industrialism. As a supervisor of work in the plant, Hank is engaged in bossing gangs of workers, dominating them by his wits, but relying in the final analysis on force. It is a blow on the head, suffered in the course of a disagreement with one of his workers "conducted with crowbars," that sends him backward in time. Both the violence that sends him and the direction of travel are antithetical to the ideas of *Looking Backward*: Bellamy dreams his reader past the invisible violence of the present to a future of perfect design; Twain hurls us backward in time, into the primitive past, through a violent confrontation between industrial labor and management.[13]

Instead of applying to the sixth century his own analysis of the violent basis of human society and the necessity of violent revolution, Hank Morgan chooses a mode of violence that belongs to the Myth of the Frontier—as modified by the experience of the Civil War. He first attempts to resolve the problem by eliminating the moral authority of the aristocracy through a symbolic confrontation—a tournament in which he will defeat representatives of the ruling class and so demonstrate the efficacy of his power and values. He arms himself for this battle with just the weapons we might expect him to use against "Indians"—a cowboy's lariat hung from a western saddlehorn, and a pair of Colt's revolvers. This confrontation combines the imagery of the tournament—both the medieval original and its nineteenth-century version—and the Wild West show. Twain had seen Buffalo Bill's Wild West in 1885 and written of it, with a shrewd understanding of the Wild West's implicit myth of American progress.

The final battle invokes images from the same source in a much more complex way. Failing to understand that bourgeois greed can spur violence as surely as romantic illusion, the Yankee has failed to anticipate the outbreak of war between Arthur's party and that of Lancelot and Modred. Failing to educate the masses "up to revolution grade," he has opened his regime to attack by the joint forces of aristocratic reaction and religious superstition. Gathering his elite corps of boys about him, he fortifies an isolated position and prepares to stand off the united forces of the aristocracy and the slavish masses. His position is entrenched, surrounded with dynamite mines and electrified barbed wire and bristling with Gatling guns—a masterpiece of nineteenth-century technology. But against him is arrayed the apparently united mass of "the English nation," peasants and chivalry alike; and his "boys," having learned modern republican patriotism at his hands, balk at making war upon the nation.

Morgan answers their objections ideologically and technologically. He declares that their real strife is not with the nation or "the people" of England, but only with the ruling clerical-chivalric class; and through the magic of modern science (specifically electricity) they will be able to effect the separation of the ruling class from the masses—and exterminate the armored chivalry with the flick of a switch. They will first have to demonstrate to "the nation" the power of Morgan's science, decimating and demoralizing the peasants but not exterminating them. As a preliminary demonstration of power, and to keep their own weapons from being used against them, Morgan orders the blowing up of all the railroads, telegraphs, workshops, and civiliza-

---

[13]Ibid., pp. 8, 65–68, 101; Bellamy, *Looking Backward*, chs. 1–2.

tion factories—a massive and instantaneous "scorched earth" in which Morgan destroys his civilization in order to save it.[14]

This is followed by the "Battle of the Sand Belt," in which Morgan's dynamite mines, electrified wire, and Gatling guns accomplish the first part of his program. The peasants are thoroughly demoralized, and "the war with the English nation" is ended. But the forces of chivalry are not so easily defeated: it is the source of their power, and of what virtue they have, that they will maintain their right to rule at all costs. Hence the only way to defeat them will be to exterminate them.

The idea of the war of extermination is the central theme of the Myth of the Frontier, and of the myths of class struggle whose origins we have been examining. The notion of an extermination restricted to the ruling class derives from the Civil War variations on this theme. Extermination or removal of the Confederate elite was suggested several times during the war. The Civil War aspect of the metaphor links the battle of the Sand Belt with Twain's southern theme; but the association of both peasants and knights with savages and primitives suggests the Indian war connection as well.

Here the Custer myth is brought into play. The original myth presented the tableaux of his defeat as an image of progressive young soldiers foundering in a sea of rampant savagery, behind which lay the fanaticism and bigotry of false "philanthropists." Falling in with Bellamy's military metaphor, Hank made his military academy, his West Point, the central institution of learning for his new elite. For them, science and military organization go hand in hand—as indeed they had done for Hank, when he exercised his Yankee ingenuity in the Colt Firearms factory. He is the commander of an elite corps of West Pointers and boys—the imagery links him closely to Custer—and with them he is proud to assert that he will challenge the whole of English chivalry to battle, just as Custer dared the entire Sioux nation to oppose him and his single regiment. Hank Morgan's reasons for pride are far more complex than those of Custer, but the kinship is apparent.

The battle that follows ironically combines both the catastrophic reading of the Last Stand and the view of the battle as a redemptive sacrifice. The catastrophic reading of the Last Stand held that it represented the possible destruction of civilization and progress by an uprising of human savagery from below. The optimistic reading emphasized the sacrificial aspect of the battle, showing that Custer's death struggle wounded the Indians and aroused the slumbering spirit of the American nation, leading in the end to revenge on the Indian and the triumph of a chastened and purified people. But the Battle of the Sand Belt combines these readings into a single dark prophecy. The progressive elite deploys its technological might and exterminates its class enemy with appalling thoroughness:

One thing seemed to be sufficiently demonstrated: our [electric] current was so

[14]Twain, *A Connecticut Yankee*, pp. 227–29 for "Wild West"; pp. 241–51 for the death of Arthur and Morgan's own Last Stand.

> tremendous that it killed before the victim could cry out . . . I believed the time
> was come, now, for my climax; I believed that that whole army was in our trap . . .
> So I touched a button and set fifty electric suns aflame on the top of our precipice.

> The sudden glare paralyzed this host . . . I shot the current through all the fences
> and struck the whole host dead in their tracks. *There* was a groan you could *hear*! It
> voiced the death pang of eleven thousand men . . . "Stand to your guns, men!
> Open fire!"

> The thirteen gatlings began to vomit death into the fated ten thousand . . . Within
> ten short minutes after we had opened fire armed resistance was totally annihi-
> lated, the campaign was ended, we fifty-four masters of England! Twenty-five
> thousand men lay dead around us.

But the political failure of Hank Morgan to raise the people as a whole to
revolution grade makes it impossible for him to leave his fortress. Although
this Custer has massacred all the Indians, his fate is the same: the Yankee falls
into a trance caused by Merlin, and his elite corps perish of a pestilence
brewed in the piled-up corpses of their slaughtered enemies.[15]

The conclusion is a blow to Bellamiac faith. Violence proves inescapable,
and the massive force of the savagery of the lower depths is canceled out by
the armed might that reason deploys; but in the end, reason itself sinks into
magic, madness, and disease through its surfeit of power and of killing. It is a
horrible vision, prophetic in many of its details of the causes and tactics of the
Great War, and of the revolutions that grew out of the exhaustion of society's
military frenzy. But it is also a brilliant and complex development of the
implications of the Custer myth and the ideology of class struggle that it
contained—one in which the Last Stand becomes a metaphor for the fate of
both savages and cavalrymen, peasants and aristocrats, proletarians and elites;
and the "Instinct of Progress" itself willingly calls upon the "Spirit of Massacre."

Twain's work uses the symbolic language of the Frontier Myth tradition,
and he shares its traditional preoccupations. But his book is not simply a
further elaboration of that tradition; it is a commentary on it, an attempt to
turn the language of myth back upon itself. Thus, it does not proffer author or
reader the kind of satisfaction mythology has to offer: it does not "naturalize"
the social dilemma by assimilating it into a vision of harmonious natural
wholeness. *Connecticut Yankee* presents the Myth of the Frontier in the form
of a tragedy. Hank Morgan is a hero because he exemplifies the entrepreneur-
ial skills and egalitarian ambitions of the Jacksonian Frontier hero, and
because he has "improved" these basic endowments by adapting them to the
task of industrial production and industrial management. He rises to the top
of his world not through favor but through merit, particularly of the managerial kind. Yet he discovers that an aristocracy of labor and of merit is still an

---

[15]Ibid., pp. 254–55. Twain's use of Gatling guns is significant, given the strong association
between machine guns and the industrialization of society. See John Ellis, *The Social History of
the Machine Gun* (New York, 1975), chs. 1–3.

aristocracy—an order dependent on political and cultural privilege; and in a society divided between privileged and dependent classes (and between rival classes of the privileged), the maintenance of social order is still dependent on force. Indeed, the essence of class privilege, both under chivalry and under Sir Boss's "new deal," is the right to a legitimate monopoly of force. Hank displaces the monopoly of chain mail and battle-ax with a monopoly of barbed wire and Gatling guns; but he cannot himself dispense with his monopoly, even though it kills him. And there is Twain as well: unable, finally, to identify himself and us uncritically with Hank Morgan; but equally unable to reject Morgan, abandon the Gatlings, and merge with the peasantry of the "English nation." To do that would be to abandon Custer for Sitting Bull and civilization for white savagery. Morgan's trap is built into the language of the myth through which he interprets his Last Stand.

Armies and Factories:
A Connecticut Yankee

Walter Benn Michaels

"Training is everything," says Mark Twain's Connecticut Yankee in an extraordinary speech that begins by asserting the absolute determination of the individual by society—"Training is everything. . . . Training is all there is to a person"—and ends by asserting the absolute autonomy of the "one microscopic atom" of a person that is "original,"[1] that is, in other words, *not* a function of training. Hence the enormity of the Yankee's opportunity—he can train an entire people—and hence the enormity of his failure—they can resist his training.

For despite its frequent proclamations of the "power of training! of influence! of education!" (180), it is with the power to *resist* training that *Connecticut Yankee* is most concerned. The Yankee's notorious reliance on violence and physical force in his efforts to "civilize" the "white Indians" of Arthurian England and his failure in these efforts are both effects of a conception of individuality that systematically denies any power at all to training, influence, and education. "A man *is* a man at bottom," the Yankee reflects happily, "Whole ages of abuse and oppression cannot crush the manhood clear out of him" (279). The man in question here has resisted the tyranny of the sixth century, but the Yankee's admiration is as great for those who resist the democratizing of the nineteenth: "English knights," he tells the faithful young products of his "man factory," "can be killed, but they cannot be conquered" (397). They cannot be conquered because no amount of physical abuse or coercion can ever produce in them the educational advance that even an acknowledgment of defeat would serve to mark. They are monuments to an individuality defined by nothing but the powers of resistance.

It is for this reason, rather than for their lack of civilization, that they are plausibly seen as "white Indians."[2] "The Indian is hewn out of the rock,"

[1]Mark Twain, *A Connecticut Yankee in King Arthur's Court* (1889; reprint ed., Harmondsworth, Eng., 1971), 161. Subsequent references are cited in parentheses in the text.

[2]In his important and illuminating *The Fatal Environment* (Middletown, Conn., 1986), Richard Slotkin describes Twain as unable "to identify himself and us uncritically with Hank Morgan; but equally unable to reject Morgan . . . and merge with the peasantry of the English nation" since to

Francis Parkman had written in 1851, "You can rarely change the form without destruction of the substance."[3] In principle ineducable, such men could only be subdued by violence. Hence, as Michael Rogin has argued, Indian hunters like Andrew Jackson identified with the Indians in the very act of—actually *by means of* the very act of—hunting them; the violence of the Indian required the violence of the Indian hunter who, in killing the Indian, became a version of him.[4] It is not hard to see a similar identification in the "withering deluge" of machine-gun fire that kills the last ten thousand "white Indians" at the end of *Connecticut Yankee*. But this massacre, so often identified by critics and historians as a critique of late-nineteenth-century industrialism— what Twain called "machine culture"—is in fact a tribute to that culture and to its machines. Indians in Progressive America were increasingly identified as paradigms of the American individualism that was understood to have created Twain's machine culture just because of the absolute inflexibility that Parkman in 1851 had predicted would cause their "ruin." Thus in Thomas Dixon's antisocialist dystopia *Comrades* (1909), it is the Indian Saka, in addition to the capitalist Colonel Worth, who emerges as a hero of "individuality":[5] having tried and failed to order him about, the socialist "Brotherhood of Man saw Saka no more for many moons, but the crack of his rifle was heard on the mountain side and the smoke of his teepee curled defiantly from the neighboring plains" (175). Morgan's recognition that *his* Indians can be neither trained nor conquered is thus a recognition of their rocklike character, and his commitment to exterminating them is not an attack on their savagery but a tribute to their individuality. Only by means of the massacre can Twain acknowledge the "microscopic atom" that is "truly me," the selfhood that cannot be altered and so must be destroyed.

Twain's Indians, however, are made out of metal, not rock. Twain's financially disastrous involvement with technology and, in particular, with that "mechanical miracle," the Paige Compositor, is well known, and just as the end of *Connecticut Yankee* is often read as a repudiation of late-nineteenth-century industrialism, it is often read also as a proleptic repudiation of the typesetter: "In bringing Morgan to death Twain was symbolically killing off

---

"do that would be to abandon Custer for Sitting Bull and civilization for white savagery" (530). The mistake here, as I see it, is to understand identification with the Yankee as identification with a certain set of values—"progressivism"—and thus to read *Connecticut Yankee* either as endorsing or repudiating or partially endorsing and partially repudiating those values. I argue below that Twain's identification with the Yankee is essentially ontological, involving a commitment not to the views he holds (about, say, civil service exams or technology) but to the self he is (a mechanical one), and thus expressing itself most powerfully in formal terms.

3Quoted in Michael Paul Rogin, *Fathers and Children: Andrew Jackson and the Subjugation of the American Indian* (New York, 1976), 115.

4Rogin's account of this process is more psychoanalytic than my summary of his account; he puts the point in Kleinian terms, citing characterizations of the Indians as infants and describing identification with them as the simultaneous experience of "longing for union with the mother and primitive rage against her" (119).

5Thomas Dixon, Jr., *Comrades* (New York, 1909), 82. Subsequent references are cited in parentheses in the text.

the machine madness which possessed him."[6] But what was most striking about Twain's involvement with the Paige was not that it took the form of an excessive (financially or ethically) and hence punishable enthusiasm for technology as such. Had Twain been backing the Paige's competition, the Mergenthaler linotype machine, he would have made the fortune he expected to make. The problem was that he chose the wrong machine, and his reasons for choosing that machine are crucial to an understanding of the individual that emerges triumphant in *Connecticut Yankee.*

The Paige Compositor, as Twain's financial savior H. H. Rogers described it many years after its final failure, "was the nearest approach to a human being in the wonderful things it could do of any machine I have ever known."[7] Unlike the Mergenthaler, which cast its own type, melted it down at the end of each run and then recast it, the Paige performed all the acts of a human typesetter—setting, justifying, and distributing individual types—automatically and, when it was working, very quickly.[8] Where the seventeen-year-old Mark Twain had been able to set only ten thousand ems a day (more proficient typesetters could do fifteen thousand), the Paige could set twelve thousand ems an *hour* (the Mergenthaler could only do about eight thousand). But it wasn't working very often for, as H. H. Rogers went on to say, its wonderful similarity to a human being was "just the trouble; it was too much of a human being and not enough of a machine. It had all the complications of the human mechanism, all the ability of getting out of repair, and it could not be replaced with the ease and immediateness of the human being."[9] With its eighteen thousand parts (still a record), the Paige would never be able to function economically; eventually, it helped drive Twain to bankruptcy. But its real significance was not so much financial as intellectual; the Paige marked a nineteenth-century highpoint in the attempt to represent human actions in metal. As a strategy for building effective machines, this proved to be a failure; the success of the Mergenthaler was a function of its bypassing what Justin Kaplan has called "the human analogy."[10] But as a thesis about what sort of thing a person is—the sort of thing that can be represented in machinery, if not a typesetter then a computer—the thinking that produced the Paige was not and has not been in any definitive way discredited: at least one segment of the artificial intelligence industry of the late twentieth century is committed

---

[6]James M. Cox, "*A Connecticut Yankee in King Arthur's Court:* The Machinery of Self-Preservation," *Yale Review,* 50 (1960): 89–102; reprinted in *A Connecticut Yankee in King Arthur's Court,* ed. Allison R. Ensor (New York, 1982), 398.

[7]Quoted in *Mark Twain's Correspondence with Henry Huttleston Rogers, 1893–1909,* ed. with an introduction by Lewis Leary (Berkeley, 1969), 26.

[8]For the best account of the Paige and of Twain's involvement with it, see Justin Kaplan, *Mr. Clemens and Mark Twain* (New York, 1966), 280–311.

[9]Ibid.

[10]Ibid., 283. Kaplan, like John F. Kasson after him, tends to emphasize what Kasson calls Twain's "anthropomorphic conception of the machine"; Kasson, *Civilizing the Machine* (New York, 1977), 204. My own interest is less in Twain's tendency to see machines as mysteriously human than in his commitment to seeing humans as essentially mechanical.

to insisting upon not bypassing the human analogy. And as a thesis about the nature of individuality—the "truly me" is the mechanical me, as immune to training as Dixon's Indians are to socialism—the Paige provided a valuable bulwark against those who really did think that training was everything and who argued, as John Dewey did in *The School and Society* (1900), that the trick to effective training was to "get hold of the child's natural impulses and instincts," "saturating him with the spirit of service," and so fitting him for life in the "larger society."[11]

Dewey here articulates the idea of a total education—an utterly "saturated" self—that Twain's imagination of the mechanical self is designed to make impossible. Indeed, progressive education, conceiving "individual mind as a function of social life," is devoted precisely to exploiting the possibilities for training neglected by an "earlier psychology," which "regarded mind as a purely individual affair" (98). The disciplinary techniques of that earlier psychology treated the individual as a self-contained entity in need of "external" control; they are replaced in the "new education" by techniques of "guidance" (17) that, instead of "forcing the child from without," attempt to shape her from within. Once you "get hold" of the child's "interests," you have no need for the tactics of "external imposition."

Dewey himself, however, manifests some reluctance to accept this account of the shift from traditional to progressive education as a shift from "forcing" the child to appealing to her "interests," not, however, because of the difficulty involved in producing an educational system that was continuously interesting but rather because of the difficulty involved in producing an educational system that wasn't. For even the disciplinary practices that are usually understood as forms of "external imposition"—keeping the child after school, giving her low marks, refusing to promote her—are in fact indirect appeals to interest or appeals to interest "in its obverse aspect": "to fear, to dislike of various kinds of physical, social, and personal pain" (29). For Dewey, then, even the most apparently coercive educational methods turn out to rely, like progressive education, on some version of the appeal to interest (turning out to be, from the standpoint of *Connecticut Yankee*, insufficiently coercive).

In education, Dewey would write some fifteen years later, "purely external direction is impossible."[12] External direction may elicit a "physical result" (as when a man is locked up to prevent him from "breaking into other persons' houses"), but we must not "confuse a physical with an educative result"—locking the man up "may not alter his disposition to commit burglary" (27). The point here is not to deny that locking a man up may be an effective way of keeping him from committing burglary; it is rather to remind us that as educators we are interested in the disposition that produces the action rather

---

[11]John Dewey, *The Child and the Curriculum, The School and Society* (1900; reprint ed., Chicago, 1956), 127, 29. Subsequent references are cited in parentheses in the text.

[12]John Dewey, *Democracy and Education* (1916; reprint ed., New York, 1963), 25. Subsequent references are cited in parentheses in the text.

than in the action itself. But, of course, locking the burglar up (or threatening to lock him up) may, after all, alter his disposition (just as threatening to keep the child after school may alter hers), so the purest negative example is action without disposition of any kind. "Suppose that conditions were so arranged that one person automatically caught a ball and then threw it to another person who caught and automatically returned it; and that each so acted without knowing where the ball came from or went to. Clearly such action would be without point or meaning. It might be physically controlled, but it would not be socially directed" (30–31). Where the physical control over the burglar's actions (his incarceration) might after all appeal to his interest (in avoiding incarceration), the physical control over the ball throwers can appeal to no interests since the ball throwers are imagined from the start as having no interests—that's what it means for their actions to be described as proceeding automatically. The ball throwers are better examples than the burglar because, while the burglar may resist education, the ball throwers are immune to it; with them, the only possible results are "physical," the only possible changes in their behavior a function of "force."

Seeking a philosophically satisfactory (although pedagogically irrelevant) alternative to progressive education, Dewey is thus driven to Twain's solution; the world of his ball throwers is the world of Twain's knights, who can be killed but not conquered because (like the ball throwers but unlike the burglar) they are immune to even the attenuated appeal to their interest implicit in the threat of violence. Since no education can be "purely external," in *Connecticut Yankee* there can be no education; schooling is redescribed by Twain as manufacture, training as production—it takes place in the man "Factory" (159) or in the "civilization-factories" (396). And the conflict between cultures is really a conflict between machines: the ones made in the Yankee's factories and that "political machine" (160), the Church; Merlin's "magic" and the Yankee's "science." As such, this conflict is intrinsically and essentially violent; because they are immune to the threat of violence, the knights are susceptible only to the fact of violence. The "microscopic atom" that is "truly me" can be altered only by being transformed (by dynamite) into "miscroscopic fragments of knights and hardware and horse-flesh" (259), uncountable "because they did not exist as individuals, but merely as homogeneous protoplasm, with alloys of iron and buttons" (396). The "error" of the old psychology, Dewey thought, was to see "no alternative between forcing the child from without, or leaving him entirely alone" (17). Seeing no alternative between the microscopic atom that is the individual and the microscopic fragments that do not exist as individuals, Twain commits himself to this "error." The triumph of social atomism in *Connecticut Yankee* is his ability to represent any transformation of the atom as its destruction. The world in which the only actions are violent ones is the world made safe for individuals.

It may be, however, that the characterization of these transformations as "violent" is as inappropriate as the language of "force" and "external imposition" turned out to be in connection with the old education's disciplinary appeals to punishment. It was inappropriate with respect to punishment because the appeal to, say, the burglar's fear of jail in no way bypasses the question of his interest; it just alters the interest that is being appealed to. And it is inappropriate with respect to the knights and ball throwers because it makes no sense to think of them as having been coerced or even externally imposed upon. Having no interests in the first place, automatic ball players can no more have their interests violated or ignored than they can have them appealed to. They can't be directed "from without" because they don't really have a within—in Dewey's terns, a machine is *all* without. Twain's mechanical Indians thus represent not only an extension but a perfection of Parkman's Indians hewn out of rock. In Parkman, the Indians' "substance" is destroyed when their "form" is altered; substance is simultaneously different from and dependent on form, and it is this difference combined with dependence that produces the possibility of violence. But in Twain, form is either absolutely identical to or absolutely independent of substance; the response of the victim is in both cases irrelevant.

Thus St. Stylite, the hermit, "bowing his body ceaselessly and rapidly almost to his feet," can be hooked up to "a system of elastic cords" and "used to run a sewing-machine" (205). The hermit is praying, but he is at the same time engaged in "one of the most useful motions in mechanics, the pedal-movement." The example is parodic but the principle—the irrelevance of what St. Stylite knows and wants to what he can be used to do—is not. Think of the difference the slide rule made to what Frederick Winslow Taylor called "The Art of Cutting Metals": "By means of these slide-rules," Taylor wrote in 1911, intricate mathematical problems "can be solved in less than half a minute by any good mechanic, whether he understands anything about mathematics or not."[13] Fitted out with a slide rule, as St. Stylite is fitted out with elastic, the mechanic can become a part in a calculating machine as St. Stylite became a part in a sewing machine.

Indeed, the mechanic is from this perspective a more extreme example of mechanization than St. Stylite, since with St. Stylite the difference between form and substance more or less corresponds to the difference between body and mind, as if the mind were immune to mechanization, whereas the slide rule makes the distinction between body and mind irrelevant. Taylor is often accused of producing a "schism" "between the mind and the body of the

[13]Frederick Winslow Taylor, *The Principles of Scientific Management* (1911; reprint ed., New York, 1967), 111. Subsequent references are cited in parentheses in the text. For helpful discussion of scientific management in relation to the more general phenomena of the efficiency movement and systematic management, see Samuel Haber, *Efficiency and Uplift: Scientific Management in the Progressive Era* (Chicago, 1964); and Daniel Nelson, *Managers and Workers: Origins of the New Factory System in the United States* (Madison, Wisc., 1975). For a powerful analysis of Taylor's importance in the restructuring of work, see Alfred Sohn-Rethel, *Intellectual and Manual Labor*, trans. Martin Sohn-Rethel (Atlantic Highlands, N.J., 1983). And for an important account of Taylorism's relation to the history of American literature and art, see Cecilia Tichi, *Shifting Gears: Technology, Literature, Culture* (Chapel Hill, N.C., 1987).

industrial workman,"[14] and the workmen in plants undergoing Taylorization routinely complained about being reduced to automata, unable to think or move for themselves. Taylor's response to such complaints was not to deny them but to generalize them: "The same criticism and objection," he argued, could be "raised against all other modern subdivisions of labor" (125). The actions of a surgeon, properly understood, were as mechanical as those of a bricklayer or metal cutter. Replacing "rules of thumb" with "rigid rules for each motion of every man"—in effect, bypassing individual judgment and substituting for it something like a slide rule—was scientific management's goal for human action at all levels. The "instruction cards" for every factory worker that became one of the hallmarks of scientific management specified not only the rules according to which work would be performed but the rules by which that work would be evaluated. The cards call, Frank Gilbreth wrote, for "a definite quality. They do not call for having the 'work done to the satisfaction' of anybody."[15] The manager's satisfaction is as irrelevant as the worker's initiative. In scientific management, management was to be as mechanical as the work it managed; the mind was as much a machine as the body. The discrepancy between what St. Stylite is thinking and what his *body* is doing thus appears most powerfully in Taylor as a discrepancy between what the mechanic is thinking and what his *mind* is doing.

Perhaps the most extreme example of mechanization, however, is the Yankee himself, whose character is so much a product of Twain's own identification with the Paige Compositor. Readers have often noted the extraordinary inconsistencies in Twain's presentation of the Yankee, for example the juxtaposition of his lachrymose sympathy for Morgan le Fay's victims and his cheerful willingness to be "reasonable" by letting her hang the band that plays that "Sweet By-and-By" so badly. Attempts to explain such inconsistencies by appealing to the complexities of the Yankee's character are unconvincing.[16] The execution of the band, like the hanging of Sir Dinadan the Humorist, is a joke, and it is a joke made possible by indifference to consistency, by a conception of character as mechanical and as thus susceptible only (but absolutely) to external change: the transformation produced by Hercules' crowbar is a prototype of the transformations produced by Mark Twain's typewriter. To put it another way, the Yankee doesn't exactly *have* a character, he *is* the character he can be described as having; he is incapable of behaving "out of character" because his character is defined by nothing but his behav-

[14]Sohn-Rethel, *Intellectual and Manual Labor*, 157.

[15]Frank B. Gilbreth, *Primer of Scientific Management* (New York, 1912), 42.

[16]Also unconvincing, in my view, are attempts to extend the analysis of the Yankee's character to his politics. John Kasson, for example, concludes his interesting discussion of *Connecticut Yankee* by claiming that the book demonstrates "how a powerful, supposedly humanitarian republican leader may betray his own ideals as he seeks to extend control over a weaker, underdeveloped nation through essentially aggressive use of his technology"; *Civilizing the Machine*, 215. Presentism aside, the trouble with this analysis is not exactly that it takes the Yankee too seriously but that it takes him seriously in the wrong way, transforming Twain's vision of mechanized (and hence rescued) individuality into a critique of the Yankee's humanitarianism.

ior. If St. Stylite and the mechanic embody the priority of form to substance, the Yankee embodies the identity of form and substance. And when the only identity is formal identity, there can be no question of consistency—only repetition or difference. To alter him is thus to destroy him but at the same time to replace him; he perfects the "immutability" of the Indian by making it mutable.

A *Connecticut Yankee* does not, then, express an attitude toward technology, either the optimistic one of a Mark Twain who loved machines or the pessimistic one of a Mark Twain who was getting nervous about the Paige Compositor and beginning to worry about the ultimate value of machine culture. Rather it embodies a commitment to the essential likeness of persons to machines, a commitment embodied also in Twain's own identification with the Paige and in his vision of himself as a kind of writing machine: "I started the mill again 6 days ago and have ground out a good average," he wrote Rogers, while waiting for news of the Paige's last try-out, "11,800 words" in a week.[17] "It is the aim of Scientific Management," Gilbreth wrote in 1912, "to induce men to act as nearly like machines as possible."[18] In the Yankee's failure, Twain predicts Taylor's success; defending individuals, he prepares them for the factory.

In Edward Bellamy's *Equality* (1897), the sequel to his phenomenally successful utopian novel *Looking Backward* (1888), the narrator asks again a version of a question he had asked in 1888: what is done with people who do not acknowledge their "social duty"[19] and refuse to join the "industrial army" that in the late twentieth century provides equal work, equal pay, and equal rights to all citizens? Bellamy's answer in 1888 to the question whether "universal military service" was "compulsory" had been first that it was more "a matter of course than of compulsion"[20] and then, less evasively, that "a man able to duty, and persistently refusing, is sentenced to solitary imprisonment on bread and water till he consents" (107). By 1897, however, bread and water—"compelling someone to work against his will by force"—has come to seem "abhorrent"; in *Equality*, such a man would be provided with seeds and tools and "turned loose on a reservation expressly prepared for such persons," a reservation corresponding, perhaps, as the voice of the twentieth century says to the nineteenth, "with the reservations set apart for such Indians in your day as were unwilling to accept civilization."[21]

The Indian here is once again a figure for the resisting individual, but the Bartleby-like refusals so admired by Twain and Dixon are condemned by Bellamy as "excessive individualism" (57) or, forgetting even the "excessive,"

[17]*Twain's Correspondence with Rogers*, 105–6.
[18]Gilbreth, *Primer*, 50.
[19]Edward Bellamy, *Equality* (New York, 1897), 41.
[20]Edward Bellamy, *Looking Backward* (New York, 1982), 70. Subsequent references are cited in parentheses in the text.
[21]Bellamy, *Equality*, 41.

as symptoms of that "incapacity for cooperation which followed from the individualism on which your social system was founded" (103). "Who has not often felt . . . as if the sense of personal identity, i.e. sense of his connection with his particular individuality, were slipping from him?"[22] Bellamy wrote in an early essay. This appeal to a "religion of solidarity" in which the individual would be reduced to "an atom, a grain of sand on a boundless shore, a bubble in a foam-flecked ocean," may be understood to express what Arthur Lipow describes as Bellamy's "deep-going revulsion against individualism in all its forms," a revulsion that motivates his attempt in *Looking Backward* "to solve the problem of the individual in modern society by the suppression of individuality and personality in the warm embrace of a bureaucratic society,"[23] an attempt that can serve as counterpoint to *Connecticut Yankee* in being an attack on the individualism Twain defends.

At the same time, however, that *Looking Backward*'s doctrine (and most of the book is doctrine, a series of lectures by the twentieth century's Dr. Leete in response to the questions of the nineteenth century's Julian West) seems to preach against individualism, what there is of its narrative works in a somewhat different direction. For when Julian West awakens after his first night in the twentieth century, he finds himself "staring about" in "anguish," "unable to regain the clew" to his "personal identity": "I was no more able to distinguish myself from pure being during those moments than we may suppose a soul in the rough to be before it has received the earmarks, the individualizing touches which make it a person" (77). The desire to lose one's identity is here matched by the fear of losing it and by the hope that one will "never know" that fear again; the society in which individualism has been eradicated is imagined as a society in which individualism has been secured.

It is this reversal, rather than the search for an alibi, that makes sense of Bellamy's claim that service in the industrial army "is more a matter of course than of compulsion." Dixon's antisocialist Indian is a hero because he lives according to "natural law" under which "no man, even the poorest, could be commanded to work by a superior power. He could always quit if he liked. He might choose to go hungry . . . but he was still master of his own person. His will was supreme. He, and he alone, could say, I will, or I will not" (307). In this characteristic defense of freedom of contract (socialism, Dixon complains, replaces "contract" with "command"), Dixon identifies individuality with the possibility of independence, and that possibility—the refusal to serve—is just what Bellamy denies. He denies it, however, not because he cannot countenance it but because, in the end, he cannot imagine it. Service in the industrial army counts in *Looking Backward* less as a choice one can make than as the ground of the choices one can make. Thus the refusal to serve seems like "suicide" (70), not a refusal on behalf of individuality but a refusal of individuality. "Nowadays everybody is a part of a system with a distinct

---

[22]Edward Bellamy, "The Religion of Solidarity," quoted in Lipow, *Authoritarian Socialism*, 45.
[23]Ibid., 162.

place and function. I am outside the system," Julian complains, "and don't see how I can get in" (137). By no means a declaration of independence, neither is this complaint a renunciation of individuality. Rather the yearning for a "distinct place" within the system (like the "anguish" induced by being unable to "distinguish" yourself from "pure being") marks the assertion of an individuality that only some "system" can make available.

In *Looking Backward*, that system is the army. Where Dixon's war hero Colonel Worth hates the army's "organization," hates "its iron laws of discipline, its cruel machinery devised for suppressing the individuality of its members" (81), the peace-loving citizens of *Looking Backward* regard its "perfect organization" as a way of producing what they call "self-devotion" (89). Divided into three "grades," which are in turn divided into two "classes," within which are "many minor distinctions of standing" (107–8), the industrial army is more committed to producing individuality than to suppressing it. But the individuality it produces is defined by difference rather than independence. What the industrial army offers is a system of finely graded distinctions, an "organization" that makes "self-devotion" possible because it defines the terms in which "self-devotion" can be pursued. Outside the system you cannot know who you are because you are not yet you—you are "pure" (i.e., undifferentiated) "being." But the system allows for differences—indeed, it consists of nothing but differences—and by making difference possible, it makes identity possible.

From this standpoint, what used to look like individuality comes instead to look like the inability to achieve individuality. After Taylor's initial presentation of "A Piece Rate System" before the American Society of Engineers in 1895, one of the discussants, admitting the virtues of Taylor's system, nonetheless waxed nostalgic for a time when scientific management was "unnecessary," when the "machine shops of this country were individual shops. . . . There was a certain community of feeling, in those days, between the boys in the shop and the master, which I think passed away when machine-shop owners became corporations, when they were managed by a board of directors who never saw the workmen, who knew nothing of them, individually, and, as I fear, cared less."[24] Taylor, however, redescribes workmen in individual shops as "workmen" in "isolation" (25), unable to profit from the scientific study of time and motion and, in this respect (strikingly enough) in exactly the same situation as workmen in "gangs." The subject of scientific management, Taylor maintains, is neither workmen in "isolation" nor workmen in "masses" but, rescued from the undifferentiation of isolation and the equal undifferentiation of the mass, the "workman as an individual" (71–72).

[24]Frederick Winslow Taylor, "A Piece Rate System," reprinted in Clarence Bertrand Thompson, ed., *Scientific Management: A Collection of the More Significant Articles Describing the Taylor System of Management* (Cambridge, Mass., 1914), 680–81. The compatibility here of the "individual" with the "community" suggests that even in nostalgia the old opposition between the individual and society was coming to seem irrelevant; community and independence become indistinguishable when confronted by "organization."

What is even more striking here, however, is scientific management's simultaneous compatibility with the defense of individualism and with the attack on it: the white Indian, defined by his resistance to "organization," mechanized, becomes the ideal factory worker; the industrial soldier, defined by nothing but his participation in the system, also becomes the ideal factory worker. Hence the appropriateness both of Herbert Croly's contradictory complaint about American individualism and of his vision of that complaint answered. The complaint was that America was both excessively and insufficiently individualistic, and the response is one that represents individuals defined by difference as individuals who have achieved independence. "Individuality is necessarily based on genuine discrimination"[25], he writes, and, "In every kind of practical work specialization . . . is coming to prevail; and in this way individuals . . . are obtaining definite and stimulating possibilities for personal efficiency and independence" (430). Discrimination and specialization clearly invoke the Bellamyite conception of individuality as difference, but Croly, rather than exchanging (as Bellamy does) independence for difference, imagines difference as providing a new basis for independence. Thus the nonunion laborer, characterized by employers as the "independent working man," is regarded by Croly as "a species of industrial derelict" (387) who, if he were a truly "independent industrial individual" would demonstrate both his independence and his individuality by joining the union" (395).

In Croly, then, as in Taylor, the opposition between attacking individuality and defending it or, more importantly, between defining it by difference (Bellamy) and defining it by independence (Twain), is overcome. This is not to say that it disappears entirely or that it never mattered in the first place. The sense that individuality was threatened helped to make possible the enthusiasm for turning men into machines; the sense that individuality was threatening helped to make possible the enthusiasm for turning men into soldiers. But the compatibility of the products is in the end more striking than the incompatibility of the motives. What emerges from the defense and the attack combined is a transformation of individuality, one in which the mechanical defense of independence becomes itself a part of the machinery that reimagines the loss of independence as the access to individuality.

[25]Herbert Croly, *The Promise of American Life* (1909; reprint ed., New York, 1965), 413. Subsequent references are cited in parentheses in the text.

Hank Morgan and the Colonization of Utopia

David R. Sewell

[A] *colonial situation* is created, so to speak, the very instant a white man, even if he is alone, appears in the midst of a tribe, even if it is independent, so long as he is thought to be rich or powerful or merely immune to the local forces of magic, and so long as he derives from his position, even though only in his most secret self, a feeling of his own superiority. The man-in-the-street will say instinctively and without experience that if the white man who goes among the negroes [sic] avoids being eaten, he will become King.

—O. Mannoni (18)

[I]f . . . it was really the sixth century, all right, I didn't want any softer thing: I would boss the whole country inside of three months.

—Hank Morgan (Twain, *Connecticut Yankee* 63)

When I was in the sixth grade my class had a unit on Aztec culture and history. As part of a follow-up exam, my teacher asked us to write a few sentences about what we would do to help Montezuma if we could travel back through time to Mexico just before the arrival of Cortés. The answer seemed obvious to me: I wrote that I would take along lots of machine guns and hand grenades and give them to the Aztecs to use against the Spaniards. Years later I first read the conclusion to Mark Twain's *A Connecticut Yankee in King Arthur's Court* with a sense of déjà vu—Mark Twain had shared my boyish fantasy of power. Only in his case it came as an adult. Around the beginning of 1885, a forty-nine-year-old Twain would jot in his notebook the vision that developed into the apocalyptic Battle of the Sand Belt: "Have a battle between a modern army, with gatling guns—(automatic) 600 shots a minute . . . torpedos, balloons, 100-ton cannon, iron-clad fleet &c & Prince de Joinville's Middle Age Crusaders" (*Mark Twain's Notebooks* 86). As finally written, the battle would be less theatrical but more grimly efficient: Hank, Clarence, and fifty-two helpers kill twenty-five thousand knights with a combination of electric fences, an engineered flood, and the inevitable Gatling guns. Arguably, there are "progressive" motives behind the anachronistic dissemination of lethal weapons that Mark Twain and I imagined, namely

Reprinted from *American Transcendental Quarterly* 3 (March 1989), 27–44. By permission of the University of Rhode Island.

resistance to hegemonic invasion and defiance of theocratic oppression, respectively. Our revisions of history are utopian to the extent that they project the substitution for an actual past of a story that is more equitable, rational, and pleasing to contemporary sensibilities. But there is something terribly disturbing about this apparent tendency of the modern imagination to make destructive weaponry the archetypal form of knowledge that the present offers the past in such a time-travel story. Why does our awareness of superiority lead us so inevitably to plot a display of force? What turns our knowledge into firepower?

Gatlings against arrows and lances: it is not hard to guess that Mark Twain's "fable of progress" displaces onto a temporal opposition the historical confrontation between Europe and the noncivilized world.[1] Long before the development of anything like modern science fiction, mysterious aliens with awesome powers populated the most widely read European and American adventure stories, tales told, unlike *The War of the Worlds*, from the point of view of the invaders: narratives of conquest, exploration, and frontier war. Hank Morgan's fireworks, bombs, and revolvers are the literary descendants of the heavy cannon which Columbus discharged during his first voyage to prove to allied Indians his ability to defeat their enemies, and of the "squibs and serpents" the young Francis Parkman fired off to impress a tribe of Ogillallah Sioux with his skill as a "fire-medicine" (Irving 128; Parkman 225–226). As I mean the epigraphs to this essay to suggest, Hank Morgan is Mannoni's man-in-the-street fortuitously placed in his own "colonial situation," and inexorably rising to become Boss of sixth-century Britain. The relation between Hank's progressivism and Camelot's backwardness is structurally identical to the dichotomy between "civilization" and "savagism" that provided nineteenth-century America with an ideology, an anthropology, and a literary myth.[2] The collapse of Hank's modernized Britain, his Pyrrhic victory at the Sand Belt, and his final defeat at the hands of the "wicked shaman" Merlin reflect almost allegorically the moral consequences of a polity of "civilization or death."[3] But the crucial implications of Hank's failure go radically beyond a mere incrimination of the abuse of political power. Hank self-destructs not in spite of but *because of* his utopianism, because the knowledge that he brings to the Middle Ages is inescapably a form of power that follows laws operating independently and mostly outside the awareness of their subject. In March 1886, shortly after he had begun work on *A Connecticut Yankee*, Twain formulated one of those laws at the beginning of an address on the labor movement: "Power, when lodged in the hands of man, means oppression— *insures* oppression: it means oppression *always*: not always consciously, delib-

---

[1]The phrase "fable of progress" is Henry Nash Smith's (*Mark Twain's Fable of Progress*).

[2]For a history of the concepts of civilization and savagism in America, see Pearce.

[3]Among the parallels between Haggard's *King Solomon's Mines* and *A Connecticut Yankee* noted by Justin Kaplan is "the figure of the wicked shaman who represents magic as well as religious orthodoxy" (146). "Civilization or death to all American savages" is recorded as an American soldier's toast during the Revolutionary War (quoted in Pearce 51).

erately, purposely; not always severely, or heavily, or cruelly, or sweepingly; but *oppression*, anyway, and *always*, in one shape or another" ("New Dynasty" 383). The "what if" postulate of the reverse time-travel plot inherently creates the colonial situation, since it is premised on the time traveler's superiority to everyone he meets in the past, a pre-eminence in technology, political theory, and even morals, that the traveler believes sanctions his exercise of power. But the time traveler is only a special case of any utopian projector who aims at replacing one system of politics or discourse with a superior one. The most radical implication of *A Connecticut Yankee in King Arthur's Court* is that utopian narrative is a variety of literary imperialism— that Utopia is always a colony.

Criticism of *A Connecticut Yankee* has sometimes proceeded as if it were enough to identify the target of Mark Twain's satire in order to decide whether the novel is in fact "utopian." If Twain's true intent was, as he says in a section of his autobiography dating from 1906, to contrast medieval life with modern civilization "to the advantage of the latter" (*Autobiography* 271), then Hank is a progressive hero whose utopian project unfortunately fails because it is sabotaged by reactionary forces. If, on the other hand, Mark Twain is writing a cautionary tale about the excesses of capitalist civilization and technology, then Hank is the blundering architect of a dystopia, an authoritarian proto-fascist.[4] Generic categorization is confounded further by the fact that Hank's "utopia" is nothing but his own nineteenth century exported backwards, whereas utopian fiction is commonly understood to describe a better society than the author's. And even if Hank's design for Britain is read as a "Utopia program" (Holmes 464), one must confront the irony of its ultimate failure (Robinson 67–69).[5]

But the attempt to assign a fixed generic label to *A Connecticut Yankee* is already frustrated, independently of interpretive questions, by Mark Twain's protean handling of genre. Like all of his full-length fiction, the novel jumbles together heterogeneous conventions, allusions, voices, and modes. Among the narrative forms that are incorporated, parodied. or even partially invented are Arthurian romance, science fiction, lost-race tales, travelogue, exploration accounts, adventure stories, slave narratives, dime novels, and ethnographic

---

[4]This interpretive dichotomy is strikingly evident in articles by Everett Carter and Chadwick Hansen that appeared during the same year. Carter relies on E. D. Hirsch's theory of hermeneutics to argue that the "probable meaning" of *A Connecticut Yankee* is "a defense of democracy, technology, and progress" (427) and that the carnage at the end is "no aberration but a conventional mode of frontier hyperbole" (432). For Hansen, Hank is a totalitarian, literally comparable to Hitler, who attributes social evil to "a scapegoat class" whose elimination will produce "utopia"; the Battle of the Sand Belt "is precisely an act of genocide" (70).

[5]Other critics who define *A Connecticut Yankee* as utopian include Khouri, Jones, Tuveson, and Winters. Among those who judge it dystopian or otherwise imperfectly utopian are Hansen, Kasson, Suvin (194–196), and Salomon (103–105). David Ketterer has noted the significant fact that when Mark Twain read Bellamy's *Looking Backward* he apparently associated it not with *A Connecticut Yankee* but with his own formally utopian sketch "The Curious Republic of Gondour" (*Science Fiction* xxxi. n. 23).

and sociological reportage.[6] More importantly, instead of writing a "classic" utopia, Mark Twain has explored the psychological and mythic origins of utopian narrative in modern Western and specifically American culture. *A Connecticut Yankee* resembles less the formal, programmatic utopias of Bellamy and Howells than it does the fantasies of exploration and conquest in Shakespeare's *Tempest*, Defoe's *Robinson Crusoe*, and Swift's *Gulliver's Travels*. What all of these thematize (or, in Swift's case, partly satirize) is the plight of the innocent castaway or exile in the face of an alien environment that he must either master or succumb to. And although the connection is farther to seek, the very genre of Arthurian romance that Twain consciously undertook to parody enacts a similar battle for mastery . . . [one] in which a man returns to do battle with the very origins of his own condition, with his historical roots. Like Gulliver's, Hank's story begins when he is transformed into the threatening Other of someone else's romance: where Gulliver is a "man-monster" to the Lilliputians, Hank is initially the prize falling to Sir Kay, who will claim "he had encountered [Hank] in a far land of barbarians," and who will describe him "as 'this prodigious giant' and 'this horrible sky-towering monster,' and 'this tushed and taloned man-devouring ogre'" (77).[7] As Gulliver's claim to humanity is stripped from him when he is alternately objectified as colossus and as plaything in Lilliput and Brobdingnag, so Hank is initially reduced through shame by the gaze of his captors when he is stripped naked and discussed "as unconcernedly as if [he] had been a cabbage" (80). But Hank's ego is far too powerful to tolerate the humiliation Gulliver must undergo in accepting and internalizing an alien view of himself. To be the passive object of gaze is a scandal to Hank. It is unsettling when a young girl dressed with Botticellian abandon treats *him* as a source of wonder:

> [T]here she stood gazing, in a sort of stupefied fascination, till we turned a corner of the wood and were lost to her view. That she should be startled at me instead of at the other man [the armored Sir Kay] was too many for me. . . . And that she should seem to consider me a spectacle, and totally overlook her own merits in that respect, was another puzzling thing. . . . (57)

To be a "spectacle" is to be an object defined by the Other's subjectivity, and Hank will not stand it for long. His resistance takes two forms. One is to turn spectacle into theatrical performance, seizing control of the "script" of intersubjective relations and defining the precise role that his audience must take. The second is to insert himself into the community by becoming a participant observer, in the manner of an ethnographer or sociologist. Imme-

---

[6]Many, but by no means all, of Twain's generic debts have been investigated. On his use of Malory, see Baetzhold (102–106) and Kordecki; science fiction, Franklin, Ketterer ("Epoch-Eclipse"; *Science Fiction* xx–xxii), and Suvin (*Metamorphoses* 193–203); the lost-race tale, Pfaelzer (103–108) and Khouri; adventure fiction, Green (23, 236–244); slave narrative, Baetzhold (151–152); dime novel, Canby (1970) and Slotkin (510–511).

[7]*Gulliver's Travels* is discussed as a possible source of *A Connecticut Yankee* in Goldman and, with more sophistication, Salomon (105). Gribben (2: 679–681) documents Mark Twain's thorough familiarity with Swift's book.

diately after dazzling a crowd of thousands by "miraculously" restoring the fountain in the Valley of Holiness, Hank resolves to disguise himself as "a freeman of peasant degree" and wander through the country making observations, mingling with the "lowliest and poorest class," in order to "inform [himself] perfectly of their every-day life and the operation of the laws upon it" (274). Critics have occasionally been bothered by Hank's shift from "active" to "passive" protagonist, but, understood rightly, his observation is merely a more subtle form of control than his overt rule of the country. We tend to be so aware of King Arthur's awkward imitation of a peasant that we forget Hank is playing a role, too: he is no less the consciously evaluating observer of inferiors than he is when beholding, for instance, a mass audience of "human beings groveling on the ground" (105) after one of his displays of craft.

Hank's closest symbolic identification is with Robinson Crusoe, and the paradox of the Crusoe story is that it abolishes the distinction between activity and passivity by making the latter an inadmissible category. The moral, for the European imagination, of Defoe's story was that civilization must and will reproduce itself in whatever locale it appears; explorer and castaway are both powered by the same teleology of discovery and taking-possession. So Hank, finding himself in a medieval castle lacking in necessary commodities, makes a well-known allusion to Defoe in resolving to supply them: "I saw that I was just another Robinson Crusoe cast away on an uninhabited island, with no society but some more or less tame animals, and if I wanted to make life bearable I must do as he did—invent, contrive, create; reorganize things . . ." (100). As Frank and Fritzie Manuel note in their magisterial study of Western utopian thought, *Robinson Crusoe* and the "robinsonades" that it engendered altered the shape of European utopian narrative by demonstrating its power to represent the actual course of history, helping to transform the utopian mode from wish-fulfillment into "an assertive proclamation" of the power of the will, making Crusoe "a kind of aggressive bourgeois Prometheus" (433).[8] Among critics of *A Connecticut Yankee*, Martin Green has gone the farthest in demonstrating the novel's descent from Defoe as a "modernist adventure" in which "the adventurer defeats the challenges he meets by means of the tools and techniques of the modern world system" (923). Arthurian romance, says Green, "is not the book's imaginative context" (236); its real subject is "modern imperalism or modernization" (237).[9]

One might object that both the Crusoe allusion and Hank's constant equation of sixth-century Britons with savages and child-like primitives[10] are

---

[8]Compare Roger Salomon's discussion of Hank's political resemblance to Crusoe as another "practicing empiricist" or "Whig bourgeois" (31). Alan Gribben details at length Twain's lifelong "fascination with Defoe's fictional castaway" (1:181).

[9]Green may be echoing Henry Nash Smith's comments that feudalism was irrelevant to the "imaginative core" of *A Connecticut Yankee* (*Mark Twain's Fable* 81) and that sixth-century Britain is "a backdrop designed to allow a nineteenth-century American industrial genius to show what he can do with an underdeveloped country" (*Mark Twain's Fable* 36).

[10]For Hank, Arthur and his subjects are "a childlike and innocent lot" (66), "white Indians" (66), "great simple-hearted creatures" (68–69), "animals" (86, 100), "savages" (86, 127, 154), the "quaintest and simplest and trustingest race" (109), "a sort of polished-up court of Comanches" (175).

simply satirical devices for deflating the pretensions of European civilization to superiority, as a decade earlier Twain had compared the French unfavorably to the Comanches ("The French and the Comanches"). But from the moment Mark Twain conceives of making Hank a missionary of the nineteenth century, he is pushed almost inexorably into reproducing the ideological confrontation between civilization and savagism. It is a conflict that Twain has already tried to deal with directly in two incomplete projects of the 1880's, a quickly abandoned novel about Hawaiian colonization and the longer fragment "Huck Finn and Tom Sawyer among the Indians."[11] By the turn of the century he would become well known as a critic of imperialists, of those he sarcastically termed the "Disseminators of Progress and the Blessings of Civilization" ("To the Person" 260), beginning in *Following the Equator* and continuing in a series of essays, newspaper interviews, unpublished sketches, and autobiographical dictations. Yet if *A Connecticut Yankee* is, as I believe, Mark Twain's most powerful indictment of imperialism, it is largely *because* Mark Twain has not yet consciously rejected the prevailing ideology and can therefore, in the person of Hank, participate in it much more freely than he ever could again— all the more so since the novel's chronological displacement serves as a kind of dreamwork that obscures latent meanings. (Indeed, Twain's first notebook entry relating to *A Connecticut Yankee* begins, "*Dream* of being a knight errant in armor in the middle ages" [emphasis added; *Mark Twain's Notebooks* 78].) In an essay like "To the Person Sitting in Darkness," Mark Twain will provide, as it were, an auto-analysis of the Battle of the Sand Belt:

> Had we better invest in this Civilization which .   storms frightened villages and cables the result to glad journals at home every day: "Chinese losses, 450 killed; *ours, one officer and two men wounded.* Shall proceed against neighboring village to-morrow, where a massacre is reported." Can we afford Civilization? (261)

No one has better glossed than this the charge Hank gives to his army concerning their knightly foes: "While one of these men remains alive, our task is not finished, the war is not ended. We will kill them all" (479). . . .

Hank . . . at one point or another compare[s] himself to Crusoe, Columbus, and Cortés, the central figures of three narrative forms often treated as distinct, but which Hank's career will demonstrate are based upon identical ideological premises. Robinson Crusoe (like Gulliver) is essentially the hero of a captivity narrative, Columbus of an exploration narrative, and Cortés of a narrative of conquest. . . [E]xploration and captivity narratives are attenuated or masked forms of the conquest account: domination, the overt object in the latter, appears at the level of discourse as a submerged motive in the former. By transforming her experience into a published account, the author

---

[11]Fred Lorch argues that Mark Twain's knowledge of Hawaiian history was a more basic source of his depiction of aristocracy than even his reading of Malory, and that Hank's character may have been suggested by early nineteenth-century Hawaiian missionaries. Martin Green looks back to the letters from the Sandwich Islands to note "the interest Twain took in the islands' cultural contrasts—between what he called 'savagery' and 'civilization' " (238). Richard Slotkin discusses "Among the Indians" as evidence that Mark Twain had assimilated the "vocabulary of the Frontier Myth" by the time he wrote *A Connecticut Yankee* (522).

of an Indian captivity, for example, is in effect saying, "Although my body was imprisoned, I remain the master of language; I (unlike my captors) am literate and can give a true account of what happened; I can define my own situation." In the first published and now archetypal American captivity story, Mary Rowlandson's *True History*, the author's most powerful discursive weapon is Scriptural language and allusion, which she uses to interpret her case as a parallel to the Babylonian Captivity. The Indians' power and autonomy can be negated when, following the Puritans' typical strategy, their attacks are construed as Providentially allowed chastisement of God's chosen people. The captivity narrative's author is always able to counter a physical humiliation with linguistic victory: the captors may have controlled the brute events, but the captive controls the story-telling.

In *The Conquest of America* Tzvetan Todorov has taught us that European triumph in the New World derived from language as much as from guns and horses, and his contemplation of the psychology of exploration and conquest casts light upon Hank Morgan's story. A central task of Todorov's book is to explain the "paradox of the understanding-that-kills," why Cortés's sophisticated comprehension of the Aztec world, which ought to have produced sympathy, led instead to wholesale destruction (127). The paradox follows inevitably from the colonist's psychology: either he sees the natives as identical equals, which leads to assimilationism, "the projection of his own values on others," or else he sees difference, which is translated into terms of superiority and inferiority. In either case, "what is denied is the existence of a human substance truly other, something capable of being not merely an imperfect state of oneself" (42). (Hank's otherwise puzzlingly inconsistent attitude toward the Britons—now seeking to make free citizens of them, now dismissing them as "human muck" [473]—illustrates the paradox nicely.) Still more relevant to *A Connecticut Yankee* is Todorov's provocative assignment of Cortés's astonishing victory to his superior mastery of communication, his strategic manipulation of symbols to enhance his political and military position. Like Hank, Cortés is a canny showman, concerned "when weak . . . to make others believe he is strong," given to "*son et lumière* spectacles with . . . horses and canons" meant to impress the Indians as evidence of his transcendent powers (Todorov 113, 115). Where language serves ritual functions for the indigenous population, for the Conquistador it is above all "a concrete instrument of action upon the Other" (123). Hank's own most constant endeavor and—temporarily—greatest triumph is to substitute his own discourse for what he finds in the sixth century, attitudes and communicative styles that are satirized throughout the novel. As the speaker of a "strong language," he bends the Malorian world to submit to his translation until it can give way no farther and erupts in violence.[12]

---

[12]See Asad for a discussion of the languages of European anthropologists, along with their conventions of representation, as "strong languages" which tend to impose themselves upon the "weaker" languages of the societies which they are used to describe.

A central metaphor for Hank's project in *A Connecticut Yankee* is provided by the physical form of the manuscript that he gives to "Mark Twain" in Warwick, a parchment palimpsest. "Under the old dim writing of the Yankee historian appeared traces of a penmanship which was older and dimmer still— Latin words and sentences: fragments from old monkish legends, evidently" (53). Mark Twain's novel is itself a palimpsest, Hank's story inscribed over Malory's *Morte D'Arthur*, traces of the original surviving with greater or lesser alteration. At the level of Twain's novel, Malory's monologic language is dialogized as it is variously framed, mocked, parodied, and questioned. But for Hank as character there is no dialogue, because he recognizes only one voice as legitimate. Hank's quest is to replace one world-view with another. He means, for example, to abolish the code of knight-errantry altogether: "I was the champion of hard, unsentimental, common-sense and reason. I was entering the lists to either destroy knight-errantry or be its victim" (430). So Hank defies Arthurian discourse at all levels, from the vocabulary and syntax of its spoken language through its narrative forms to its semiotic of dress, ritual, and ceremony. Just before Hank resolves to destroy knighthood, for instance, Mark Twain juxtaposes two texts describing the upcoming tournament, from the Camelot newspaper Hank has begun publishing. The first is King Arthur's formulaic proclamation of the fight between Sir Sagramour and The Boss, filled with archaisms and Anglo-Norman legal phrases; the second is Clarence's breezy country-paper account of the upcoming fight (428–429). To read it is to realize that Hank has already destroyed chivalry without firing a shot, merely by subjecting it to a point of view that ignores its claim to authoritative discourse. Nor is Clarence's role in the novel as the most active disseminator of Hank's language accidental. Clarence, from the time Hank wins him over as an ally, is the indispensable native interpreter, La Malinche to Hank's Cortés, won over to the ideology of his powerful mentor and ultimately acquiescing in the destruction of his own people.[13] His adoption of The Boss's vernacular is one of Hank's true successes in Camelot.

Hank's knowledge is never neutral; his Yankee "know-how" is presented as active force from the beginning of his tale, where it is immediately conjoined with violence. "[I] learned to make everything . . . it didn't make any difference what; and if there wasn't any quick, new-fangled way to make a thing, I could invent one" (50): so, Hank tells us, he became a factory superintendent. The second paragraph opens with an apparent non sequitur: "Well, a man like that, is a man that is full of fight—that goes without saying" (50). If we look for the antecedents of "like that" in the first paragraph we find nothing but the qualities of practicality and inventiveness, which must accordingly be equated with aggressiveness. Hank's combativeness is connected not only with his

---

[13]La Malinche "does not simply submit to the other . . . she adopts the other's ideology and serves it in order to understand her own culture better . . . (even if 'understanding' here means 'destroying')" (Todorov 101). Martin Green calls Clarence a "development of [Defoe's] Friday figure" (243).

know-how in the mechanical arts, but with his skill at dialectic as well. In the fervor of an argument, Hank can easily lose sight of his putative desire to be helpful, as in the curious episode at Marco the charcoal-burner's house. Frustrated in his attempt to win an audience of peasants and petits bourgeois over to his doctrine of free-trade economics, he takes revenge upon his principal opponent, Dowley the blacksmith, with a convoluted Socratic argument that forces Dowley into confessing to a de facto capital crime for which his auditors are legally obliged to inform on him.

I have elsewhere described this passage in terms of the "polemical misunderstanding" that Hank wields in refusing to comprehend Dowley's faith in the fixity of values (Sewell 127; 133–135). What strikes me on reconsideration is how well, in fact, Hank *does* understand Dowley's reasoning: "What those people valued was *high wages*; it didn't seem to be a matter of any consequence to them whether the high wages would buy anything or not" (373). Hank's sophisticated grasp of "primitive" economics is illustrated even better in a remarkable passage that Twain originally placed near the beginning of chapter 31 but deleted in manuscript:

> To him [the protectionist], a dollar is a dollar, it doesn't make any difference whether you can buy anything with it or not. If he had been Robinson Crusoe, *he* wouldn't have kicked the bag of gold coin aside when *he* was getting things out of the wreck to use on the desert island. . . . No, the gold coin was *money*, and he would have lugged it ashore, sure; for to his mind money isn't simply a shadow which represents value, a substance, it's the *thing* itself. (*Connecticut Yankee* 677)

The Crusoe reference is apt, for Twain is contrasting Crusoe's "civilized" semiotics (gold is pure symbol) with a "primitive" idolatry of gold as something with inherent power. Dowley's idol is high wages. Realizing this, Hank's impulse is to smash the idol—or, more precisely, the idolater himself. The "first statesman of the age, . . . the best informed man in the entire world," Hank smarts at being "apparently defeated in argument by an ignorant country blacksmith!" (374). The lesson is over; the logomachy begins. Metaphors of violence proliferate: "struck below the belt" (374), "hit a man . . . hit him a lifter" (374), "knocked them absolutely dumb!" (375), "I judged he was hit" (378). The trap Hank springs when he demonstrates that Dowley has confessed to a serious crime is a "smasher," a "blow [that] came crashing down and knocked him all to rags" (379), a "pile-driver" (382). Reduced to silence, Dowley and his friends finally launch a fistfight against their incognito ruler—democratic Boss and aristocratic King allied against peasants—which ends in an image I find more unsettling than the carnage during the Battle of the Sand Belt:

> [R]eeling with exhaustion . . . they kept right on, hammering away with what might was left in them. Hammering each other—for we stepped aside and looked on while they rolled and struggled, and gouged, and pounded and bit, with the strict and wordless attention to business of so many bulldogs. (384)

Hank has, for the moment at least, divided and conquered his foes. Yet these are the same men whom Hank has just feasted, and upon whose honesty and manhood he has founded his hopes of instituting universal suffrage in Britain (346). We have here, it seems to me, a compact parable illustrating Todorov's paradox of the movement from assimilationism to exclusion, figured as a struggle for control over the terms of argument. Those who cannot be converted or "reasoned with" are deprived of reason, turned into speechless animals, and turned against one another.

Hank, having failed to convince Dowley that his economic theory is faulty, manages in reprisal to lead the blacksmith through a careful cross-examination into admitting that his personal practice is at odds with the economic rules of his society. (The blacksmith has carelessly acknowledged that he sometimes pays his workers more than the set legal wage.) While Hank's contentions that prices are arbitrary and, implicitly, that wages should not be fixed are "correct" from the viewpoint of free-market economics, his argumentative procedure violates interpersonal trust. . . .

It is irrelevant for my purposes that the "real" object of Hank's economic debate is the protective tariff policy of the Republican Party in the 1880's. As figured in *A Connecticut Yankee* it is no longer a political debate between equally powerful parties, but the demolition of inferior knowledge by superior. José Rabasa's comment on Cortés's use of dialogue as a tool of conquest is apt: "The equation *discourse is violence . . .* refines the commonplace *knowledge is power;* it displaces the formulation of the problem from misuse of information to an integral view of knowledge as a form of domination, of control" (132). Hank knows what advantages his knowledge entails. "Look at the opportunities here for a man of knowledge, brains, pluck and enterprise to sail in and grow up with the country. . . . I was no shadow of a king; I was the substance. . . . My power was colossal . . ." (109). Unlike Gulliver in Lilliput, Hank needs no physical superiority to be a colossus, for his strength is, as he would boast to his opponents before the Battle of the Sand Belt, in his *mind*, "a force against which mere animal might might [not] hope to prevail" (480).

Hank is a special kind of colossus in Camelot: he is a father, *the* father ("The Boss") in a land of children—a "nursery" (69)—where, he says, there is "not a man who wasn't a baby to me in acquirements and capacities" (109). From Swift's Gulliver, a phallic father in Lilliput (recall the soldiers' awed gaze up his breeches) and a helpless infant in Brobdingnag, to H. G. Wells' childlike Eloi, to Arthur C. Clarke's transcendent children in *Childhood's End*, utopian fiction reflects anxiety over the relation between history and parenthood. This is especially the case when a time-travel plot is involved, when the question "what would it be like to go back in time and give birth to oneself?" generates a master-plot revolving about a primal scene fantasy (Penley 72). In *A Connecticut Yankee* the Oedipal tendency of the time-travel narrative takes a very specifically American political form: that supplanting of the father which is regicide, whether actual or symbolized in the form of revolution. For all of Twain's care to preserve Arthur himself from satirical diminishment, and despite Hank's admiration of the King's heroism in the smallpox-hut, it is impossible not to see that Hank has purposely usurped Arthur's paternal role, turning the erstwhile King into a child to be tutored.[14] Yet, as we have seen, he proves to be an equivocal parent. After lavishing food upon Marco and Dowley, he ends up fighting them. He leads to their death in Merlin's Cave "fifty-two fresh, bright, well educated, clean-minded young British boys" (472) whom he refers to and addresses as "my boys" (473, 475). Twenty-five thousand of the childlike knights lie dead around them. One recalls the central riddle Michael Rogin investigates in his book on Andrew Jackson: "What meaning can be given to a policy of death and dispossession, centrally important to American development, which is justified by the paternal benevolence of a father for his children?" (9), as well as one of his solutions: "Indians were the bad children on whom whites projected their own aggressive expansionism" (122). Thanks to the paradoxes of time travel, Arthur and his knights can be imagined now as repressive fathers, now as primitive children who must be disciplined. Hank enacts *both* the myth of Oedipus and the myth of Cronus, at the same time and upon the same victims. Mark Twain's comic formulation of the time-loop paradox of self-generation is signally revealing: with his civilization booming along, Hank says, "I was getting ready to send out an expedition to discover America" (444). But for Hank to travel along this Möbius strip is to become the Old World that he has spent the novel repudiating. To cut the Möbius strip by attempting to end Arthurian history is no better: no Arthur means no England means no America.

Hank Morgan—alone but powerful, convinced of his own superiority in knowledge—acts confidently on his belief that he can reform the sixth century and effectively revise history. He is, in the final analysis, a colonizer of time. Consequently *A Connecticut Yankee* becomes a cautionary tale about any utopian impulse that seeks to supplant actual or yet-unrealized history with what it considers a superior version, an improved order of things. Our imaginary explorations into the past and future are not encounters with the actual stuff of history, but with our own fantasies, projections, patterns, and languages. Naive utopianism is therefore liable to an objection that has been leveled against colonialist literature: it is "essentially specular: instead of seeing the native as a bridge toward syncretic possibility, it uses him as a mirror that reflects the colonialist's self-image" (JanMohamed 65). Perhaps in

---

[14]CF. Johnson: "The civilization that Hank would create requires the overthrow of fathers, of monarchy, of reality. He would have the sons of Arthur catch up into themselves the prerogatives and powers of the fathers—become their own fathers, with the powers of generation amplified to such an extent that they can create themselves" (30). Dan Beard's illustration for the opening page of chapter 9, "The Boss," captures perfectly the infantilization of Arthur, showing him standing slightly more than knee high nextto Hank (*Connecticut Yankee* 118). (Freudians will take care to remark the comparative sizes of the swords the two men are wearing.)

his transition from mocking Sandy to loving her Hank begins to accept the Other as an authentic subject, but in destroying chivalry he is destroying the conditions that made her possible in the first place, and so must lose her. Only in his final delirium does he represent Camelot as an "original text," his lost world, the locus of the only dialogue that really matters to him, but by then it is too late: he has already effaced it by inscribing over it the map of his own self-reflective Utopia.

Works Cited

Asad, Talal. "The Concept of Cultural Translation in British Social Anthropology." *Writing Culture: The Poetics and Politics of Ethnography.* Ed. James Clifford and George E. Marcus. Berkeley: University of California Press, 1986. 141–164.

Baetzhold, Howard G. *Mark Twain and John Bull: The British Connection.* Bloomington: Indiana University Press, 1970.

Berthold, Dennis. "The Conflict of Dialects in *A Connecticut Yankee.*" *Ball State University Forum* 18:3 (1977): 51–58.

Budd, Louis J. *Mark Twain: Social Philosopher.* Bloomington: Indiana University Press, 1964.

Canby, Henry Seidel. *Turn West, Turn East: Mark Twain and Henry James.* Boston: Houghton, 1951.

Carter, Everett. "The Meaning of *A Connecticut Yankee.*" *American Literature* 50 (1978): 418–440.

Franklin, H. Bruce. "Mark Twain and Science Fiction." *Future Perfect: American Science Fiction of the Nineteenth Century.* Ed. Franklin. Rev. ed. New York: Oxford University Press, 1978. 375–381.

Green, Martin. *Dreams of Adventure, Deeds of Empire.* New York: Basic Books, 1979.

Gribben, Alan. *Mark Twain's Library: A Reconstruction.* 2 vols. Boston: G. K. Hall, 1980.

Hansen, Chadwick. "The Once and Future Boss: Mark Twain's Yankee." *Nineteenth-Century Fiction* 28 (1978): 62–73.

Holmes, Charles S. "*A Connecticut Yankee in King Arthur's Court:* Mark Twain's Fable of Uncertainty." *South Atlantic Quarterly* 61 (1962): 462–474.

Irving, Washington. *The Life and Voyages of Christopher Columbus.* Ed. John Harmon McElroy. The Complete Works of Washington Irving 11. Boston: Twayne, 1981.

JanMohamed, Abdul R. "The Economy of Manichean Allegory: The Function of Racial Difference in Colonialist Literature." *Critical Inquiry* 12 (1985): 59–87.

Johnson, James L. *Mark Twain and the Limits of Power: Emerson's God in Ruins.* Knoxville: The University of Tennessee Press, 1982.

Jones, Joseph. "Utopia as Dirge." *American Quarterly* 2 (1950): 214–226.

Kaplan, Justin. *Mark Twain and His World.* New York: Simon, 1974.

Kasson, John F. "Technology and Utopia." *Civilizing the Machine: Technology and Republican Values in America, 1776–1900.* New York: Grossman, 1976. 181–234.

Ketterer, David. "Epoch-Eclipse and Apocalypse: Special 'Effects' in *A Connecticut Yankee.*" *New Worlds for Old: The Apocalyptic Imagination, Science Fiction, and American Literature.* Garden City: Anchor, 1974. 213–232.

——, ed. *The Science Fiction of Mark Twain.* Hamden, Connecticut: Archon Books, 1984.

Khouri, Nadia. "From Eden to the Dark Ages: Images of History in the Work of Mark Twain." *Canadian Review of American Studies* 11 (1980): 151–174.

Kordecki, Lesley C. "Twain's Critique of Malory's Romance: *Forma tractandi* and *A Connecticut Yankee.*" *Nineteenth-Century Literature* 41 (1986): 329–348.

Lorch, Fred. "Hawaiian Feudalism and Mark Twain's *A Connecticut Yankee in King Arthur's Court.*" *American Literature* 30 (1958): 50–66.

Mannoni, O. *Prospero and Caliban: The Psychology of Colonization.* Trans. Pamela Powesland. London: Metheun, 1956.

Manuel, Frank E., and Fritzie P. Manuel. *Utopian Thought in the Western World.* Cambridge: Harvard University Press, 1979.

Parkman, Francis. *The Oregon Trail.* Boston: Little, 1872.

Pearce, Roy Harvey. *Savagism and Civilization: A Study of the Indian and the American Mind.* Rev. ed. Berkeley: University of California Press, 1988.

Penley, Constance. "Time Travel, Primal Scene, and the Critical Dystopia." *Camera Obscura: A Journal of Feminism and Film Theory* 15 (1986): 67–84.

Pfaelzer, Jean. *The Utopian Novel in America, 1886–1896: The Politics of Form.* Pittsburgh: University of Pittsburgh Press, 1984.

Rabasa, José. "Dialogue as Conquest: Mapping Spaces for Counter-Discourse." *Cultural Critique* 6 (1987): 131–160.

Robinson, Douglas. *American Apocalypses. The Image of the End of the World in American Literature.* Baltimore: Johns Hopkins University Press, 1985.

Roemer, Kenneth M. *The Obsolete Necessity: America in Utopian Writings, 1888–1900.* Kent, Ohio: Kent State University Press, 1976.

Rogin, Michael Paul. *Fathers and Children: Andrew Jackson and the Subjugation of the American Indian.* New York: Knopf, 1975.

Rowlandson, Mary. *A True History of the Captivity and Restoration of Mrs. Mary Rowlandson.* London, 1682. Facs. ed. The Garland Library of Narratives of North American Indian Captivities 1. New York: Garland, 1977.

Salomon, Roger B. *Twain and the Image of History.* New Haven: Yale University Press, 1961.

Sewell, David. *Mark Twain's Languages: Discourse, Dialogue, and Linguistic Variety.* Berkeley: University of California Press, 1987.

Slotkin, Richard. *The Fatal Environment: The Myth of the Frontier in the Age of Industrialization, 1800–1890.* New York: Atheneum, 1985.

Smith, Henry Nash. *Mark Twain: The Development of a Writer.* Cambridge: Harvard University Press, 1962.

———. *Mark Twain's Fable of Progress: Political and Economic Ideas in "A Connecticut Yankee."* New Brunswick: Rutgers University Press, 1964.

Suvin, Darko. *Metamorphoses of Science Fiction: On the Poetics and History of a Literary Genre.* New Haven: Yale University Press, 1979.

———. *Victorian Science Fiction in the UK: The Discourses of Knowledge and of Power.* Boston: G. K. Hall, 1983.

Todorov, Tzvetan. *The Conquest of America: The Question of the Other.* Trans. Richard Howard. New York: Harper, 1982.

Tuveson, Ernest Lee. *Redeemer Nation: The Idea of America's Millennial Role.* Chicago: University of Chicago Press, 1968.

Twain, Mark. *The Autobiography of Mark Twain.* Ed. Charles Neider. New York: Harper, 1959.

———. *A Connecticut Yankee in King Arthur's Court.* Ed. Bernard L. Stein. The Works of Mark Twain 9. Berkeley: University of California Press, 1979.

———. "The French and the Comanches." *Letters from the Earth.* Ed. Bernard DeVoto. New York: Harper, 1962.

———. *Mark Twain's Notebooks and Journals.* Ed. Robert Pack Browning, Michael B. Frank, and Lin Salamo. Vol. 3 (1883–1891). Berkeley: University of California Press, 1979, 3 vols. to date. 1975–.

———. "The New Dynasty." Rpt. in Paul J. Carter, Jr. "Mark Twain and the American Labor Movement." *New England Quarterly* 30 (1957): 382–388.

———. "To the Person Sitting in Darkness." *Europe and Elsewhere.* New York: Harper, 1929. 250–272.

Winters, Donald E. "The Utopianism of Survival: Bellamy's *Looking Backward* and Twain's *A Connecticut Yankee.*" *American Studies* [Kansas] 21 (1980): 23–38.

Roxana's Plot

Carolyn Porter

Many critics of *Pudd'nhead Wilson* have agreed on the extraordinary power
of Roxana as a character, while others have attended more to her problematic
behavior, such as the radical changes in her demeanor, her white supremacist
attitudes, and her capacity for both cruelty and tenderness, and have offered
a variety of explanations either to defend or to attack Twain's portrayal. The
critical response shows a marked tendency, however, to use her sexuality to
account for both Roxana's power and the problems she raises as a character.[1]
For example, in the most compelling and nuanced analysis of the novel as a
whole, James M. Cox calls Roxana "the primary force in the world she serves"
and underscores that force as "sexual." He traces a circuit of power in the
novel's plot structure originating in the white, male lust of the Southern
slaveholder. What "explains Roxana's power," according to Cox, is the "submerged lust" of the white male, whose "passion" is transferred "from the
white wives to the slave mistresses." Roxana serves as the repository of "the
guilt of their repressed desires," so that "their guilt is objectified in her
repression." Her son, Tom Driscoll, thus becomes "the avenging agent who
carries back across the color line the repressed guilt which has gathered at the
heart of slavery." Therefore, Tom's assassination of his foster father, Judge
Driscoll, is the thematic center of the plot, and his "murder suggests the
anarchy which the white society has by its own action released upon itself." As

Reprinted from *Mark Twain's Pudd'nhead Wilson: Race, Conflict, and Culture* ed. Susan K.
Gillman and Forrest G. Robinson (Durham, NC: Duke University Press, 1990), pp. 121–36.
Copyright Duke University Press, 1990. Reprinted by permission of the publisher.

[1]For example, while calling Roxana Twain's "most fully realized female character," Arlin Turner
argues that "through her, in the clearest instance in all his fiction," Twain "acknowledged sex to be
an element in human relations." Frederick Anderson sees her as "Twain's most successful female
protagonist," pairing her with the Aunt Rachel of "A True Story" to suggest that Twain apparently
"required the distance provided by color to establish and sustain the vulgar quality of life in
female character." One of the most impressive critiques of Twain's characterization of Roxana is
also based on this assumption that her power is fueled by her sexuality. According to Arthur G.
Pettit, it is Twain's ambivalence toward the powerfully sexual black woman of his imagination that
accounts for Roxana's "bewildering" role changes from "black shrew" to "tragic mother figure."
Twain "used blacks and mulattoes," Pettit argues, "to express sexual feelings that were prohibited
by white standards of propriety," and Roxana's contradictory behavior reflects Twain's inability to
cope with such feelings. Thus her "wound up with two Roxana's," Pettit suggests, a "near-white
one, . . . and a much darker Roxana." See *Pudd'nhead Wilson and Those Extraordinary Twins*,
ed. Sidney E. Berger (New York: W.W. Norton, 1980), 275, 285, 351–54.

Cox tracks the transmission of guilt and desire *from* the white male *through* the black female and *back onto* the white male, he also tracks power from its "origin" in the white, male "lust out of which [Tom] was created" down to Roxana, who is only the "immediate source" of Tom's "dark force." If "the power of those who rule has been transferred to those who serve," its origin remains marked at the site of the white, male father, and its final restoration is secured by the "dark comedy" of Pudd'nhead Wilson's ascent to the position of authority left vacant by Judge Driscoll's death. The oedipal pattern, in which white males hold, lose, and then regain power, is fulfilled by David Wilson's story, which is itself plotted along a circuit of power originating with and returning to the white male. "Having precipitated the crisis," Cox notes, David Wilson concludes the plot he has himself "set in motion by his own idle remark to Roxy" when he unveils Tom Driscoll as both black and a parricide.

It is this dual status, of course, which makes Wilson's plot resolution a case of "disjunctive irony." He exposes the killer in the community's midst, but by the same act he exposes that community's "secret history" of miscegenation. Thus the indictment of the society implicit in Wilson's exposure of Tom Driscoll as "black" is finally deflected and its threat recontained by the restoration to the status quo it effects by convicting him as a killer. Accordingly, both Wilson and his plot are "repressive," serving to recontain and deny the "erotic motive" buried in the adultery which is the "primal action . . . from which the entire plot originates."[2]

I have rehearsed Cox's argument at such length because it seems to me that he delivers the definitive analysis of the novel's plot, insofar as it can be understood to originate in the white, male desire, repression, and guilt of the Southern slaveholding class, and to culminate in the simultaneous exposure and repression of that origin. He delivers as well a definitive diagnosis of the novel's flaws as a product of that same repression operating through the plot machinery centered in *Pudd'nhead Wilson*. Within the terms of his argument, both the analysis and the diagnosis are wholly persuasive. Yet those terms themselves are grounded in an essentially Freudian framework marked by oedipal struggle and a focus on repressed male sexual desire that is significantly limited and limiting in its treatment of Roxana. Such a framework accounts splendidly for David Wilson's plot as a repressive mechanism, but it cannot finally account for the fact to which Cox himself testifies when he says that "Only Roxana has the power to create drama and to become the primary force in the world she serves."[3]

Such a statement underscores every reader's sense that Roxana generates a good deal of the energy that moves the often creaky machinery of the novel forward. If we focus on Roxana as "primary force," even as a kind of prime

---

[2]See James M. Cox, "The Ironic Stranger," in Clemens, *Pudd'nhead Wilson*, 259–67. For a fuller version, see Cox's *Mark Twain: The Fate of Humor* (Princeton. N.J.: Princeton University Press, 1966), chap. 10, 222–46.

[3]Cox, "The Ironic Stranger," 262.

mover of events in the world she serves, then the repressive function that Cox accurately attributes to *Pudd'nhead Wilson's* plot looks rather different. What makes that plot's censorship visible becomes less a matter of its success at repressing Roxana's sexuality than its *failure* wholly to recontain the disruptive force of what amounts to another plot—Roxana's plot.

In order to account for Roxana's resilient power, which suffers repeated deflection and suppression only to return in new guises and disguises, we need to attend to her status as mother. "Mother" is to be understood here not as a "natural" but as a social identity defined in Roxana's case by a set of particular legal, social, and cultural codes that make the slave mother at once antebellum America's most tragic victim and potentially one of its most powerful subversive agents.

No doubt the axiomatic problem of the Southern black woman stereotyped as "Jezebel" (to borrow the label used by the historian Deborah White) plays a critical role in Roxana's troubled creation, but the critical focus on her sexuality has obscured her status as mother and underestimated the force of the anxieties unleashed in both Twain and his readers by a figure who is both sexual and maternal. The opposition Jezebel / Mammy in the antebellum South repressed a great deal of social and psychic conflict and confusion among the white slaveowning classes. As with the analogous oppositional stereotypes of the black man as rapist / Uncle Tom, an ideologically secured psychic defense operates to force the Other into two contradictory, interdependent, and equally mystified positions. Such either / or stereotypes only point to the excluded middle that they repress.

This region has been, of course, partly colonized by literary convention as the site of the "tragic mulatta" who signals and represses at once the fact that slave women were sexual objects of desire in the eyes of their white masters. And clearly, Roxana's status as a mulatta is crucial to Twain's story. But in order to assess what makes it crucial, we need to see it within the context that Hortense Spillers has described. For Spillers, the mulatta is a figure of containment for white culture; what in reality threatens exposure—the physical evidence of miscegenation—is culturally recontained by a defensive sign deployed as an "alibi, an excuse for . . . otherness," as Spillers calls it. A term that "designates a disguise, covers up . . . the social and political reality of the dreaded African presence," *mulatta* or *mulatto* serves as a "semantic marker" that "exists *for others*—and a particular male other," according to Spillers. As a mulatta, Roxana certainly exposes the "covert tradition" of miscegenation, but her serial ordeal as a mulatta *mother* intent on saving her son exposes much more. Typically, the mulatto is a son or daughter who undergoes a crisis upon discovering a black or mulatto mother. Roxana is—first and last—that mother. Indeed, her status as a mulatta is established only to be immediately refocused by her status as a slave mother.[4]

---

[4]Quotations from Spillers taken from lecture delivered at the University of California, Berkeley, November 1987. Twain explored the theme of the "tragic mulatto" more fully in the original manuscript of the novel before he separated the "tragedy" of *Pudd'nhead Wilson* from the "farce"

Roxana is introduced as a set of contradictions: she sounds black, but looks white; "majestic" in "form and stature," fair-complexioned, she has a "heavy suit of fine soft hair," but it is "concealed" by a "checkered handkerchief"; "sassy" among her black friends, she is "meek and humble" among whites. These contradictions result from that "fiction of law and custom" that officially resolves them by dictating that "the one-sixteenth of her which was black out-voted the other fifteen parts and made her a negro." Thus Roxana's invisibly "mixed blood" matters not at all to her cultural, social, or legal identity. What matters—as Twain immediately reports—is that "she was a slave, and salable as such," and her child "too, was a slave."[5] In short, Roxana's white appearance is a plot device in the story of a slave mother and her child. Indeed, it is the central plot device, a tragic equivalent to "those extraordinary twins" in the "suppressed farce" that Mark Twain said he "pulled out by the roots" from the mother-text of *Pudd'nhead Wilson* (119). But it is her son's mulatto status, more than Roxana's, which invites Twain's brief exploration of the plight of the "tragic mulatto" faced suddenly with news of a black mother.

By attending, then, to Roxana as the slave mother, we can gain access to that blurred, confused, and anxiety-producing region of the excluded middle repressed by the binary, Jezebel / Mammy (a space of contradiction too often sutured over in white culture by the figure of the tragic mulatto). What comes into and out of focus in Twain's portrayal of Roxana is a region where mothers are sexual, slaves are powerful, and women are temporarily out of (and thus in) control. Roxana's agenda as a protagonist is set by her status as a slave mother, but in pursuing that agenda, she exposes not only the falseness of the Mammy / Jezebel opposition, but also the inadequacy of either "Mammy" *or* "Jezebel" to contain or represent the slave woman. The partitioning of sexuality from motherhood that is implicit in much of the critical response to Roxy is undermined in the novel itself, and thus such critical analysis cannot account fully for either Roxana's power or her problematic behavior. Indeed, that partitioning is a defense against what Twain was unable entirely to defend against—a slave mother wielding a subversive power in ways that threaten both narrative and social control.

From this viewpoint, *Pudd'nhead Wilson*'s coherence is undermined not by the dissociation of Roxana's character from a plot that operates to repress her sexuality, but rather by a struggle between the unsuccessfully suppressed slave mother's story and the story of the white fathers whose oedipally grounded plot Cox makes so lucid. In other words, *Pudd'nhead Wilson* is the scene of conflict between a repressive paternal plot and a subversive mater-nal one.

---

called *Those Extraordinary Twins*. On these revisions, see Hershel Parker, "*Pudd'nhead Wilson*: Jack-leg Author, Unreadable Text, and Sense-Making Critics," in *Flawed Texts and Verbal Icons: Literary Authority in American Fiction* (Evanston, Ill.: Northwestern University Press, 1984), 115–46.

5Clemens, *Pudd'nhead Wilson*, 8–9. All further references are to this edition, and will be cited in the text.

Before exploring Roxana's plot, I should make clear the severe limits within which its subversive power emerges. Roxana's remarkable series of strategems to save her son do not, finally, succeed. No matter how powerfully Roxana wields the forces she learns to appropriate from the white patriarchy, her son is finally sold down the river. The plot I wish to foreground here is one that only emerges temporarily, in what might be called the artificially induced gap between the white slaveowning patriarchy's *threat* of such a sale, and its final enforcement of that threat twenty-three years later. Roxana's "plot" exposes contradictions in the white, slaveowning patriarchy, signaling a potentially explosive negative power to thwart and undermine its rule, but her plot has no power to *alter* that rule itself, and more pointedly, it has no power to deflect that rule's crushing force on the slave mother's bond with her child.

In Roxana's plot, the primal action is not adultery, but childbirth. The first event recorded in this plot is also the first event recorded in the novel; in chapter 1, after describing Dawson's Landing and its "chief" citizens, Twain reports of Percy Driscoll, "on the first of February, 1830, two boy babes were born in his house; one to him, the other to one of his slave girls, Roxana by name" (5). But it is not until Roxana switches these two "boy babes" that her plot proper gets under way. No doubt, she acts in response to a threat from above, the threat of her son being sold down the river. However, it is worth noting that the threat is not immediate; she is not guilty of the recent petty theft to which her fellow slaves have confessed and for which they, not she or her child, are going to be sold. Her master's act, in other words, is technically what starts the plot rolling, but only technically. It is Roxana's ability to understand the threat posed by this incident that leads to her radical response.

It is also worth noting how radical a response it is. Provided with motive and opportunity, she is also endowed with the courage to commit an act so violent in its implicit threat to her society that it is unthinkable, and so invisible. The children's striking resemblance, and their white appearance, coupled with the fact that no one can tell the difference between them save Roxana, provide opportunity only. The threat of her child's ultimate loss provides motive only. What we can easily fail to notice is that Roxana's act requires a will so strong, and a calculating mind so acute, that it can conceive of a "plot" so "beyond the pale" that it cannot even strictly be called criminal. The law cannot forbid it because the law cannot imagine it. When the "law" in the shape of Pudd'nhead Wilson, detective manqué, is finally forced to imagine it, the discovery requires the modern "scientifics" of fingerprinting, and even with this tactical aid, Wilson remains thoroughly befuddled until the very last moment.

The mainspring of Roxana's plot lies in the implications of the exchange with which it begins. When Roxana switches the children, she commits two subversive acts: she reduces the real Tom to slavery, and she creates a new "Tom" by renaming her son. As Evan Carton has persuasively argued, "her attempt to save one twin by dooming the other reiterates the structure and the illusion of the society it challenges." What Carton calls the "paradoxical imitative character of her enterprise" indeed haunts it from the outset, but it does so in ways that subvert as well as reiterate the white slaveholding patriarchy.[6]

This dimension of Roxana's endeavor comes into view if we attend first to her son's translation from slavery to freedom and the terms on which the novel invites us to understand it. Roxana acts to save her own son from a fate not only worse than death, but also functionally equivalent to it. From beginning to end, the novel enforces this equivalence between death and being sold down the river. When she conceives her plan, at the story's outset, Roxana is on the way to drowning both herself and her child to save the latter from being sold down the river. At the story's end, Tom is saved from life imprisonment by being restored to his status as property and sold down the river. As Richard Chase, among others, has noted, "down the river" serves as the novel's version of hell, and throughout the story, it is clear that there is little difference between death and slavery in the Deep South.[7]

As Orlando Patterson has argued, part of what makes slavery a form of "social death" is its status as a commutation of an actual death sentence.[8] The slave "lives" under the continuous threat of a death to which she or he is nonetheless socially condemned. Because the slave can always, in principle, be killed by the master, the slave's life is always conditional on that master's consent that he or she live. In *Pudd'nhead Wilson*, this condition is foregrounded when Roxana perceives the threat posed by Percy Driscoll's decision to *refrain* from selling her fellow slaves down the river *this time*. She understands that her very life, and that of her son, is permanently conditional—a commuted death sentence that can always be revoked at the master's will. For the slave, what this means is that survival depends upon remaining alienable. Roxana's fellow slaves express heartfelt gratitude at being sold, but not sold down the river. In terms of the novel's identification of death with being sold down the river, they preserve their lives by remaining alienable. This logic is pervasive. Percy Driscoll's treatment of his slaves is echoed at the end of the novel: "As soon as the Governor understood the case, he pardoned Tom at once, and the creditors sold him down the river" (115). The novel closes as it opens, with a pardon followed by a sale.

In this light, Roxana's opening gambit needs to be understood not only as a reiteration of the white patriarchy's structural inequality, but also as a specific

6"*Pudd'nhead Wilson* and the Fiction of Law and Custom," in *American Realism: New Essays*, ed. Eric Sundquist (Baltimore: Johns Hopkins University Press, 1982), 86.

7See Clemens, *Pudd'nhead Wilson*, 244.

8See Orlando Patterson, *Slavery and Social Death: A Comparative Study* (Cambridge, Mass.: Harvard University Press, 1982), esp. chap 2, 35–76. In addition to Winthrop Jordan's *White over Black: American Attitudes Toward the Negro, 1550–1812* (Baltimore: Penguin, 1969), useful sources on the cultural, legal, and political contexts of miscegenation in the United States are Michael Grossberg, *Governing the Hearth: Law and the Family in Nineteenth-Century America* (Chapel Hill: University of North Carolina Press, 1985), 136ff. and Marylynn Salmon, *Women and the Law of Property in Early America* (Chapel Hill: University of North Carolina Press, 1986), esp. 211ff.

imitation of the white master's power to enforce that inequality in the form of social death. Comprehending her permanently alienable status as itself predicated on a threat of death permanently in force, Roxana first seizes power over her life and that of her child by deciding to end them both. She then finds a way of commuting this double death sentence when she conceives her design to "save" her son. She thereby institutionalizes a power over her son that imitates the slaveholder's dominant position as commutator of a death sentence that he can always revoke. But if Roxana seizes the power to commute the metaphoric death sentence of being sold down the river, she clearly still lacks the power to enforce that threat.

This is hardly surprising. After all, no matter how violently subversive, Roxana's secret act is, it remains—and *must* remain, to have its immediately intended effect—secret.[9] Further, Roxana remains a slave. What is surprising is that twenty-three years later she is able to enforce the threat implicit in her deed, to exploit its actual consequences in terms that, for a while, at least, transform her imitation of the master's power into an active appropriation of it.

In order to understand this turnabout, it is necessary to explore the relation of killing to selling in the slave economy of social death as it operates in this novel, so as to see—what Patterson fails to see—how the slave mother is specifically positioned in and by that economy.

The complexity of the analogy between killing and selling is revealed by the novel's technically flawed ending. As everyone has noticed, in order to sell Tom down the river at the end, and thus restore him to his status quo ante, Twain must "forget" that Tom's double, Chambers, has already been sold and Percy Driscoll's estate thereby credited with the money Judge Driscoll paid for him. Because there is one slave whose exchange value is already accounted for, in this view, the sale of a second under the same name is redundant—a gratuitous addition made necessary by Twain's desire to underscore what George Spangler aptly calls a "parable of property."[10]

Yet what counts as contradiction on the surface of Twain's plot is quite consistent with the rules of property and exchange as they operate in Roxana's plot, where the economy's operation is experienced by the slave. Here, the condition of alienability is definitive, as Roxy demonstrates when she allows Tom to sell her back into slavery. Legally, she may be "free," but actually, she can always be sold and resold. In this economy, the same person can clearly be sold twice, that is, for a double profit. All that is necessary is that the person be designated "black." In Roxana's case, as she notes, it is her speech that identifies her as black despite her white skin. In Tom's case, it is finally his fingerprint that identifies him as black, despite his white speech *and* his

---

[9]The question of whether it must remain a secret to her son, once he is old enough to hear it, is begged by Twain's account of Tom's upbringing as a white master. But the question is answered differently by Faulkner in the story of Charles Bon. See *Absalom, Absalom!* (New York: Vintage, 1936).

[10]See George M. Spangler, "*Pudd'nhead Wilson:* A Parable of Property," in *Pudd'nhead Wilson,* 295–303.

white skin. But in both cases, all that is required for a person to be placed on the sale block, to be alienable, is proof of a specific racial identity. What makes Tom's sale at the end possible as well as logical, then, is an extension of the principle of the slave's alienability in terms of his or her name, or more accurately, the lack of one.

The real anomaly of Tom's sale lies deeper—in the perception that two bodies have been sold under the same name. From the slave's perspective as always-alienable property, once his racial identity is proven, "Tom" has no identity at all as a person. This is clear from the fact that he loses his patronymic surname. As Roxy tells him "you ain't *got* no fambly name, becaze niggers don't *have* 'em" (41). If racial identity is "a fiction of law and custom" and thus manipulable by and subordinate to capital, so is the identity that depends upon, and is represented by the "name of the father." Once reduced to nameless property, that is, two bodies can occupy the same alienable identity. This point is, in fact, demonstrated at the book's outset by Roxy's exchange of the babies and helps to explain why the exchange lacks symmetry. If Roxana "saves" her son from sale, she simultaneously places her master's son, potentially, on the sale block, an exchange that does not free anyone. Because the legally defined distinction between "free" and "slave" seems so absolute, it is easy to assume that Roxana's original exchange of the free Tom and the enslaved Chambers operates on a one-to-one ratio. If one is free, the other is a slave, and vice versa. But this ratio holds no more firmly within the economic system than it does within the racist society. If both children in the end become niggers, the one legally and the other culturally, this outcome is consistent with the contaminating force of a system of property and exchange value that replicates the contamination of nigger blood. Once a slave, always a slave. Once a nigger, always a nigger—even to the fifth generation in Tom's case. In other words, the exchange of A for B, as David Wilson later refers to the original Tom and Chambers, is no simple act of turning A into B and B into A so that the two can be returned to their original condition by a legal decision. Instead, it turns the free Tom (A) into the slave Chambers (B) and yet, despite Roxana's continual efforts, B ultimately reverts to B. Tom's reversion to the status of alienable property is always, from the moment of his un-naming, a potential threat.

In short, the symbolic form that the threat takes for Tom is the erasure of his surname. Without that name, he is subject to the slave's condition, in which death is either exchanged for alienability or else accepted as the only alternative to it. It is the lack of the name that accords a paternally founded identity that matters here. Accordingly, the exchange of the names, "Tom" and "Chambers," which designates a one-to-one exchange of two identities for each other, is functionally a chimera and is irrelevant in a system in which all that matters is the presence or absence of "Driscoll." This point is underscored by the striking contrast between what is at stake in Wilson's loss of "David" for "Pudd'nhead" and what is at stake for either Tom or Chambers in the loss or gain of "Driscoll."

Roxana's power to erase that name provides her with the leverage to appropriate and turn the white master's power against him. She has, of course, exercised this power over the real Tom Driscoll at the outset. But in blackmailing her son, she threatens to repeat her own initial erasure of "Driscoll" from the real Tom's name by un-naming the false Tom. The power she calls upon here enables her to complete the imitation of the white master by enforcing the threat of death he wields, and this power emerges as a result of her status as a slave mother as dictated by the antebellum slave code.

Because this code observed the Roman rule of matrilineal descent, in which the child follows the "condition" of the mother, no matter what the father's status, a slave mother, in giving birth, delivered her child into slavery. It is this rule, among other unwritten laws, that Roxana subverts when she inserts her son into the patrilineal, and patriarchal, system, in which he becomes the "heir of the house" (15). In one sense, this is a re-insertion because her son's father is a member in good standing of the white master class to which Roxana, in effect, returns her son. As a changeling, Tom thereby temporarily escapes his maternal legacy of slavery and social death and eventually devotes his attention to retaining his paternal legacy of a surname and the property accompanying it. But (in this context at least) the fate of the newly enslaved Chambers, whose name has been erased, designates the hidden power that eventually displays itself in Roxana's aggression against the white patriarchy. A crack in the patriarchy is opened to view on the site of the slave mother's body as the locus of miscegenation, a gap that opens because of the patriarchy's legal recognition of the slave mother as the source of her child's *lack* of identity. If in giving birth, the slave mother condemns her child to social death and the status of always-alienable property, that birth blots out the father and thereby condemns the child to an always-alienable condition marked by a lack of surname. Thus, within the slave family, the slave child is automatically made into property, and the slave father is automatically rendered legally impotent. The body of the slave mother, meanwhile, is the putatively passive conduit that the white master uses to castrate the slave father and appropriate the slave child as always-alienable property.

That, in any case, is how the system was supposed to function. But as the work of social historians—not to mention black women novelists—has abundantly demonstrated, slave mothers *and* fathers actively and often effectively combated the corrosive effects of this system on the slave family. (Despite which, the discussion of the "Black Matriarchy" and its sins never seems to stop.) Roxana's is neither a stereotypical nor a real slave family, but her case can perhaps help reveal the flaw in a system predicated on the slave mother's passivity. In Roxana's blackmail plot, we find that mother appropriating as power the negation of the father enacted by the son's birth. What makes this possible is also what makes it radically subversive: the father is a white master (as, in this case, is the son, at least on the face of it). But this subversive power exercised in succession over two "white" sons (one, "real", one "false"), in revenge for "two centuries of unatoned insult and outrage" (39), is blighted by the subtext of horror that emerges in the fate of two "black" sons, and the condition of the mother that fate exposes. It is difficult, as well as painful, to separate these two sides of Roxana's plot, but it is necessary to do so in order to grasp the plot's implications.

If in her initial switching of the children, Roxana erased the real Tom's paternal identity, she returns twenty-three years later, recognizing her power to erase that of the false Tom. If we translate real / false to "white / black" or master's son / slave's son, she has already, of course dealt this blow, sub rosa, against the master's son. Having given birth to her son, Roxana saved him from the fate his birth decreed. By appropriating the matrilineal descent rule, she suspended its negative power in regard to her son; at the same time, she exercised that power over the master's son. If she can blot out one father, she can blot out another. But now, the negative power implicit in the slave mother's position becomes explicit, as the repressed returns literally with a vengeance. Roxana has recognized her power not only to erase the name of the father by identifying her son, but also to threaten with death the white master who is her son by exposing him as her son. The slave mother's power to negate paternal identity, both disclosed and suspended at the moment Roxanna exchanged the babies, is now unleashed and aimed not only at Tom, but also through him at the white patriarchy, against which Roxana turns the same threat on which its power relies.

More specifically, until Roxana's return, all that Tom has to lose is his inheritance. After her return, and her revelation of his origins, he stands to lose his name and, symbolically, his life as well. By exploiting his fear of the first loss, Roxana is able to make good her threat of the second. And by exploiting his fear of the second, she is able to siphon a livelihood from the Judge's coffers. She thereby wreaks her revenge *on* Tom for mistreating her, and *through* him, on the white masters whose crimes she wants to avenge. Tom's life now depends upon providing for her survival, as befits the slave's relation to his master. Of course, because Roxana's extorted funds depend upon Tom's retaining his legacy, and thus upon his remaining in the judge's good graces, they both remain subject to the white master. Yet *within* this patriarchal system, Roxana has opened a rift that enables her revenge, and through Tom, she creates havoc in Dawson's Landing.

The whole show, of course, is a bluff. Roxana cannot prove that she is her son's mother. Like all bluffs, hers can work only by not being called, but that it works for so long is testimony not only to Roxana's shrewdness as a "blackmail" artist whose manipulation of Tom makes him seem almost smart on occasion, but also to the obliviousness of the white masters whose social structure she subverts. That it works for so long testifies particularly to the remarkable blindness of David Wilson; Roxana knows Wilson to be her chief adversary from the start, but it takes him forever to see her as his.

Indeed, all the white fathers lack personal force, to put it mildly. Essex ("Tom's" real father) is—significantly—no more than a name. Percy Driscoll, his next "father," dies bankrupt, his finances having apparently gone into decline soon after his own son's birth. As for Judge Driscoll, his central identity lies in his reputation as a gentleman. He can swing elections, but he is too "infatuated" with Tom to exercise any genuine authority over him (93). The story of how Chambers acquires the name "Tom Driscoll's nigger pappy" suggests that effective paternal power might reside in the vacant position of the black father, were the "black" son allowed to become a father, that is, possess a name. This incident also foreshadows the relation between Tom and the Judge. Like the Judge, who keeps believing Tom despite Tom's repeated failure to make good on any of his promises to reform, Chambers believes Tom when he says he is drowning and thus "unfortunately"—as Twain says— saves his life. Tom then stabs Chambers, and when that fails to kill him, Tom tries to have Chambers sold down the river. When Judge Driscoll buys Chambers in order to "prevent" this "scandal," he ironically "saves" his brother's real son from the death that such sale implies. When the white patriarchs act in this novel, they act blindly. Further, the Judge's primary means of eliciting our respect is his friendship with David Wilson, the "true son" who finally names his "father's" killer and assumes his "rightful" position of authority in Dawson's Landing.

But Wilson, if we bracket his calendar, *is* a pudd'nhead. His intelligence is proven, and his ascension to authority vindicated in the end, but only after what amounts to Twain's extended humiliation of him as a detective who is remarkably dull-witted when it comes to reading his evidence. Most noteworthy is his persistent and blundering confusion over the identity of the "young woman" in Tom's room, "where properly no young woman belonged," and his search for this "mysterious" girl's fingerprints, despite his faith that a "gentleman" like the Judge "could have no quarrels with girls" (97). Roxana, certainly, has a "quarrel" with the class represented by the Judge, and in light of this fact, Wilson's "pudd'nheadedness" reflects the white masters' blindness to the violent power of the black woman in its midst. Tom wears his mother's clothes to disguise his movements as a thief and to cover his getaway as a murderer, and so Pudd'nhead Wilson pursues the clue of the mysterious woman in black. But what is a red herring on the novel's surface points to a vital truth at its center: Roxana, as a "black" woman, has turned Tom into her instrument for revenge. Figuratively, the knife that Tom uses to kill the Judge is an extension of the knife Roxana holds on Tom when she forces him to accompany her home in St. Louis. That none of the appointed authorities of Dawson's Landing imagine this is hardly surprising. That Wilson fails to see it suggests that the superior intelligence that Dawson's Landing has marginalized all those years may be somewhat overrated.

Aggressive and shrewd, the Roxana who deceives Wilson and rules Tom, advising him in his thievery while forcing him to "behave" more effectively than any of his fathers, ought to present a gratifying spectacle, not least because with Tom as her agent, running in and out of houses and dressed in her clothes, Roxana has everyone in Dawson's Landing thoroughly baffled and confused. But as any reader of *Pudd'nhead Wilson* can attest, gratification is hardly the word for our responses to this novel. To account for this, we need to attend to the other side of the slave mother's unique position as the locus of negation. Roxana's status as "imitation white" provides the precondition for her campaign of vengeance, a campaign that exposes a critical gap in the slave economy of social death, a gap that opens precisely on the site of the mulatto mother. What enables her attack on the white patriarchy is that she can turn the power inscribed on the slave mother's body—the power to negate the slave father—back on the white father. But this radical displacement entails the alienation of that father's "white" son as well, a fact that serves Roxana's purpose only insofar as Tom is that "white" son. But of course, "Tom" is not Percy Driscoll's "white" son. He is Roxana's "black" son.

Consequently, what looms up behind Roxana's vengeful subversion of the white fathers is the fundamental and unchanging horror of the condition that motivates it—the slave child's "natal alienation" from his mother, and her foredoomed loss of him. In the excruciating chapter 4, for example, in which Twain describes Tom's childhood culminating in "an abyss of separation" between Roxana and "her boy," the abyss in question is not simply that which opens as the master-slave relationship overtakes and destroys the mother-child bond. Several ideologically charged and contradictory codes (e.g., the black Mammy and her white charge and the white mother's love of her child) circulate through the story told in this chapter, but none wholly deflect the horror of the situation they both describe and obscure—that of the slave mother condemned to the loss of her child. Beneath the confusions of real / false and white / black lies the distinction "my son" / "his son," and the erasure of two white fathers' names entails the destruction of two "black" sons' lives. Satirizing the Southern ideology that exalted the Mammy's devotion to her white owner's children as well as theirs to her, Twain displays Roxana as full of "impotent rage" at Tom, and Tom as an irredeemable little bully to her. Twain includes a hilarious account of Tom as a "bad baby" that must have rung as true to the mothers of Twain's day as it does to those of ours, but the humor is corroded throughout by the racist implications it inevitably fosters. Likewise, when he appeals to the white culture's sanctification of the mother, Twain both satirizes this ideology, calling Roxana a "doting fool of a mother," whose son becomes her "master, and her deity," and yet invokes its cultural force by depicting Roxana's fall "from the sublime height of motherhood to the somber deeps of unmodified slavery," as Tom's "chattel" and "dog." What makes this chapter so painful to read is what both destabilizes Roxana as a character and generates the entire novel's radically disjunctive tone. In appealing to such codes to tell the story of a black mother's alienation from a "white" son become a "master," Twain's chapter exacerbates the horror of the slave mother's plight as not only the victim, but also the reproducer of social death. What is represented explicitly as a double-bind blocking the immediate avenues of revenge implicitly refers us to the violently severed bond between slave mother and child.

That is, because she is "imitation-white," as Chambers tells her, Roxana can subvert the matrilineal rule of descent, but only at the cost of losing her son entirely. By disowning him, she makes him free but no longer hers. Once the maternal bond to him is worn thin by his mistreatment of her, she is faced with the fact that to "own" Tom as hers, even if she could prove her claim, would make him a slave, subject to being sold down the river—the very fate from which she had set out to save him. But, as we have seen, Roxana finds a way out of this impasse; by threatening to "own" him before the Judge, Roxana can bring vengeance on him as well as on the white masters. What she cannot do is "save" her son, for the dilemma she faces with regard to her "white" son—to own him is to make him a slave—uncannily reiterates precisely the slave mother's constitutive double-bind: to give birth is to inflict social death. In other words, to give life to her child is to condemn him to death: it is this contradiction—so brilliantly explored in Toni Morrison's *Beloved*—which reveals what the economy of social death that Patterson describes entails for the slave mother. And it is this logic which Roxana's plot both resists and horribly confirms. If to blot out one father means that you can blot out the other, the same negativity entails that any child you have you must lose. From the opening moment when she decides to drown her child, to the closing one in which he is sold down the river, death is the slave mother's predetermined legacy that Roxana tries to, but finally cannot, abort. The choice she confronts at the outset, between seeing her son sold away or killing him herself, in retrospect collapses; from her position, death is not merely the equivalent of being sold down the river, but identical to it.[11]

From this vantage point, the space of the narrative opened up between Percy Driscoll's threat of sale and his creditors' final enforcement of that threat twenty-three years later may be figured as a space pried open between the jaws of a vise. In a sense, what keeps those jaws from closing for so long is the continual substitution of alienability for death that Roxana negotiates. For example, Chambers becomes alienable so Tom can "live"; Roxana sells herself back into slavery to save Tom; and Tom must find the money to buy Roxana back in order to save his life. Because the white slaveowning masters continue to buy and sell, and the "inventory" remains intact, they remain blindly aloof from the feverish strategems we observe going forward around them. Like Percy Driscoll, as a class they are too concerned with their speculations to notice any substitutions in the specific bodies that are the vehicles of their capital. Recall that no matter how much Roxana's second owner may admire her, he is quite satisfied to be reimbursed for her loss. From the white slaveowning class's viewpoint, the slave's life *is*, quite literally, his or her alienability as property so that the "erroneous inventory" held responsible for

---

[11]In fact, the collapse of difference between death and alienability has already been accomplished for her. When her efforts to exploit the exchangeability of death for alienability culminate in her own sale down the river, her experiences there can be read as narrativing the metaphorical relation between killing and selling, relocating it along a metonymic axis where her sale and her death threaten to achieve a cause-effect relationship.

the judge's murder is corrected to everyone's satisfaction by Tom's final sale down the river. But from Roxana's viewpoint, that sale is her son's death, snapping the vise shut forever.

Roxana's plot, then, drives in two directions at once. Most explicitly, it operates to subvert the white patriarchy. The plot device of an "imitation white" slave mother focused Roxana as a slave mother of 1850 through the lens of the 1890s, with its "one-drop" rules, its lynchings, Jim Crow laws, and *Plessy v. Ferguson* two years away. Roxana's power to erase the name of the father thus emerged and enabled Twain to assault, humiliate, and expose the white Southern gentleman, to attack virulently the slave society he had ruled and the racist society he had bequeathed and still ruled. Thus, Cox is quite right to identify the novel's target as the white Southern patriarchy. What needs to be added is that it is the matrilineal rule of descent reinscribed on the mulatto mother that makes Roxana such a powerful weapon in Twain's arsenal. The negating power that the white patriarchy has invested in the body of the slave mother backfires here. If the white fathers have used the slave mother to erase the name of the black father, Roxana turns this negating power back onto the white fathers. Insofar as it is a matter of revenge against the white fathers, then, Roxana's subversive power is appreciable. But insofar as it is a matter of sons rather than fathers, her plot backfires on Roxana herself. If what the slave code termed "the condition of the mother" enables Roxana to blot out the white father, it also compels her to blot out the "black" son—*her* son, for whose sake she had acted in the first place.

On the one hand, Roxana's plot foregrounds the radical difference in the fates of the two sons in order to drive home the moral idiocy of that "fiction of law and custom" that enforces the color line. But on the other, it also exposes the similarity in their fates; for the slave mother, that is, both fates are "killing." The slave mother's constitutive double-bind is thus explosively revealed, but corrosively recontained by the *Pudd'nhead Wilson* plot. This, I believe, is why Roxana as a character is thoroughly contradictory in herself— and destabilizing to the entire novel.

It is not only Roxana's sexual force that must be repressed. Nor is it only a question of Pudd'nhead Wilson finally bringing down the curtain on Roxana's career as an "imitation" master. Most fundamentally, what gives Roxana's plot its radical and disruptive force lies in the contradiction at its heart—a contradiction we can imagine Twain violently warding off even as it looms up more powerfully all along—the contradiction between a power to negate, but one unleashed from within—and brutally reinforced as—the slave mother's negated position. This contradiction might account for, although by no means redeem, the well-known moments in the novel that provoke a kind of moral vertigo in the reader, such as Roxana's appeal to "white folks'" example to justify her exchange of the babies, her infamous genealogy speech, or the scene in which she excoriates Tom for his cowardice and blames the nigger in him. Such an account would require another essay, but I could suggest how we might proceed. For me, one of the worst among many moments in

Pudd'nhead Wilson comes in the courtroom scene, when Roxana cries out, "De Lord have mercy on me, po' misable sinner dat I is!" and the clock strikes twelve. In some nightmarish version of Cinderella, Roxana is reduced to the rags of a racial stereotype. And rather than a prince, she finds in Twain a stern judge who condemns her in the final chapter as the recipient of a pension from "the young fellow upon whom she had inflicted twenty-three years of slavery" (114).

There is no way to read this and other comparable passages without succumbing to a kind of ethical nausea. But there may be a way to account for such passages by suggesting that the aggression Roxana's plot unleashes in Twain's text is driven out of control by the horror that provokes it, so that Twain gives in to the temptation to turn that aggression against Roxana herself. As black women in this country have always known and have testified repeatedly, this would not be the first or the last time that the black mother got blamed.

Mark Twain and Homer Plessy

Eric J. Sundquist

The carnivalesque drama of doubling, twinship, and masquerade that constitutes *Pudd'nhead Wilson* and its freakishly extracted yet intimately conjoined story, "Those Extraordinary Twins," is likely to remain misread and controversial in estimations of Mark Twain's literary achievement as long as the work's virtual mimicry of America's late-nineteenth-century race crisis is left out of account. Readers have, of course, often found a key to the novel's interpretation in the notorious "fiction of law and custom" that makes the "white" slave Roxy legally "black" by allowing one-sixteenth of her blood to "outvote" the rest (8–9).[1] Like so many parodic moments in the book, however, Twain's joke about voting speaks not simply to general anxieties about miscegenation but more particularly to the deliberate campaign to disfranchise blacks and strip them of legal protections that was underway by the early 1890s. Built of the brutal artifice of racial distinctions, both American law and American custom conspired to punish black men and women in the post-Reconstruction years, and Twain's bitter failed fiction, verging on allegory but trapped in unfinished burlesque, has been thought to participate in the black nadir without artistically transcending it or, conversely, without reaching its broader historical implications. . . .

Preoccupied with relevant but improperly construed issues of aesthetic unity and verisimilitude, critics have typically missed the primary ways in which *Pudd'nhead Wilson* (1894) and its attached tale of the Italian Siamese twins involves itself in the dilemma over national discrimination against blacks that would reach its authoritative constitutional expression two years later in the Supreme Court ruling in the case of *Plessy v. Ferguson*, while mirroring as well the equally volatile issue of anti-immigrant nativism.

Although the court's landmark ruling in favor of the doctrine of "separate but equal" was only handed down in 1896, Homer Plessy's case had been pending since January of 1893, after being carried up from the Louisiana Supreme Court to the high court on a writ of error. Despite the manifold thematic and figurative entanglements between *Plessy v. Ferguson* and

Reprinted from *Representations* 24 (Fall 1989), 102–27. © 1989 The Regents of the University of California. By permission.

[1]Parenthetical page numbers refer to the Norton Critical Edition of *Pudd'nhead Wilson and Those Extraordinary Twins*, ed. Sidney E. Berger (New York, 1980).

Pudd'nhead Wilson, it is not necessary to argue that Twain had specific knowledge of the case as it came before the Court. It is quite likely for several reasons that he did; but more to the point is the fact that *Plessy* brought to a climax the series of Supreme Court decisions, legislative maneuvers, and developments in sociological theory that had already created the atmosphere in which his wrenching text was composed. The central irony of Homer Plessy's deliberately staged challenge of Louisiana's segregated train car law lay in the fact that he was seven-eighths "white"—like Twain's Roxy and her son Tom, he was "black" only by the fictions of law and custom—and his case therefore tied together the radical decline in black civil rights that had occurred since Reconstruction and the fanatical adherence to "one-drop" definitions of negritude that had begun to engulf the South and much of the nation by the mid 1890s. Twain's tale, in which color hallucination, separation and reversal, and the freakish alliance of bodily selves in the twins' story play such critical roles, is a fitting gloss on the nation's rush toward racial extremism in law, in science, and in literature, and its propensity to define equal protection under the Constitution in such a way as to render the black population invisible or, what was more fantastic, to define color itself not by optical laws but by tendentious genetic theories that reached metaphysically into a lost ancestral world.

Changing "itself from a farce to a tragedy" during his process of composition (as Twain, not quite honestly, explained his method of composition), *Pudd'nhead Wilson* and the story of the twins comically dramatized national policy in which farce and tragedy were indistinguishably conjoined, like black and white in the mulatto body or like the Italian "freak of nature"—separate but equal in name and by law but hardly so in fact (119). The story's endless play on the problems of doubling reflects Twain's own interest in questions of identity, dream selves, and dual personalities, which readers have rightly connected to his partly suppressed fascination with miscegenation and racial doubles.[2] More specifically, it corresponds to an array of dualisms comprising the contemporary American racial trauma: theories of miscegenation and "blood" contamination that polarized the races and divided the mulatto identity; sectionalism and the evident cultural, economic, and legal reunion of North and South that was underway by the 1890s; the conservative drift in constitutional law that created distinct notions of national and state citizenship, with a consequent decay in legal protection of civil rights; and pervading all, the dual layering of antebellum and post-Reconstruction (or Old South and New South) ideologies, the recreation of the dynamics of slavery in new masquerade that Twain adumbrated here, as he had in *Adventures of Huckleberry Finn,* by imposing upon antebellum dramatic action an allegory of the 1880s and 1890s.

By the time of *Pudd'nhead Wilson,* the painful and farcical attempt by

[2]See, for example, Justin Kaplan, *Mr. Clemens and Mark Twain* (New York, 1966), 341–47; Arthur G. Pettit, *Mark Twain and the South* (Lexington, Ky., 1974), 141–72; Evan Carton, "*Pudd'nhead Wilson* and the Fiction of Law and Custom," in *American Realism: New Essays,* ed. Eric J. Sundquist (Baltimore, 1982), 82–94.

Huck and Tom to "set a free nigger free"—as Huck described the charade of Jim's mock liberation into which Twain cast his most penetrating critique of the collapse of Reconstruction ideals—had become a nightmare of tautology. Blacks were free according to the law; but the law, as Twain understood clearly, was more than ever in the process of reenslaving them. Reflective of, if not overtly caused by, growing Northern concern about the freed black population, the sequence of court rulings that prepared the way for the decision in *Plessy* broke down the legal gains blacks had made during Reconstruction largely by giving Southern, states-rights rule precedence over national civil rights protection. The "dual" citizenship that in effect allowed the reconstitution of aspects of chattel slavery in a system of segregation subverted black freedom at the same time that it fired the debate over whether it was environment (the world of social construction) or instinct (the laws of "nature") that created seemingly separate racial characteristics. Both in Twain's novel of racial crisis and in the rising national penchant for Confederate nostalgia, the 1850s and the 1890s, the South and the North, and white and black became freakishly twinned in the failure of freedom. Taking on the voice of corrupted legalism that rules his tale of artificial identity, Twain himself, Southern imposter and pudd'nhead author, stands in mocking yet deadly serious judgment over materials that refused to cohere—materials that, like the destructive constitutional decisions from which they undoubtedly in part borrowed their grim energy, were themselves a "monstrous 'freak,'" a "twin-monster" (169–70) of skewed intentions and betrayed ideals. A full understanding of *Pudd'nhead Wilson* must therefore trace the intricate relationship between Twain's fascination with questions of psychological and racial doubling, and the pervasive dualisms in Jim Crow race theory and the laws of segregation.

Plessy's appeal of the lower court ruling against him to the Louisiana Supreme Court brought forth from Justice Charles Fenner the key ingredients of the eventual United States Supreme Court ruling. Like Justice Henry Billings Brown, who wrote the majority opinion in *Plessy*, Fenner chose the path of anachronism, for his decision was based in one instance on a case decided prior to the enactment of the Thirteenth and Fourteenth Amendments, prior, in fact, to the Civil War. Fenner took his language from an 1867 case in which a Pennsylvania Jim Crow railroad regulation was upheld by a court that appealed to racial differences "resulting from nature, law, and custom" and that declared that, "following the order of Divine Providence, human authority ought not compel these widely separated races to intermix." In the antebellum case cited by Fenner and Brown as precedent, Lemuel Shaw, chief justice of the Supreme Court of Massachusetts and Herman Melville's father-in-law, wrote in a decision upholding school segregation in *Roberts v. City of Boston* (1849) that racial "prejudice, if it exists, is not created by law and probably cannot be changed by law."[3] . . . Henry Billings

---

[3]Charles Fenner, *Ex parte Homer A. Plessy*, 45 La. Ann. 80 (1893), reproduced in Otto Olsen, *The Thin Disguise* (New York, 1967), pp. 71–74; Fenner cites the Pennsylvania Supreme Court in

Brown [also] appealed to "established usages, customs and traditions of the people" in his *Plessy* opinion and held that "legislation is powerless to eradicate racial instincts or to abolish distinctions based upon physical differences," that whatever equality is afforded in political and civil rights, "if one race be inferior to the other socially, the constitution of the United States cannot put them upon the same plane."[4] . . .

Like *Pudd'nhead Wilson*, a text obsessively devoted to problems of legal rights, evidence, codes of authority, and the interplay of "natural" and artificial laws, and culminating in a melodramatic burlesque of a trial that sets right subverted racial roles and boundaries, *Plessy v. Ferguson* was at once a mockery of law and an enactment of its rigid adherence to divided, dual realities. What *Plessy* brought to fruition was the long assault on the Fourteenth Amendment that had begun with the *Slaughterhouse Cases* of 1873, in which the Supreme Court first held, in a verdict on the surface not pertaining to black civil rights but in a manner critically destructive of those rights, that the amendment provided "dual" citizenships—national *and* state—and so carefully circumscribed federal protection of rights transcending state oversight as to make national citizenship virtually meaningless. . . . For example, *United States v. Reese* (1876), *United States v. Cruikshank* (1876), and *United States v. Harris* (1883) all undermined federal jurisdiction in cases involving Southern mob violence against blacks, in particular those attempting to exercise voting rights. Separating national from state rights, the court insisted that, while it could prevent a *state* from abridging civil rights, only states themselves could prevent *individuals* from denying blacks their rights. Corresponding to the end of Reconstruction, the establishment of such a federal-state duality had the effect of drawing a stark color line. As Frederick Douglass noted in 1880, "The citizenship granted in the Fourteenth Amendment is practically a mockery, and the right to vote, provided for in the Fifteenth Amendment, is literally stamped out in the face of government."[5] . . .

John Marshall Harlan's famous dissent in *Plessy* built on his view, already articulated in the *Civil Rights Cases*, that federal allowance of discrimination did indeed constitute a "badge of servitude" and a resurrection of "slavery" in the form of the "sinister legislation" states were able to pass.[6] But the meaning

---

Westchester R. R. Co. v. Miles, 55 Penn. St. 209 (1867), and Lemuel Shaw, *Roberts v. City of Boston*, 5 Cush. 198 (1879). For Shaw's decision in the Sims case, see *Thomas Sims's Case*, 61 Mass. 285 (1851).

[4]Henry Billings Brown, *Plessy v. Ferguson*, 163 U.S. 537 (1896), reproduced in Olsen, *Thin Disguise*, 108–12.

[5]Frederick Douglass, quoted in Loren Miller, *The Petitioners: The Story of the Supreme Court of the United States and the Negro* (New York, 1966), p. 114.

[6]John Marshall Harlan, *Plessy v. Ferguson*, in Olsen, *Thin Disguise*, 113–21. Harlan's position reverted toward Lemuel Shaw's in 1899, however, when he wrote the majority opinion in *Cumming v. Richmond County Board of Education*, 175 U.S. 528, which upheld separate but equal schools. Both an advocate of black rights, in most cases, and a conservative defender of property rights, Harlan betrayed an unusual mix of attitudes. Harlan's evolution. as Kluger points out, from a former slaveholder to a convert to the cause of civil rights is not entirely unlike

of such slavery was more effectively spelled out in Albion Tourgée's brief, which distinguished in antebellum terms between simple chattelism and the black person's "legal condition of subjection to the dominant class, a bondage quite separable from the incident of ownership." As a "defenceless and despised victim of the civil and political society," Tourgée argued, the slave was "in bondage to the whole white race as well as to his owner." Chattelism might be gone, Tourgée concluded, but the Supreme Court decisions culminating in *Plessy* would clearly have reestablished black bondage to the dominant class. Just as Henry Billings Brown recurred to Lemuel Shaw in writing the majority opinion, Harlan echoed the plaintiff's argument advanced by Charles Sumner in the *Roberts* case—that Boston's Jim Crow schools violated central American principles. "We abjure nobility of all kinds," said Sumner, "but here is a nobility of the skin. . . . We abjure all privileges of birth; but here is a privilege which depends solely on the accident [of] whether an ancestor is black or white."[7] Superimposing 1849 on 1896, the arguments of *Plessy v. Ferguson* recreated caste distinctions that violated American principle, the legacy of the Civil War, and the process of Constitutional amendment. Likewise superimposing the 1840–50s on the 1890s, Twain's Tom Driscoll, a disguised aristocratic master exposed as a slave, echoes Charles Sumner in asking the pertinent question: "Why were niggers *and* whites made? What crime did the uncreated first nigger commit that the curse of birth was decreed for him? And why this awful difference between white and black?" (44).

Not just the caste division enunciated in *Dred Scott* but the more insidious aspects of slavery itself would reappear under the forms of segregation that began to flourish in the 1890s as the words *white* and *black* acquired newly powerful, separate meanings and "nobility of skin" took on subtleties in some respects more extreme than those regnant in the Old South. In point of fact, the racist underpinnings of the New South, as Twain well knew and dramatized with such fierce passion in *Pudd'nhead Wilson*, required the creation of an Old South myth that in most ways exceeded historical reality. By 1890, the myth received the blessing of the North; the Republican party had given up attempts to break the Democratic "Solid South," and the largely Northern, Republican Supreme Court ruled consistently on the side of the capitalistic development that the New South hoped to attract.[8] In Twain's recreated antebellum world, replete with the gaudy aura of nobility and fabricated genealogies worshipped not only by the white masters but by their black

---

Twain's response to childhood memories of slaveholding and postwar turmoil; it might be "traceable to the brutalities he saw inflicted upon Negroes in his native Kentucky during the post–Civil War years—beatings, lynchings, terror tactics beyond any conceivable justification." See Richard Kluger, *Simple Justice* (New York, 1975), p. 81.

[7]Albion Tourgée, *Brief for Homer A. Plessy*, in Olsen, *Thin Disguise*, 80–103; Charles Sumner, *Roberts v. City of Boston*, reprinted as "Equality Before the Law," in *Complete Works*, vol. 3 (1900; reprint ed., New York, 1969),81.

[8]Stanley P. Hirshson, *Farewell to the Bloody Shirt: Northern Republicans and the Southern Negro, 1877–1893* (Bloomington, Ind., 1962), 78–258, passim.

slaves as well, the code of Southern gentlemen appears to be at odds with or to despise recourse to law. In the New South, however, the code and the law were approaching identity to the extent that the code was based on racial or genealogical purity, and mob pressure dictated the legal suppression of black political rights. The aristocratic code of the Old South, part of the stage machinery of *Pudd'nhead Wilson,* was central to the "fiction" created by the New South, not least because it imagined a time when the question of black legal rights had been virtually meaningless. In the new order, white supremacy "outvoted" black rights at the polls and in the courts until, in *Williams v. Mississippi* (1898), the first state disfranchisement case to come before the Supreme Court, the legal definition of duality gave a free hand to individual and communal racism. Confronted with Mississippi's 1890 suffrage law, which excluded various convicted criminals, required a poll tax, and finally demanded that the prospective voter read and interpret a section of the state constitution—an act clearly liable to official abuse—the Court replied that such codes did not deny equal protection or, "on their face, discriminate between the white and Negro races." Specifically, Justice Joseph McKenna wrote, it was not shown that the administration of such laws "was evil but only that evil was possible under them."[9]

At the same time, blackness outvoted whiteness in the blood, and "one-drop" ideology drove mulattoes toward blacks—or, in the case of those who were light enough to pass, toward a masked existence among whites. Lynching peaked in the early 1890s, as Twain was writing, and national campaigns against it were sparked by Ida B. Wells's powerful 1892 editorials on lynching for the *Memphis Free Speech* and the *New York Age,* reprinted as a pamphlet entitled *Southern Horror: Lynch Law in All Its Phases.* Revived schemes for the deportation of blacks to colonies in Africa or Latin America were further evidence of the white desire for separation. Fears of increased black criminality and degeneration created the paradoxical situation in which racist exclusion and black alienation fed imitatively upon one another, creating—as Twain a few years later would write of lynching—a "mania, a fashion; a fashion which will spread wider and wider, year by year, covering state after state, as with an advancing disease." In Twain's imagined world of *Pudd'nhead Wilson,* the power of imitative behavior can, as in Roxy's case, destroy the slave's awareness of her own oppression or her recognition that her son has been transformed by her own hand into her abusive master; in the "United States of Lyncherdom," as Twain called it, the power of imitation can define roles of black submission, roles of black segregation, and ultimately roles of black destruction.[10] The imitative behavior that spread disfranchisement laws to state after state during and after the 1890s, and decimated black economic and

---

[9]Joseph McKenna, *Williams v. Mississippi,* 170 U.S. 213 (1898), quoted in Kluger, *Simple Justice,* 67–68.

[10]Mark Twain, "The United States of Lyncherdom," from *Europe and Elsewhere,* in *The Portable Mark Twain,* ed. Bernard DeVoto (New York, 1968), 586.

social rights in the process, thus gave to lynching a figurative dimension that made it all the more virulent. . . .

Even though he did not perhaps deserve the description of genius or hero, the history of the legal battle for black civil rights culminating in *Brown v. Board of Education* would recognize not Albion Tourgée but John Marshall Harlan as the "fool" half a century ahead of his time. Still, it is Tourgée's arguments that bear most precisely on the legal and racial figurings of *Pudd'nhead Wilson*. His attempt to drum up national support for the case with a vigorous newspaper campaign primarily in the North and through the efforts of the National Civil Rights Association (or NCRA, which he had established in 1891, with George Washington Cable among others on its executive board) met with strong and immediate early success. Given Twain's relationship with Cable, strained though it was by the early 1890s, and given too his general interest in the promotion of black rights, it is probable that Twain was well acquainted with Tourgée, his writings, and his civil rights efforts. Disagreement among various race leaders over tactics, conservative attacks, and Southern physical intimidation of blacks undermined the organization, however, and by the time *Plessy* was heard the NCRA hardly existed; the atmosphere of race hatred had heightened, not abated, as Tourgée had hoped; and his errand before the court seemed more foolish than ever. Nevertheless, Tourgée's arguments were of great, if sometimes ironic, importance. In addition to detailing the mechanisms by which Jim Crow reconstituted the essence of slavery—the slave being in "bondage" to the entire white race, not just the property of a single owner—Tourgée turned the property argument on its head . . . by insisting that the Louisiana segregation law had deprived Plessy of his property, which in this instance was vested in his "reputation of being white." "Indeed," Tourgée asked, is whiteness "not the most valuable sort of property, being the master-key that unlocks the golden door of opportunity?" Apparently hoping to fool the property-minded judges into recognizing an element of color that would destroy Jim Crow by rendering it chaotic, Tourgée opened himself to the irony that such an argument would in reality protect only those who could pass—the mulatto elite—and define equal protection just as restrictively and negatively as the Court already had, only locating it at a different mark on the color line. Whatever its merit in protecting the rights of at least the mulatto elite, the brevity of this portion of his argument suggests that Tourgée had, by 1896, recognized its foolishness. Even so, it underlined the hallucinatory character of the Jim Crow laws that were ushered in by *Plessy*, which over the next half a century would reach such extremity that Tourgée's further speculations on the color line were not in the least foolish: "Why not require all colored people to walk on one side of the street and the whites on the other? Why may [the state] not require every white man's house to be painted white and every colored man's black?" As Tourgée saw, there was no logical end to such discriminations, and Brown's reply that they must be "reasonable" was nothing to the point. The primary question, in Tourgée's view, was "not as to the *equality* of the privileges enjoyed, but *the right of the State to label one citizen as white and another as colored."* In holding indeed that "a single drop of African blood is sufficient to color a whole ocean of Caucasian whiteness"—to *outvote* it—the Supreme Court called Tourgée's bluff and exposed the nadir of the new segregationism.[11] . . .

Segregation into dual halves of society, as in dual standings before the law, left blacks and whites in significant ways more divided than they had been during slavery, with blacks, as Tourgée argued, again in bondage to a dominant white class. "Equal" and "separate" were twinned by law but in reality arranged in a hierarchy. Likewise, the widening gulf between colors swallowed into an abyss those whose very bodies were marked by the violation of racial barriers. Escape from . . . the mulatto's dual status lay not in identity or unity but in segregation, not in "equal" but in "separate" existence as it came to be defined by mob rule and by courts of law. Thus, when Pudd'nhead Wilson translates mob opinion into the rule of law at the conclusion of Twain's novel, he simultaneously reveals the hidden "nigger," the white man with black blood, and moves to the apex of the townspeople's values. Recasting his joking irony about the halves of an "invisible dog" into the final revelation of racial law, Wilson reverses the "election" and "verdict" that early on voted him a fool and carries out his original threat against that dog—to kill his half (5–6). Exposed at last as the "miserable dog" (103) to which he has been compared by Roxy, Wilson, and even himself throughout the novel, Tom is condemned for the crime of murder but punished for the crime of being black when he is sold down the river as part of the estate's inventory. And his other half, Chambers, like the innocent but nonetheless dead half of the hanged freak in "Those Extraordinary Twins," is "killed" as well by being thrust into a ruling class to which he cannot by habit belong.

The fear of "mongrelization" that pervaded radical rhetoric about miscegenation imputed bestiality to blacks but suggested also that, in their rise toward political or social equity with whites, blacks were at best able only to "imitate" the requisite manners and intelligence of civilized society. Playing on the imitation of "forms" and "habit" that Twain said could be concreted into "automatic," "unconscious," and "natural" behavior (19), stock minstrel scenes and racist literature denied the priority of environment in forming character and satirized black pretensions to manners, learning, or political sophistication. Twain's inquiry into imitation as a component of character reaches no very satisfactory judgment about the ratio between instinct and training in the case of Tom Driscoll; but just as imitation defined the era's promotion of racist stereotypes and its proliferation of legal sanctions against "black blood," so the imitation of white manners by blacks underscored the legal drive to prevent any true imitation of white rights. The danger that imitation might actually lead to the acquisition of political and social graces or to economic gains

---

[11]Tourgée, *Brief for Homer A. Plessy*, in Olsen, *Thin Disguise*, 83, 97–98.

became uncanny in the figure of the mulatto: was he "white," or did he, like Tom Driscoll, adopt a pattern of imitative behavior that suppressed the " 'nigger' in him" (73)? The mulatto concentrated the problem of racial doubling insofar as he could be said to imitate or parody, but not to own, the property of whiteness. The *de jure* dual citizenship that made for *de facto* racial dualism left the mulatto a "freak" of natural law, while the spread of segregationist thought and policy made the light mulatto an uncanny reminder that blackness both *was* and *was not* visible and whiteness both *was* and *was not* a form of property with legal significance.

The theme of imitation, which circulates through *Pudd'nhead Wilson* so as to define patterns of behavior, violence, and judicial practice, is lodged most provocatively in the thematic dialogue between the Italian "freaks" and their Jim Crow counterparts, Roxy and Tom, the "imitation niggers." The "two stories tangled together," producing "no end of confusion and annoyance," Twain would claim in comic defense of his flawed tales, until the "doings" of Pudd'nhead and Roxy "pushed up into prominence" the character of Tom and the three of them took over a "tale which they had nothing at all to do with, by rights." The result was the notorious "literary Caesarian operation" by which Twain separated his two stories, pulling the freak story "out by the roots" and thus himself giving twin birth to the freak tale and to its racial double (119–20). The figure of the maternal body unites Twain and Roxy in the "doings" that produce both Tom—Roxy's son by the shadowy, off-stage aristocratic figure, Colonel Cecil Burleigh Essex—and Tom's story, a fantasy union in which Twain recapitulates the sins of the white fathers within the authorial body of the black mothers. Becoming (black) mother as well as (white) father to his illegitimate mulatto heir, Twain brings to the surface of consciousness apprehensions he had once intimated in his well-known response to William Dean Howells's review of *Roughing It*. "I am as uplifted and reassured by it," Twain wrote Howells, "as a mother who has given birth to a white baby when she was awfully afraid it was going to be a mulatto." Drawing perhaps on his recorded dream fantasies about black female sexuality, Twain's authorial imitation of master-slave miscegenation lodges in his own body the sexual and racial doubleness at the heart of his story, and it provides a double connection—a Siamese linkage—to the two imperfectly separated tales, illuminating the double imitation in which Tom and Roxy themselves are engaged as actors in the stage play of Twain's social critique. In Roxy and Tom is centered the paradox of alienation and imitation. They strive to, and physically *do*, imitate the white masters, Tom by actually becoming one—to such an extent, in fact, that he is willing to sell Roxy *down* river to raise money for his debts. But the subtleties of the color line render them all the more different for being nearly the same in their possession of the property of whiteness Like the ironic outsider, Puddn'head Wilson, who in his first encounter with the townspeople appears an "uncanny" spectacle (5), and even more like the "uncanny apparition" of the Siamese twins (125), the imitation niggers literally embody a violation of the "laws" of nature and call forth the uncanny fright that Freud assigned to the double: "something which ought to have remained hidden but has come to light."[12] Tom's blackness, like Tom's very existence as a character, is revealed by Twain's participation in the "tragedy" of miscegenation, by his willingness to incarnate in his act of writing the coupling of slave and master while at the same time standing judicially, ironically detached in the role of his foolish hero, Pudd'nhead Wilson.

When Tom is brought to light at the conclusion of the novel, his whiteface disguise is removed and his blackness revealed. Although Twain in his original manuscript had allowed Tom to realize, when Roxy reveals his identity, that the "nigger" in him was not genetic but the Lamarckian result of "decades and generations of insult and outrage," whereas his "white blood" was "debased by the brutalizing effects of a long-drawn heredity of slave-owning" (191), such rational meditation is inexplicably deleted from *Pudd'nhead Wilson*, where all that can come to light is the hidden mark of blackness, the "nigger" in Tom. As the "imitation nigger" that Tom becomes as the slave Roxy's son, he is a parody of himself and of those "blaspheming colors" sported by the Siamese dandies (127). Like the freak, the mulatto was held by some social theorists to be an unnatural hybrid, destined to die out through a failure of reproduction—a perversion of the organic development toward higher, more pure racial forms—while to others he represented the most potent contaminating danger to those forms. The mulatto in effect became the scapegoat for contemporary Confederate apologists, the master's conjunction of property and reproduction; but he also therefore symbolized the "enslavement" of the white race to its past sins, an enslavement Twain's authorial involvement in the process of miscegenation self-consciously doubled. This relationship of dependence and servility, rewritten in the aftermath of Reconstruction to imitate, if not recreate, antebellum slavery, is also what Twain dramatizes in the figure of the twins. In one of the shreds of their Siamese form left unrevised in *Pudd'nhead Wilson* Twain designates their sideshow exploitation in Europe as "slavery" (28). In the twins' story itself Angelo finds normal men to be "monstrosities" and "deformities," and their separateness an "unsocial and uncanny construction," but he still desires "that he and his brother might become segregated from each other" (136–37). The farcical exchanges of control over their body between Angelo and Luigi mimics both the mulatto's dilemma and the South's. In *Pudd'nhead Wilson*, the twins are separated (the liberal segregationist solution), but in "Those Extraordinary Twins" they are hanged (the radical racist solution).

Twain's twins were Italian, and he modeled them to some extent on the Tocci brothers, late nineteenth-century Siamese twins who like Angelo and Luigi had two heads and four arms but only two legs. Yet he drew as well for

---

[12]*Mark Twain–Howells Letters*, ed. Henry Nash Smith and William M. Gibson, 2 vols. (Cambridge, Mass., 1960), 1:10–11; Sigmund Freud, "The Uncanny," in *Standard Edition of the Complete Psychological Works*, trans. and ed. James Strachey et al., 24 vols. (London, 1953), 17:241.

the *meaning* of the twins for his novel on his 1868 comic sketch about the famous Chang and Eng, "Personal Habits of the Siamese Twins." In Twain's postwar imagination the twins became a mock replica of sectional strife: Eng fought on the Union side and Chang on the Confederate: they took each other prisoner and were exchanged for one another as prisoners by an army court. Their marriages and drinking are subject to Twain's comic eye, as in "Those Extraordinary Twins," and although he fails to mention that Chang and Eng were also slaveowners, the irony of that fact had obviously become far more suggestive by the 1890s when the uncanny spectacle of the freak came back into his writing.[13] By then, the twins' bodily servility pointed not just to the conjoined intimacy of white and black but also to the uncanny resurgence of antebellum manners and social theory in late nineteenth-century life, the freakish doubling of reactionary myth in contemporary postures. The fratricidal conflict that Twain turned into burlesque in 1868 had by 1894 become organized along racial lines, with South and North increasingly allied against the black man—tied to him as though by physiology (as in many cases he was) yet anxious to be cleanly separated. The explicit return of latent Civil War models of fratricidal intimacy to Twain's consciousness, along with the authorial embodiment of miscegenation itself, paralleled the uncanny doubling in race law whereby the courts, as in *Plessy*, appealed to antebellum case law that should have been long dead and buried but now returned from repression to "reinvent" slavery under new legal sanction.

Chang and Eng were Twain's original model for the figure of twinship that yokes the extraordinary twins to Tom and Chambers or to Tom as mulatto, but the more physiologically apt Tocci brothers were an even better model. In addition, the fact that Angelo and Luigi are Italian is far from insignificant. In anti-immigrationist thought of the 1880s and 1890s Italians were widely thought, on the basis of their "color," their reputed criminal activities, and their comparatively low standard of living, to be among the most degraded of immigrants, and their willingness to mix with blacks brought forth excited nativist charges that new immigrants would further "mongrelize" America's racial stock. The Italian twins' blurring of the color line has an even more specific force in *Pudd'nhead Wilson*. Besides satirizing the aura of nobility and culture that surrounds the gentleman twins, Twain also capitalized on the common stereotype of Italians as criminals especially adept in the use of knives and prone to impassioned violence and vengeful assassination. The climax of such anti-Italian feeling, in fact, came in New Orleans just the year before Homer Plessy set out to test the segregated train car law. When a jury failed to convict a group of Italians on trial in 1891 for the murder of a New Orleans police superintendent, supposedly because of his efforts' to bring Mafia members to justice, a rioting mob of several thousand attacked the

[13]Mark Twain, "Personal Habits of the Siamese Twins," in *Sketches, New and Old* (New York, 1875), 273–79; see also Leslie Fiedler, *Freaks: Myths and Images of the Second Self* (New York, 1978), 204–18.

prison and lynched eleven of the suspects. The case created a national sensation, with the prosecution complaining that it was impossible to get convictions against the Mafia because of their strict code of honor, while politicians and periodicals lined up to defend or attack the mob's makeshift execution of the "assassins" and the atmosphere of lawlessness and "bloody duels" that some said had made it possible. Most importantly, the lynchings ignited a diplomatic crisis when Secretary of State James Blaine refused to grant redress to the families of the victims, some of whom were Italian citizens, or guarantee the indictment of the mob (President Harrison finally offered redress some months later). The administration's logical but unsatisfactory contention was that the controversy came about because of the Italian government's inability to understand the "dual nature of our government"— that is, its division into federal and state jurisdiction.[14] The incident grew briefly into a serious war scare and . . . the subsequent national outburst of militant patriotism had an important effect on the process of reunion between North and South that would reach its peak in the Spanish-American War at the close of the century. In dramatic demonstrations of loyalty, Union and Confederate veterans' groups pledged cooperation against the Italian enemy if war should come. Journalists and politicians alike called for sectional unity in the face of the seeming threat from abroad and the purported fifth-column danger within. The lynchings and their aftermath gave South and North a further opportunity for reunion—again over what was perceived to be the criminality of "lower" races.[15]

Writing most of *Pudd'nhead Wilson* and its appended burlesque at his villa in Italy or on trips back and forth to the United States, Twain might be imagined to have deliberately cultivated the deadpan voice of his protagonist and the detached irony evident in his opening "Whisper to the Reader," with its bogus rhetoric of authentically rendered courtroom scenes and legal language, and its absurd mockery of antique cultural traditions. Such ironic distance on the problems of American race relations and the New South is certainly present in the tale, but it is inconceivable that Twain was not impressed by the Italo-American crisis and the light it cast on the blurring of the color line caused by non-Anglo immigrant races. The Italian twins, in their Siamese version, define the conjunction of black and white that Twain located in the bodies of Roxy and Tom. As immigrant figures they simultaneously bridge the gaps between white and black, and between North and South, further segregating one pair while unifying the other.

The rhetoric of ironic distance with which Twain opens *Pudd'nhead Wilson* must be taken as his defense against direct implication in the emotional pain

14John E. Coxe, "The New Orleans Mafia Incident," *Louisiana Historical Quarterly* 20, no. 4 (October 1937): 1066–1110; Maldwyn Allen Jones, *American Immigration* (Chicago, 1960), 266.
15J. Alexander Karlin, "The Italo-American Incident of 1891 and the Road to Reunion," *Journal of Southern History* 8, no. 2 (May 1942): 242–46.

of the tale, a disguise, like Tom's color, that covers a latent and incriminating truth that will be revealed at the end of the tale. Provisionally separated from America (and his own personal financial troubles), Twain nevertheless came back in his foreign twins to just the problem his own black changeling would pose when he revised his novel and lodged the problem of doubling not in the now separated twins but in the now "Negro" Tom and his slave Chambers. Angelo and Luigi, both of them charged with the crime of kicking Tom Driscoll when only one is guilty, are exonerated in confusion by a court that refuses to "imitate other courts"; but when their paralyzing double election to the board of aldermen cannot be resolved by court after court, the citizens lynch "one" of the twins (149, 169). Lynching, that is, takes the place of or approximates the justice of the courts. Twain, as we have seen, would later claim that lynching thrives on imitative behavior, something his novel had already shown to apply to the whole range of human attitudes and actions, including his authorship, and something the Supreme Court cases that laid the groundwork for his satire had shown to be key to its own decisions, as one after another the civil rights cases destroyed the gains of Reconstruction by mimicking antebellum law and carefully dividing black from white.

"Imitation is the bane of courts," remarks the judge in "Those Extraordinary Twins" before condemning the hung jury for failing to convict Angelo-Luigi and thus setting free a being with "a hidden and grisly power for evil," by which crime after crime may be committed with no way to separate the guilty one from the innocent (153–54). In *Pudd'nhead Wilson* it is the Siamese-like secret mulatto Tom who, disguised in blackface and a woman's clothing, commits undetected crimes (93–94). His ultimate crime, the murder of the judge, is committed with the knife of the Italian twins against a man whom Twain had originally thought to cast as Tom's actual father and whom he loosely modeled on his own father, John Marshall Clemens, both a slaveholder and a sometime judge, his name, like that of John Marshall Harlan, an echo of past heroic justice. Judge Driscoll, in any case, is the book's symbolic father in his relationship to Tom, Chambers, and Roxy, as well as in his upholding of the *code duello* and the laws of aristocratic prerogative. Despite Twain's own suppression of evidence, as it were, the murder thus follows a logic of revenge. In James Cox's words, Tom becomes "the avenging agent who carries back across the color line the repressed guilt that has gathered at the heart of slavery." More than that, he carries the antebellum world into the post-Reconstruction world in yet another way. In playing out the parricidal rebellion of the black slave against his master-father—or, if his disguise as a woman or his role as Roxy's son is taken into account, as the slave avenging the master's sexual abuse—Tom fuses the Old South and the New by dramatizing the reversal in meaning miscegenation underwent after emancipation. Between 1863 and 1890 the fact of slaveholding miscegenation by white masters and the fear of black slave rebellion were together transformed into the specter of black crime and contamination—the Negro as mongrel or "beast."[16] The imitation white Tom, now like a minstrel performer masquerading in the disguise that parodies his hidden slave status, becomes in effect the mulatto killer of contemporary race theory. In blackface and women's clothing, however, his part includes the maternal authorial disguise adopted by Twain himself, divided as ever between exposing Tom as a "nigger" and participating in his revenge against the aristocratic Southern fathers. Twain's double participation in the plot of his novel thus imitates the Siamese-like entanglement he attributes to his characters. Separate but equal, his twin, paradoxical inclinations toward black vengeance and racist suppression must lie at the heart of his novel's flawed form as well as its dangerously comic representation of Reconstruction's tragic failure.

Tom's crime with the knife momentarily implicates the Italians, already considered "assassins" because of his slander of them. As in late nineteenth-century America, however, it is the black man who is found to be most liable to criminal guilt. Twain leaves unsettled the question of whether it is the "nigger" in Tom that leads to the killing, though as allegory it can be read no other way. Likewise, Tom's traits of laziness, criminality, and cowardice, which Roxy herself ascribes to his hidden race, may be a sign either of aristocratic degeneration or of blackness as defined by the radical thesis and the minstrel stereotype. But the stereotype itself is enforced by a disturbing negative imitation in the scene where Tom's newly acquired eastern mannerisms are burlesqued by a black bell ringer: the black man plays the minstrel to mock the white man who, secretly black, is playing a mannered role that he does not yet know to be a role (24). When Twain adds to this Tom's knowledge of his blackness and his blackface disguise during the murder, his inquiry into imitation reaches a crisis, for Tom's worst traits, like his "color"—or like the guilt of the Italian twins before the jury—can be traced neither to birth nor to training alone, neither to black nor to white. As Twain says of Tom's remorse over his "uncle's" killing, "He was playing a part, but it was not all a part" (99).

Tom's identity belongs neither to his whiteness nor to his blackness; and the novel, like the law of the land in Jim Crow America, leaves him unprotected, stranded between dual worlds of jurisdiction neither of which is responsible for his acts or for his rights. The hero of the novel has no trouble convicting Tom— convicting him both of murder *and* of pretending to be a white man. Tom's sale down the river indicates which is the worse crime, or at any rate demonstrates that the murder follows from the masquerade. The

---

[16]Pettit, *Mark Twain and the South*, 17; James M. Cox, *Mark Twain: The Fate of Humor* (Princeton, N.J., 1966), 232. See also Henry Nash Smith, *Mark Twain: The Development of a Writer* (Cambridge. Mass., 1962), 174: "From the standpoint of imaginative coherence Judge York Leicester Driscoll is the father of Tom just as clearly as Roxy is his mother. But Mark Twain places the unmentionable fact of sexual intercourse between master and slave at two removes from the actual story—first by making Roxy, Tom's mother, the slave of the shadowy brother of Judge Driscoll at the time of Tom's birth; and then by the further precaution of creating an even more shadowy figure, Colonel Cecil Burleigh Essex, to be his father."

value of Tom's whiteness as a kind of "property" does him no more good than it did Homer Plessy; the court recognizes only his blackness, in which property is not self-possession or identity but a sign of the rights of others. Consciously tying his own flawed art to the courtroom theatrics of David Wilson, Twain engaged in a ghostly reduction of the world of the novel to a stage play of parodic codes and habits in which the law dressed as one more player, and in his identification with Wilson Twain admitted his complicity in restoring to order the plantation myth subverted by Roxy's act and Tom's role.

The road to reunion of North and South required both the reinvention of the Confederate myth in the cultural domain and the reactionary readings of constitutional law carried out by legislatures and the Supreme Court. In his reply to Cable's "The Freedman's Case in Equity," the popular Southern writer Thomas Nelson Page had argued, at just the time Twain was writing *Pudd'nhead Wilson*, that in the encroaching struggle against a rising Negro population, "The only thing that stands today between the people of the North and the negro is the people of the South."[17] Page's plea for state rights and Southern control of the "Negro problem" met with increasing favor in the North during the 1890s. It needed and received the assent and support of figures like Pudd'nhead Wilson, who can be read both as an outsider to the South and, ultimately, as its most admired representative, the one who most embodies its cherished codes and racial values. Taken "on trial" (169) by Twain as a "fool" who exposes the town's pretensions and failure of ironic insight, Wilson, it might be said, matures into an eloquent spokesman for Jim Crow. If Tom Driscoll was his Homer Plessy, Twain's Pudd'nhead representative of the law was no Albion Tourgée or John Marshall Harlan but rather the rising voice of segregation. Convicting the black man of imposture as a white gentleman, Wilson's miraculous revelation of Tom's identity restores the community's subverted aristocratic order, much as the overturning of Reconstruction and its accompanying civil rights legislation restored an antebellum racial hierarchy in the new dress of Jim Crow. Crossing geographical as well as chronological boundaries, Wilson is the sign of sectional reunion in law and in culture. His voice of irony, not unlike Twain's own deadpan voice, modulates from critique to accommodation. Both separated from and yet intimately tied to the story whose conclusion he creates, Pudd'nhead-Twain freakishly twins in himself both the racist inclinations bred in him since birth and the countering condemnations of racism that are the better part of his conscience. In Twain's novel, fiction and law imitate one another, and the greatest challenge, in the end, is to separate "racism" from its parodic critique.

---

[17]Thomas Nelson Page, "The Negro Question," in *The Old South: Essays Social and Political* (New York, 1892), 284.

The Lie of Silent Assertion:
Late Twain

Forrest G. Robinson

[Mark Twain's] most balanced assessment of what he recognized as an ineluctable fact of human social experience appears in his essay "On the Decay of the Art of Lying," which he presented for discussion at the Historical and Antiquarian Club of Hartford in 1882. Though his tone is frequently inclined to archness, there is little evident irony in the axiom that forms his point of departure. "No fact is more firmly established," he declares, "than that lying is a necessity of our circumstances." He is more playful in his insistence that lying is "a Virtue," in suggesting that the art of lying deserves "careful and diligent cultivation," and in the declaration that "an awkward, unscientific lie is often as ineffectual as the truth." It would be impossible, he goes on, to

> *live* with an habitual truth-teller; but, thank goodness, none of us has to. An habitual truth-teller is simply an impossible creature; he does not exist; he has never existed. Of course there are people who *think* they never lie, but it is not so—and this ignorance is one of the very things that shame our so-called civilization. Everybody lies—every day; every hour; awake; asleep; in his dreams; in his joy; in his mourning; if he keeps his tongue still, his hands, his feet, his attitude, will convey deception—and purposely.

Persuaded of the inevitability of deception, Mark Twain proceeds to weigh its uses and abuses. Lies are to be valued or condemned according to the pleasure or pain they produce. Thus on one side, "courteous lying is a sweet and loving art, and should be cultivated"; on the other, "an injurious truth has no merit over an injurious lie. Neither should ever be uttered" (XX, 361–64).[1]

Such indulgent, gently playful distinctions form a brief prologue to the more circumstantial, more deliberate discussion of what Mark Twain calls "the

Reprinted from *In Bad Faith: The Dynamics of Deception in Mark Twain's America* (Cambridge, Mass.: Harvard University Press, 1986), pp. 212–37. Copyright © 1986 President and Fellows of Harvard College. Reprinted by permission.

[1]Parenthetical references for "On the Decay of the Art of Lying" and "My First Lie, and How I Got Out of It" refer to *The Writings of Mark Twain, Author's National Edition*, 25 vols. (New York: Harper and Brothers, 1907–18). Subsequent parenthetical references are to *The Mysterious Stranger*, ed. William M. Gibson (Berkeley: University of California Press, 1970).

silent lie—the deception which one conveys by simply keeping still and concealing the truth." This brand of deceit is a variety of bad faith.[2] A silent lie is the mute refusal to acknowledge an awkward reality. Because it is silent, such deception betrays both an impulse to deny, and an impulse to deny that a denial has occurred. Such double denials go unobserved by deceiver and deceived because the silent lie conforms to and even reinforces an acceptable construction of reality. Most significant perhaps, "simply keeping still and concealing the truth" was evidently on Mark Twain's mind in 1882, and it was a topic that he could approach in a mood of good-humored acquiescence. Although his example is graphically exemplary of the perils of lying silently, the essayist is nonetheless quite positive in his address to a world in which "lying is universal—we *all* do it; we all *must* do it" (XX, 364–67).

This playful, precariously balanced point of view is rarely in evidence during the years that followed the publication of *Huckleberry Finn*. As his career wore on, and as experience and reflection combined to darken his perspective on the world, Mark Twain surrendered increasingly to feelings of contempt for "the damned human race." Thus his essay, "My First Lie, and How I Got Out of It," which appeared in 1899, is parallel in much of its substance, but hardly in its tone, to the earlier "On the Decay of the Art of Lying." Once again, Mark Twain proceeds from the assumption "that all people are liars from the cradle onward, without exception." People begin "to lie as soon as they wake in the morning, and keep it up, without rest or refreshment, until they go to sleep at night." Deceitfulness is the very essence of human nature, and it is so by virtue of an "eternal law." Since man "didn't invent the law," he is not responsible for its effects; "it is merely his business to obey it and keep still." This act of concealment, he goes on, is "the lie of silent assertion; we can tell it without saying a word, and we all do it" (XXIII, 146–47).

The lie of silent assertion is the silent lie all over again, but with some important new features. While a silent lie is any mute refusal to acknowledge the truth, the lie of silent assertion is the concealment of the knowledge that humans are by nature incapable of truthfulness. All people lie all the time, but they lie first in denying this law of their nature. It is also clearly implied that the vast majority fails to recognize that deceitfulness is the inexorable law of human nature. So comprehensive is their self-deception that they actually imagine themselves honest. . . .

Mark Twain's further elaborations on the lie of silent assertion—or what we may be tempted to call the lie of truth—lend substantial confirmation to this

[2]Robinson writes earlier: "Bad faith as I have defined it is a frequently benign cultural phenomenon involving the acquiescence in manifest departures from law or custom. Bad faith features the deception of self and other in the denial that such departures have occurred, and bears the clear implication that humans will sometimes permit what they cannot approve so long as their complicity is submerged in a larger, tacit concensus. Thanks to potent prohibitions against their acknowledgement, the operations of bad faith are most often unconscious and unobserved; the act of denial is itself denied." See Robinson, *In Bad Faith: The Dynamics of Deception in Mark Twain's America*, p. 211. [Ed.]

parallel. He goes on to highlight the intimate connection between the lie of silent assertion and civilization. "In the magnitude of its territorial spread, it is one of the most majestic lies that the civilizations make it their sacred and anxious care to guard and watch and propagate." He dwells at length and quite bitterly on the way in which the lie of silent assertion at once generates and confers legitimacy on a world of lesser frauds and deceits. For one who comprehends the situation, it is an effort to try "to make it appear that abstention from lying is a virtue. . . Why should we help the nation lie the whole day long and then object to telling one little individual private lie in our own interest to go to bed on?" Most significantly of all, however, and at the dead center of Mark Twain's reflections on civilization and "the nation," is the clear and emphatic association of the lie of silent assertion with the crime of slavery. Thus in his primary illustration of the "majestic lies" of civilization he declares:

> For instance: it would not be possible for a humane and intelligent person to invent a rational excuse for slavery; yet you will remember that in the early days of the emancipation agitation in the North, the agitators got but small help or countenance from any one. Argue and plead and pray as they might, they could not break the universal stillness that reigned, from pulpit and press all the way down to the bottom of society—the clammy stillness created and maintained by the lie of silent assertion—the silent assertion that there wasn't anything going on in which humane and intelligent people were interested. (XXIII, 147–49)

The lie of silent assertion explains what is otherwise inexplicable, how civilized people committed to freedom and justice and human equality and Christian love are able, either as active or passive participants, Southerners or Northerners, to witness the inhuman spectacle of race–slavery in their midst without registering any apparent concern or discomposure. Mark Twain assumes, as I do, that racism and slavery have always been an intolerable cultural contradiction in America, and that the pervasive lie of silent assertion . . . is oblique but unmistakable testimony to an abiding, profound uneasiness with these realities of our history and common life. This impossible acquiescence in the delusion that there isn't "anything going on in which humane and intelligent people" are interested is just as surely an enduring American phenomenon as it is an enduring crux in our understanding of *Huckleberry Finn*. The novel continues to speak to our condition because it makes us mindful of the legacies of race–slavery in our midst; but it is a great favorite with us, an American "classic," in good part because it seems to invite the dismissal or disavowal of as much of its darkness as we cannot bear to own. *Huckleberry Finn* draws us close to a harsh center of our reality, and we follow willingly, unthreatened by more discomposure than we can comfortably manage because the narrative enables the relatively effortless reader recapitulation of its lie of silent assertion. . . .

It is one key to the cultural authority of *Huckleberry Finn* that at a number of levels it enables the retreat to an illusion of resolution where none has occurred. For Mark Twain and Huck and many readers, the frustration and the guilt that attach to Jim's example and continuing predicament are variously submerged in Tom's "evasion." One way or another, we are all complicit with the egregious young romantic, and our uneasiness on that score registers in a certain discomfort with the novel's conclusion, and in an impulse to try the story just one more time. . . . Mark Twain never came close to repeating this powerful, complex imaginative enactment of this twisted strand of his culture's bad faith. In his numerous subsequent treatments of racism and slavery he either seemingly stumbled on to the topic at the very end of literary fragments, or he attempted, never with much success, to withdraw to a safely detached perspective on his material. The subject either surfaced suddenly and quite unmanageably from the midst of promising projects, or it defied his attempts to frame it in a coherent philosophical perspective. In either case, the inevitable result was an incapacity to finish what he had started, and, further, an incapacity to conceal that failure in evasive illusions of resolution.

Perhaps the most telling example of the first of these characteristic failures is "Which Was It?" a long fragment of a novel recounting the nightmare of disaster dreamt by George Harrison, a rich, respected family man. The narrative does not reach the point at which the dreamer awakens to relief; rather, it terminates just as Jasper, an ex-slave, turns the tables on the degraded Harrison and begins to settle his people's "long bill" of revenge "agin de low-down ornery white race."[3] Having reached this nadir in the dream section of his tale, Mark Twain stopped, leaving the white sleeper forever face to face with the nightmare of retribution poised on the dark side of his waking reality. In trying to account for this oddly suggestive ending, it may not be altogether fanciful to suppose that the line of Mark Twain's narrative drew him all unawares—as his narratives were wont to—into a confrontation with one of his own, and his culture's, deepest fears. So compellingly real was that horrific, unlooked-for prospect that it entirely eclipsed the original comic plot and declared itself de facto the proper, if not the consciously intended, end of the story. Viewed in this way, "Which Was It?" is a record of the failure of the lie of silent assertion to restore consciousness to its waking reality—in fact, its dream—of respectable affluence. It is also an oblique acknowledgment of the unbearable human terms of that all-white dream, and a warning, aptly embodied in the strangely complete incomplete story, against straying from the shelter of bad faith into the glare of too much truth.

"Which Was It?" bears the suggestion that Mark Twain was increasingly prone, as the years wore on, to gravitate toward a perspective on American history and culture that featured racism and slavery in bold if very somber relief. This is quite clearly the drift of *Huckleberry Finn*, though in that novel, as in nothing else Mark Twain wrote, the ostensible conclusion is

---

[3]*Which Was the Dream?* ed. John S. Tuckey (Berkeley: University of California Press, 1968), p. 415.

merely the last of many evasions of a proper resolution. "Which Was It?"
amounts to a version of the same thing, a single turn on the same repeating
cycle, except that it actually achieves the resolution that *Huckleberry Finn*
seems bound for, but at the same time cancels the dark, deeply sought, more
deeply obstructed conclusion by presenting itself as incomplete. If the lie of
silent assertion in *Huckleberry Finn* is the permanent deferral of an irresist-
ible ending, then "Which Was It?" tells the same lie by lodging that ending in
an unfinished replica of the original bad faith plot of human liberation.
Neither text tells a complete story; in both the fact of incompleteness is the
formal symptom of a pervasive lie of silent assertion; and the texts taken in
tandem arrive at the resolution that bad faith obstructs in each taken sepa-
rately.

Such partial renderings of a persistent train of personal and historical
reflection figure prominently among the fragmented literary remains of Mark
Twain's later years. And let me emphasize that it was an incomplete story, one
cut short again and again in bad faith, that Mark Twain had to tell. His
message, both as an individual and as a definitive culture-bearer, is the
deferral of a reckoning with the full, painful implications of race–slavery.
Incomplete literary works that "end" in truncated disclosures of this cultural
pathology gather toward the full revelation of what is secretly known, only to
resubmerge it in their formal literary status as negligible fragments. This
telling incapacity to completely tell is manifest in "The Stupendous Procession," an unfinished allegory of civilized prospects at the opening of the
twentieth century. Modern imperialist powers, bearing emblems of their
territorial conquests, appear one after the other, until the spotlight falls,
where it remains until the piece breaks off, on America. Indeed, it is clear
that the sins of the European countries are of secondary interest to Mark
Twain; his primary object is to review in vivid symbolic detail the errors of his
own nation. The emphasis is everywhere on the cynical declension from
founding ideals, and toward the end the focus comes more and more to rest
on American racism as it descends on the citizens of our imperial acquisitions.
A contemporary version of ante-bellum slavery is the sad lot of those peoples
unfortunate enough to fall within the orbit of the Christian civilization of the
United States. Having reached this general perspective on American corruption at home and American racist imperialism abroad, the unfinished manuscript closes with an angry summary of the moral state of the nation. Banners
are imagined

> scattered at intervals down the long procession, and glinting distantly in the
> sunlight; some of them bearing inscriptions of this sort:
>   ALL WHITE MEN ARE BORN FREE AND EQUAL." *Declaration of Independence.*
>   "ALL WHITE MEN ARE AND OF RIGHT OUGHT TO BE FREE AND INDEPENDENT."
> *Ibid.*
>   14th Amendment: "WHITE SLAVERY SHALL NO LONGER EXIST WHERE THE AMER-
> ICAN FLAG FLOATS.

> "Christ died to make men holy,
> *He* died to make white men free."

(Battle Hymn of the Republic. "He" is Abraham Lincoln.)
"GOVERNMENTS DERIVE THEIR JUST POWERS FROM THE CONSENT OF THE GOV-
ERNED WHITE MEN." *Declaration of Independence.*

Finally, the Statue of Liberty appears with its "torch extinguished and re-
versed," Old Glory passes, "furled, and draped with crêpe," and over all looms
the "SHADE OF LINCOLN, towering vast and dim toward the sky, brooding
with pained aspect over the far-reaching pageant."[4] The thrust of this concluding indictment could not be more clear: American imperialism in the new
century merely repeats, on an international stage, the tragic domestic drama
of the century just passed. Nothing has been learned; there has been no moral
progress; the present and future are bound to recapitulate the intolerable
contradiction of race–slavery in the land of freedom and equality.

Mark Twain effectively silenced his public voice by leaving "The Stupendous Procession" unfinished and unpublished. The same censor enforced the
suppression of publicly unspeakable declarations on the same subject in the
long, but also unfinished "The Refuge of the Derelicts." Reflecting on one
such pronouncement, Isabel V. Lyon, Mark Twain's secretary, records in her
journal for March 21, 1905:

> Tonight Mr. Clemens read a very interesting unpublishable sketch. Unpublishable
> because it is what an old darkey says of the universal brotherhood of man—& how
> it couldn't ever be, not even in heaven—for there are only white angels there & in
> the old darkey's vision the niggers were all sent around to the back door. It's a
> wonderful little sketch but it wouldn't do for the clergy. They couldn't stand it. It's
> too true.[5]

The manuscripts of *The Mysterious Stranger*, closely related variations on
the theme of human enslavement to history, the will of God, evolution, and
the Moral Sense, came to a similar end. The "Schoolhouse Hill" fragment, by
far the shortest, breaks off quite abruptly, almost in midstride. According to
William M. Gibson, the editor of *The Mysterious Stranger* manuscripts, this
sudden standstill is itself something of a mystery. "Why Mark Twain let this
story lapse after a moderately promising beginning when he had dozens of
ideas for continuing it is problematical" (9), Gibson concedes. We may begin
to account for this otherwise puzzling circumstance by observing that "Schoolhouse Hill" is the only version of the story set in the ante-bellum South,
and thus the only version to include American slavery among its examples of
the manifold constraints on human liberty. Indeed, the narrative ends just as
the slaves, uncle Jeff and aunt Rachel, begin to grow familiar with No. 44, the

---

[4]*Mark Twain's Fables of Man*, ed. John S. Tuckey (Berkeley: University of California Press,
1972), pp. 418–19.
[5]As quoted by Tuckey in his Introduction to *Mark Twain's Fables of Man*, p. 9.

angelic witness to mortal degradation. It seems likely that the Hannibal installment on his somber theme, once it began to surface in its full range of personal and social implication, was more than Mark Twain could bear to pursue. Confronted once again with the sharp cutting edge of the tale he was bound, as if by blind compulsion, to tell, he withdrew abruptly to his own lie of silent assertion.

Let me turn [next] to "The Secret History of Eddypus, The World-Empire," yet another of the significantly incomplete writings that Mark Twain produced during the last years of his life. "The Secret History" offers itself as an attempt made in 2901 A.D. to develop an account of the rise and fall of civilization that occurred one thousand years earlier. This attempted historical reconstruction rests heavily on "Old Comrades," a book by Mark Twain, the ancient Bishop of New Jersey, and the only fully reliable written record to have survived the destruction of libraries that inaugurated the long interval of barbarism. As John S. Tuckey suggests, the Eddypus fragment sets forth a cyclical conception of history in which mankind struggles to draw itself "out of ignorance and slavery to gain freedom and knowledge, only to be led by its own cowardice and greed into fooling away its chances and being returned to its chains." Tuckey goes on to develop the parallels between "The Secret History" and *What Is Man?*, which was published in a limited, anonymous edition, and the *Autobiography*, which was written for posthumous publication. Among other things, Tuckey observes, these are all "suppressed" works, not-so-confident gospels in which Mark Twain spoke his mind only to disguise or conceal what he had to say.[6] Like *Huckleberry Finn*, "The Secret History" thematizes suppression; it records a struggle to recover a usable past from beneath a millenial lie of silent assertion. Moreover, in the late fragment, as in the novel, the act of telling recapitulates the denial of precisely the truth that the tale reveals. Huck cannot say what the narrative shows: that Jim is not really free. "The Secret History" draws the same general conclusion from the unfolding narrative of the rise and fall of modern civilization. Despite the great hope engendered by the Enlightenment and the political revolutions at the end of the eighteenth century, the liberation of "the mind and soul" that ensued was a faint flicker in a sea of darkness. The sole illustration of this sweeping overview with which the fragment terminates is the prophesy, ventured by "wise men" in the young Republic, of "the early extinction of slavery in America." This bright prospect came to naught because of the cotton bonanza that followed in the wake of advances in agricultural technology. Slavery became extremely profitable, with the result that it "was gratefully recognized by press, pulpit and people, all over the land, as God's best gift to man."[7] Thus "The Secret History" fragment draws to a close with an image of America withdrawing into a national lie of silent assertion about its peculiar institution. The bad faith, Mark Twain insists, is American ("all

6Ibid., pp. 18, 20–24.
7Ibid., pp. 380–82.

over the land"), not Southern; and he is equally clear, as early sections of the manuscript demonstrate, that race–slavery is the primary cultural ingredient in the subsequent imperialist adventures that bring this brief dream of freedom to its final, nightmarish conclusion. Civilization, he reflects, "was a sham at home and only laid off its disguise when abroad."[8]

The Eddypus fragment contains a coherent argument about the relationship between the bad-faith cultural pathology of race–slavery and the course of American empire. At the same time, however, it participates in the leading symptom of the disease it professes to deplore by failing to speak out against race–slavery in a forcefully complete, public manner. Rather, it retreats to the lie of silent assertion in making its last words indefinite, not definitive. "The Secret History" is in bad faith in the additional sense that it tends to submerge its moral outrage in a coolly detached perspective on its subject matter. More specifically, Mark Twain sets his portraits of slavery and civilization in a deterministic framework that makes no room for human design in the unfolding pattern of history. "Individuals do not project events," he argues; "individuals do not make events; it is massed *circumstances* that make them. Men cannot order circumstances, men cannot foresee the form their accumulation will take nor forecast its magnitude and force." Thus while he emphasizes that slavery is a cruel contradiction in America, he characterizes the failure of its prompt and timely abolition as a leading example of "the fell way in which the plans and foreordainings of men go down before the change-making orderly march of the serried battalions of blind Circumstance."[9] Where Circumstance rules, the argument implies, there is no human responsibility, and therefore no occasion for guilt or the laying of blame. . . .

Determinism serves Mark Twain in "The Secret History" as "the Territory" serves Huck Finn, as a refuge from what he knows, and wants to forget, about his own complicity in the crime against black people. It is a lie of silent assertion which works well enough to permit the engagement with the consuming topic, but not well enough to sustain closure, or to conceal the fact that engagement without closure is precisely what the strategy is designed to produce. The determinist argument fills many pages, and it appears to be the primary thrust of the unfinished treatise, but it does not soften Mark Twain's perception of slavery as cruel and contradictory, nor does it cool the angry irony that flows through his concluding characterization of slavery as "God's gift to man." In fact, the moral outrage has not really subsided at all. But it appears in a frame of discourse so apparently incomplete as to invite critical neglect, and otherwise so philosophically detached as to seem untroubled by guilt.

Mark Twain did not settle naturally or comfortably into detached philosophical points of view on anything. He was constitutionally ambivalent, passionate, and much too independent and willful to repose for long in

[8]Ibid., p. 327.
[9]Ibid., pp. 379–80.

systematic perspectives, let alone narrow determinisms. A little philosophy
served him well enough in his evasions of fear and guilt, but he was at least
now and then capable of recognizing his rational excursions for what they
were. A moment of such penetration occurs toward the end of "My First Lie,
and How I Got Out of It," when he lapses into the exact species of bad faith
that his essay has exposed and vigorously denounced. From the beginning of
"My First Lie," it will be recalled, Mark Twain includes himself in an
enlightened minority of perspicacious witnesses to the operations of bad faith.
A member of this group is distinguished not only because he is aware that it is
"the eternal law" of human nature to lie constantly, but also because that
knowledge does nothing to inhibit his natural inclination, even when he
deceives "his fellow-conspirators into imagining that he doesn't know that the
law exists. It is what we all do—we that know. I am speaking of the lie of
silent assertion; we can tell it without saying a word, and we all do it—we that
know" (XXIII, 147). Membership in this elite devolves upon those who understand the dynamics and the awesome dominion of unacknowledged—and, for
the vast majority of people, unrecognized—deception in human experience.
What such insiders perceive, beyond the law of their nature, is the bleak,
pathological dimension of the culture of bad faith—a civilization blinded by
the lie of silent assertion to its profound deviation from its proudest human
values. Mark Twain goes on to identify American slavery and the contemporary outbreak of imperial oppression as the premier expressions of the lie of
silent assertion, and to inveigh against them. But then, having developed this
commendable position, he concludes with what must seem a striking reversal:

> To sum up, on the whole I am satisfied with things the way they are. There is a
> prejudice against the spoken lie, but none against any other, and by examination
> and mathematical computation I find that the proportion of the spoken lie to the
> other varieties is as 1 to 22,894. Therefore the spoken lie is of no consequence, and
> it is not worth while to go around fussing about it and trying to make believe that it
> is an important matter. The silent colossal National Lie that is the support and
> confederate of all the tyrannies and shams and inequalities and unfairnesses that
> afflict the peoples—that is the one to throw bricks and sermons at. But let us be
> judicious and let somebody else begin.
>
> And then—But I have wandered from my text. How did I get out of my second
> lie? I think I got out with honor, but I cannot be sure, for it was a long time ago and
> some of the details have faded out of my memory. I recollect that I was reversed
> and stretched across some one's knee, and that something happened, but I cannot
> now remember what it was. I think there was music; but it is all dim now and
> blurred by the lapse of time, and this may be only a senile fancy. (XXIII, 156).

To be sure, this is mimicry of bad faith, a self-conscious burlesque of the lie
of silent assertion in action. But we take the humor seriously because it
works, quite conspicuously by design, to displace the timely, morally urgent
discussion that precedes it. His self-conscious mimicry notwithstanding, Mark
Twain is in earnest in moving to empty consciousness of what it knows about
human deceitfulness. His impulse to conceal this knowledge thus extends in
its application not merely to his co-conspirators, but to himself as well; in

effect, the member of the select "we that know" betrays a longing to join ranks with those that don't. And for good reason. As "My First Lie" clearly shows, the knowledge that it is "the eternal law" of human nature to lie does nothing to relieve the knower from guilt about his lying. To the contrary, that knowledge is the source of suffering, for it brings its possessor face to face with what he is powerless to respect or change in his own makeup. "We that know" are unwilling witnesses to what they quite perversely regard as their own degraded complicity in widespread human suffering. The vast majority of people, those who don't know about the lie of silent assertion, are all liars with dirty hands, but they live in blissful ignorance of what is, by the terms of "My First Lie," their natural condition. Indeed, it is the fullest expression of their compliance with the natural that they are totally and irreversibly self-deceived on the score of their constitutional deceitfulness. They believe that lying is wrong, and in this they are profoundly misguided; but they are saved from themselves by the unshakable conviction that they are essentially honest. "We that know" are equally persuaded of the moral obligation to tell the truth, but they frame that assumption in the consciousness that it is definitively characteristic of their species to lie. In the upshot, since the knowledge of their natural condition and the pressure of their unnatural morality are utterly incompatible with each other, it follows that peace of mind can result only from the severance of the conscious link between the two. Thus it is that Mark Twain beats a retreat from his painful awareness of his true nature to a righteous illusion of self that conforms to his eccentric moral prepossessions. Having penetrated to the core of their own and their culture's lie of silent assertion, it is the natural impulse of "we that know" to retell that lie, to their peers and to themselves, almost as soon as its existence and implications are recognized.

The long concluding passage from "My First Lie" is striking in a number of related ways. On one side, of course, it clearly anticipates young Satan's contemptuous treatment of the Moral Sense in *The Mysterious Stranger*. We are reminded, too, that the American jeremiad in the hands of a Colonel Sherburn, or of the Mark Twain who presides *in propria persona* over "My First Lie" and "The United States of Lyncherdom," may serve as the instrument of an unacknowledged disposition to be "satisfied with things the way they are." Less obviously perhaps, Mark Twain's bad-faith decision to "be judicious and let somebody else begin" to face the truth echos the consensus among the villagers in *Tom Sawyer*, who

> had a strong desire to tar-and-feather Injun Joe and ride him on a rail, for body-snatching, but so formidable was his character that nobody could be found who was willing to take the lead in the matter, so it was dropped. He had been careful to begin both of his inquest-statements with the fight, without confessing the grave-robbery that preceded it; therefore it was deemed wisest not to try the case in the courts at present.[10]

[10]*The Adventures of Tom Sawyer*, ed. John C. Gerber et al. (Berkeley: University of California Press, 1980), p. 108.

In a variety of guises, and viewed from a variety of points of view, the lie of silent assertion was from the very beginning a staple of Mark Twain's perspective on the world. It is evident here not only in the "judicious" retreat from morally responsible behavior, but also in the familiar suggestion that the main line of argument has been lost ("I have wandered from my text"). Alleged failures of memory and appeals to old age serve in the same way to draw attention away from the central, morally compelling business at hand. Philosophical determinism or dream, judicious temporizing or bad-faith affirmations of a degraded status quo, and the fading and blurring of vision caused by removes in space or time—all of these apparently very different states of mind involve detached points of view, equally detached, even resigned, tones of voice, and betray in the aggregate a pronounced inclination to back away from experience, to obscure or submerge or totally strike from the mind what cannot be tolerated at close range. They are the furtive mental postures, in short, of the lie of silent assertion, and they appear with increasing frequency in Mark Twain's writing toward the end of his career. . . .

The *locus classicus* in this vein is, of course, *The Mysterious Stranger,* a collection of fragments in which a consummate stranger, an angel, the innocent young nephew of Satan, offers an assessment of man's estate. The leading feature of his commentary is determinism, the notion that humans are without choice in the formation of their behavior, and thus without responsibility for what they do. It follows, young Satan argues, that men and women are fools if they blame themselves for what they regard as their sins. In a degraded but totally determined world, guilt is the pinnacle of folly, and prayer for early release into the oblivion of insanity or death is the highest mortal wisdom.

The argument from necessity is a measure of the chasm that separates young Satan from his human companions, and it helps to account for his serene indifference to the spectacle that he surveys. He is unthreatened by any suggestion of a personal kinship with humanity, and he is apparently confident in the view that the mortal predicament, though replete with foolishness and pain, is blameless and inevitable. Looking through the angelic stranger to his maker, we recognize Satan's detachment and resignation as manifestations of Mark Twain's longing. The angel's serene indifference is the expression of his author's enduring wish to arrive at a settled philosophical remove from his own deep sympathy and guilt over human suffering. Since we are all slaves to necessity, his argument clearly implies, our anguish is misplaced and should be set aside. . . .

Determinism relieves guilt at the price of obliterating choice. The freedom to choose, on the other hand, may in principle imply the potential for moral progress; but for Mark Twain such prospects invariably succumb in practice to the perverse play of man's fallen nature, and thus to the shackles of conscience and bad faith. Because he recoiled from the implications of both perspectives on human enslavement, Mark Twain could neither finish his story nor set it aside. Instead, his attitude swings, with Satan's, between intervals of detached indifference and periodic eruptions of angry condemnation. In such latter phases, of course, the futility of retreat to angelic detachment becomes manifest, and the implied philosophical solution to the moral—and esthetic—dilemma collapses into the problem. Were Satan's indifference to the mortal predicament a plausible solution, then he would maintain it. But he cannot. Nor, on the other hand, is he content to stand for long in wrathful judgment of a species whose fallen nature Mark Twain knew best from a long lifetime's self-scrutiny. The problem, we perceive, is the fundamental incompatibility between the writer's assumptions about human nature and the kind of freedom—from nature, history, conscience, others, and by implication, perhaps, from the God that young Satan's uncle disobeyed—that he attempts to confer on his angelic hero. The longing for such freedom is manifest in the conception of the extraordinary stranger; but its frustration is equally clear in the failure to embody that conception in a complete, coherent story.

It may be that in Satan we catch a glimpse of Mark Twain's groping rebellion against culture itself, against the compulsion to abide by the rules of what is, "we that know" recognize, a fiction, a fabrication. The denial of culture's constructedness is the grand progenitor of all subsequent bad faith denials, and the first and heaviest link in an endless chain of lesser, often benign, sometimes unbearable, but obligatory lies of silent assertion. Rather more narrowly, Satan is a manifestation of the urge D. H. Lawrence detected at the center of American culture, to be masterless, totally free of restraints. Most demonstrably, however, Mark Twain's obsession with an elusive, ungraspable conception of freedom expresses the frustration endemic to a culture committed to the principle that humans are created free, equal, and deserving of dignity, but which is burdened at the same time with a history that records the continuous, widespread, violent, and unabating disregard of those ostensibly sacred ideals. . . .

The apparent incoherence of *The Mysterious Stranger* finds its order in a revolving cycle of incompatible opposites engendering and canceling each other. The story has no ending because it is precisely the nature of this circular pattern to continue to rotate, to forever fail to achieve the resolution it forever seems to promise. Such perpetual motion has its source in a consciousness that is itself deeply divided. Espousal of determinism suddenly gives way to notions of free will, indifference to advocacy; the approach to the ideal collapses in unprincipled self-indulgence; and so on. But the division is not merely between the stages of consciousness; it is within them as well. The appeal to laughter bends simultaneously to prospects of reform and license; the right-minded punishment of the slave-trader is also cynical showing off. In due course, the guilt caused by the regular betrayal of shameful ulterior motives leads, in the name of stern philosophical truth, to the detection of necessity at work within the persistent oppositional structure. This step manifestly recapitulates the pattern it ostensibly seeks to break, and thus propels the cycle forward. But it is an especially decisive step because it illustrates that the consciousness at work in *The Mysterious Stranger* reacts to the revelation of its capacity for self-deception—to a glimpse of the selfish ends served by its high-minded intentions—by retreating to the illusion that such hapless duplicity is necessary, inevitable, and thus outside the range of its control or responsibility. The result is a pattern of consummate bad faith, in which the simultaneous push and pull of righteous and selfish motives propels consciousness through constant repetitions of the withdrawal to determinism and temporary repose, all the while deflecting attention away from the endlessly deferred reckoning with the theme of human freedom. Ironically, the revolving lies of silent assertion in the foreground obliquely dramatize the more comprehensive, pathological bad-faith evasion that they serve primarily to obscure. *The Mysterious Stranger* thus enacts and reenacts the fragments of a story that Mark Twain could not put aside, but that he could not bear to tell in full. As a way out where there was no way through, he contrived to retreat in symptomatic bad faith to the illusion of a perpetual cycle of necessary, irreducible indeterminacy.

Chronology of Important Dates

1835   Samuel Langhorne Clemens born November 30 in Florida, Missouri, to John Marshall Clemens (1798–1847) and Jane Lampton Clemens (1803–90); one of four children.

1839   Moves with family to Hannibal, Missouri, a port town on the Mississippi River north of St. Louis.

1848   Following father's death in 1847 begins work as an apprentice and typesetter for Hannibal newspapers.

1851   Publishes first sketch, entitled "A Gallant Fireman," in the *Hannibal Western Union*, published by his brother Orion Clemens.

1853   Begins four years of work as a printer in St. Louis, New York, Philadelphia, and Cincinnati.

1857   Becomes a cub pilot on the Mississippi River. Brother Henry Clemens killed in steamboat explosion. Publishes a satire in the *New Orleans Daily Crescent* based on the pilot Captain Isaiah Sellers, from whom he would later claim to have gotten the pseudonym Mark Twain.

1859   Licensed as steamboat pilot; works on river until 1861.

1861   Joins Confederate militia unit the Marion Rangers but deserts after several weeks. Goes west with Orion, who has been appointed secretary of the Nevada Territory.

1862   While prospecting, speculating, and traveling writes western sketches for newspapers in Iowa, Nevada, and California.

1863   First adopts the pen name Mark Twain. Becomes a correspondent for the *San Francisco Morning Call*.

1865   Publishes "Jim Smiley and His Jumping Frog" in *New York Saturday Press*.

1866   Tours Sandwich Islands (Hawaii) as reporter for the *Sacramento Union*. Begins career as public lecturer. Moves to New York as correspondent for the *San Francisco Alta California*.

1867   Sails on cruise ship *Quaker City* for tour of Europe and Holy Land as travel reporter for the *Alta California* and the *New York Tribune*. Upon return to United States meets Olivia (Livy) Langdon. Publishes *The Celebrated Jumping Frog of Calaveras County and Other Sketches*.

1869   Publishes *The Innocents Abroad; Or, The New Pilgrim's Progress* based on European tour. Buys interest in *Buffalo Express*.

1870   Marries Livy Langdon and lives in Buffalo; they eventually have four children.

1871   Moves to Hartford, Connecticut, spending many summers in Elmira, New York.

1872   Publishes *Roughing It* based on life and travels in West.

1873   Publishes *The Gilded Age* with co-author Charles Dudley Warner. Travels in Europe and continues busy public lecture schedule.

1874   Moves into newly constructed ornate mansion in Hartford, near Harriet Beecher Stowe's home.

1875   Publishes "Old Times on the Mississippi" (later incorporated into *Life on the Mississippi*) in the *Atlantic Monthly*.

1876   Publishes *The Adventures of Tom Sawyer* and begins writing *Adventures of Huckleberry Finn*.

1878   Travels in Europe until following year.

1880   Publishes *The Tramp Abroad* and *1601*, a bawdy burlesque. Continues work on *Adventures of Huckleberry Finn*.

1882   Publishes *The Prince and the Pauper*. Travels on the Mississippi River to gather material for a book.

1883   Publishes *Life on the Mississippi*. Breaks off sporadic work on *Adventures of Huckleberry Finn*.

1885   Goes on lecture tour with southern author and civil rights advocate George Washington Cable. Finishes and publishes *Adventures of Huckleberry Finn*.

1889   Publishes *A Connecticut Yankee in King Arthur's Court*.

1891   Moves to Europe, where he travels and lives off and on until 1900.

1892   Publishes *The American Claimant*.

1894   Paige Typesetting Machine, in which Twain had invested large amounts of money for more than a decade, fails, as does a publishing house of which he is part owner, leaving him bankrupt. Publishes *Pudd'nhead Wilson and Those Extraordinary Twins* and *Tom Sawyer Abroad*.

1895   Begins year-long world lecture tour to pay his debts. Publishes *Tom Sawyer, Detective*.

1896   Publishes *Personal Recollections of Joan of Arc*. Despondent over the death by meningitis of daughter Susy.

1897   Publishes *Following the Equator*, based on his lecture tour.

1899   Publishes "The Man That Corrupted Hadleyburg."

1900   Returns to New York. Produces further anti-imperialist writings such as "To a Person Sitting in Darkness" (1901) and continues work for next decade on many speculative and pessimistic manuscripts, most of which will remain unpublished at his death, including *The Mysterious*

Stranger, "Letters from the Earth," "The Great Dark," "Papers of the Adam Family," "The Damned Human Race," and "Which Was It?"

1903   Moves to Italy, where Livy dies the following year.

1905   Publishes *King Leopold's Soliloquy*.

1906   Publishes *What Is Man?* Begins relationship with Alfred Bigelow Paine, his first biographer, who later edits and publishes *Mark Twain's Letters* (1917), *Mark Twain's Speeches* (1923), *Europe and Elsewhere* (1923), *Mark Twain's Autobiography*, 2 vols. (1924), and *Mark Twain's Notebooks* (1935).

1908   Moves to Redding, Connecticut.

1910   Dies on April 21; buried in Elmira, New York.

Notes on Contributors

RICHARD BRIDGMAN, retired Professor of English at the University of California, Berkeley, is the author of *Traveling in Mark Twain* (1987), *Dark Thoreau* (1982), *Gertrude Stein in Pieces* (1970), and *The Colloquial Style in America* (1966).

LOUIS J. BUDD is James B. Duke Professor of English, Emeritus, at Duke University. He is the founding president of the Mark Twain Circle of America, and his books include *Our Mark Twain: The Making of His Public Personality* (1983), *Mark Twain: Social Philosopher* (1964), and, as editor, *Critical Essays on Mark Twain, 1867–1910* (1982) and *Mark Twain's Collected Tales, Sketches, and Essays* (1992).

JAMES M. COX is Professor of English Emeritus at Dartmouth College. He is the author of *Mark Twain: The Fate of Humor* (1966) and *Recovering Literature's Lost Ground: Essays in American Autobiography* (1989). He has also published extensive essays on Emerson, Hawthorne, Stowe, Howells, James, Hemingway, Frost, and Faulkner.

SUSAN K. GILLMAN teaches World Literature and Cultural Studies at the University of California, Santa Cruz. She is the author of *Dark Twins: Imposture and Identity in Mark Twain's America* (1989) and is currently working on a book entitled *The American Race Melodrama, 1877–1915.*

LAURENCE B. HOLLAND (d. 1980), a Professor of English at Princeton University and the Johns Hopkins University, was the author of *The Expense of Vision: Essays on the Craft of Henry James* (1964), and the editor of *The Norton Anthology of American Literature* (1979) and *Who Designs America?* (1966).

WALTER BENN MICHAELS is Professor of English at the Johns Hopkins University. He is the author of *The Gold Standard and the Logic of Naturalism* (1987), the editor of *The American Renaissance Reconsidered* (1985), and a co-author of volume 3 of the forthcoming *Cambridge History of American Literature.*

CAROLYN PORTER teaches American Literature at the University of California, Berkeley. The author of *Seeing and Being: The Plight of the Participant Observer in Emerson, James, Adams, and Faulkner* (1981), she is currently serving as Co-Director of the American Studies Program at Berkeley and completing a book on gender and the American novel.

ARNOLD RAMPERSAD is Woodrow Wilson Professor of Literature at Princeton University. He is the author of *Melville's Israel Potter: A Pilgrimage and Progress* (1969), *The Art and Imagination of W.E.B. Du Bois* (1976), and the two volume *Life of Langston Hughes* (1986–1988).

FORREST G. ROBINSON teaches in American Studies at the University of California, Santa Cruz. His books include *In Bad Faith: The Dynamics of Deception in Mark Twain's America* (1986) and, most recently, *Love's Story Told: A Life of Henry A. Murray* (1992) and *Having It Both Ways: Self-Subversion in Western Popular Classics* (1993).

JOHN SEELYE is a Graduate Research Professor at the University of Florida, Gainesville, in the field of American Studies and the director of the university's Center for the Study of Children's Literature. The author of numerous critical books and two novels, his most recent work is *Beautiful Machine: Rivers and the Republican Plan, 1755–1825* (1991). He has an anthology of short stories of the Old West forthcoming from Viking Penguin.

DAVID R. SEWELL, formerly Associate Professor of English at the University of Rochester, lives in Tucson, Arizona. He is the author of *Mark Twain's Languages: Discourse, Dialogue, and Linguistic Variety* (1987).

RICHARD SLOTKIN is Olin Professor and Director of American Studies at Wesleyan University. His books include *Regeneration Through Violence: The Mythology of the American Frontier, 1600–1860* (1973), *The Fatal Environment: The Myth of the Frontier in the Age of Industrialization, 1800–1890* (1985), and *Gunfighter Nation: The Myth of the Frontier in Twentieth-Century America* (1992).

DAVID L. SMITH is Associate Professor of English at Williams College and is currently completing a book entitled *Racial Writing, Black and White.*

ERIC J. SUNDQUIST is Professor of English at the University of California, Los Angeles. His books include *To Wake the Nations: Race in the Making of American Literature* (1993), *The Hammers of Creation: Folk Culture in Modern African-American Fiction* (1992), and *Faulkner: The House Divided* (1983).

Bibliography

Anderson, Frederick, and Kenneth M. Sanderson. *Mark Twain: The Critical Heritage.* New York: Barnes and Noble, 1971. *A collection of reviews, articles, and essays on Twain from the beginning of his career through the mid-twentieth century.*

Beaver, Harold. *Huckleberry Finn.* London: Unwin Hyman, 1987. *A thorough reading of the novel in historical, biographical, and cultural contexts, with attention to its reception and critical heritage.*

Blair, Walter. *Mark Twain & Huck Finn.* Berkeley: University of California Press, 1960. *A study of Twain's early career, especially the influences that culminated in* Adventures of Huckleberry Finn.

Bridgman, Richard. *Traveling in Mark Twain.* Berkeley: University of California Press, 1987. *An analysis of Twain's national and international non-fiction travel writings.*

Budd, Louis J., ed. *Critical Essays on Mark Twain, 1867–1910.* Boston: G. K. Hall, 1982. *A collection of early reviews, articles, news stories, and other writings about Twain.*

———. *Mark Twain: Social Philosopher.* Bloomington: Indiana University Press, 1964. *An interpretation of Twain's social theories as represented in essays and fiction.*

———. *Our Mark Twain: The Making of His Public Personality.* Philadelphia: University of Pennsylvania Press, 1983. *A study of Twain's public personality, lecture career, and celebrity.*

Cardwell, Guy. *The Man Who Was Mark Twain: Images and Ideologies.* New Haven, CN: Yale University Press, 1991. *An interpretation of Twain's work as the product of unresolved familial and psychological conflicts.*

Champion, Laurie, ed. *The Critical Response to Mark Twain's* Huckleberry Finn. New York: Greenwood Press, 1991. *A collection of essays covering the history of the novel's reception and analysis.*

Cox, James M. *Mark Twain: The Fate of Humor.* Princeton, NJ: Princeton University Press, 1966. *A study of Twain's language, narrative style, and humor from biographical and formal perspectives.*

Cummings, Sherwood. *Mark Twain and Science.* Baton Rouge: Louisiana State University Press, 1988. *An interpretation of Twain's use of scientific theories in his novels and speculative writings.*

Davis, Sara deSaussure, and Philip D. Beidler, eds. *The Mythologizing of Mark Twain.* Tuscaloosa: University of Alabama Press, 1984. *A selection of essays devoted to aspects of Twain's career, public performances, and popular reception.*

Doyno, Victor A. *Writing Huck Finn: Mark Twain's Creative Process.* Philadelphia: University of Pennsylvania Press, 1992. *A contextual study of Twain's composition of* Adventures of Huckleberry Finn.

Emerson, Everett. *The Authentic Mark Twain: A Literary Biography of Samuel*

Clemens. Philadelphia: University of Pennsylvania Press, 1984. *An interpretation of Twain's life principally in light of his major writings and public appearances.*

Fishkin, Shelley Fisher. *Was Huck Black?: Mark Twain and African-American Voices.* New York: Oxford University Press, 1993. *An interpretation of the African American sources of Twain's vernacular in the context of nineteenth-century literary and ethnographic practice.*

Foner, Philip. *Mark Twain, Social Critic.* New York: International Publishers, 1958. *A Marxist interpretation of Twain's work in social criticism.*

Gibson, William M. *The Art of Mark Twain.* New York: Oxford University Press, 1976. *A study of Twain's major writings from a formal and thematic perspective.*

Giddings, Robert, ed. *Mark Twain: A Sumptuous Variety.* Totowa, NJ: Barnes and Noble, 1985. *A collection of essays by British critics on various of Twain's writings, with particular emphasis on his social criticism.*

Gillman, Susan. *Dark Twins: Imposture and Identity in Mark Twain's America.* Chicago: University of Chicago Press, 1989. *An analysis of psychological problems of identity and disguise in Twain's writings and lectures, with particular attention to his more speculative works.*

———, and Forrest G. Robinson, eds. *Mark Twain's Pudd'nhead Wilson: Race, Conflict, and Culture.* Durham, NC: Duke University Press, 1990. *A collection of essays on* Pudd'nhead Wilson *interpreted in social, legal, and historical contexts.*

Gribben, Alan. *Mark Twain's Library: A Reconstruction.* 2 vols. Boston: G. K. Hall, 1980. *A study of Twain's reading and the sources of his ideas and themes throughout his career.*

Hill, Hamlin. *Mark Twain: God's Fool.* New York: Harper and Row, 1973. *An interpretation of Twain's late career and writings, in particular his philosophical pessimism.*

Inge, M. Thomas, ed. *Huck Finn Among the Critics: A Centennial Selection.* Frederick, MD: University Publications of America, 1985. *A collection of early and modern essays on the novel gathered on the occasion of its centennial celebration in 1985, with a very extensive annotated bibliography.*

Kaplan, Justin. *Mr. Clemens and Mark Twain.* New York: Simon and Schuster, 1966. *The major biographical interpretation of Twain and his works in a detailed historical and cultural context.*

Krause, Sydney J. *Mark Twain as Critic.* Baltimore, MD: Johns Hopkins University Press, 1967. *An analysis of Twain's journalism and essays on literature, authors, and social themes, including unpublished work.*

Kruse, Horst H. *Mark Twain and Life on the Mississippi.* Amherst: University of Massachusetts Press, 1981. *A study of the sources, composition, and interpretations of* Life on the Mississippi.

Lauber, John. *The Inventions of Mark Twain.* New York: Hill and Wang, 1990. *A biographical study of Twain focusing on his many personae, his financial problems, and his methods of writing.*

———. *The Making of Mark Twain: A Biography.* New York: Noonday, 1985. *A biographical study of Twain's early career.*

Leonard, James S., Thomas A. Tenney, and Thadious Davis, eds. *Satire or Evasion?: Black Perspectives on Huckleberry Finn.* Durham, NC, 1992. *A collection of recent essays, by African-American critics, devoted to questions of race and racism in* Adventures of Huckleberry Finn, *with annotated bibliography.*

Lynn, Kenneth S. *Mark Twain and Southwestern Humor.* Boston: Little, Brown,

1959. *A study of the sources of Twain's humor in the vernacular tradition of the old Southwest, with significant attention to formal and social themes.*

Marotti, Maria Ornella. *The Duplicating Imagination: Mark Twain and the Twain Papers.* University Park: Pennsylvania State University Press, 1990. *A study of Twain's writings that were unpublished in his lifetime, now held in the Mark Twain Papers at the University of California, Berkeley.*

Pettit, Arthur G. *Mark Twain and the South.* Lexington: University of Kentucky Press, 1974. *An interpretation of Twain's relation to the South and racial themes in his published work, journals, and notebooks.*

Robinson, Forrest G. *In Bad Faith: The Dynamics of Deception in Mark Twain's America.* Cambridge, Mass.: Harvard University Press, 1986. *A study of moral compromise and ethical contradiction in Twain's writing, focusing principally on* The Adventures of Tom Sawyer, Adventures of Huckleberry Finn, *and late works.*

Salomon, Roger B. *Twain and the Image of History.* New Haven: Yale University Press, 1961. *An analysis of Twain's social criticism and uses of history in his fiction.*

Sattelmeyer, Robert, and J. Donald Crowley. *One Hundred Years of Huckleberry Finn: The Boy, His Book, and American Culture.* Columbia: University of Missouri Press, 1985. *A wide-ranging collection of essays gathered on the occasion of the centennial of* Adventures of Huckleberry Finn.

Sewell, David R. *Mark Twain's Languages: Discourse, Dialogue, and Linguistic Variety.* Berkeley: University of California Press, 1987. *An interpretation of Twain's vernacular language and narrative style in a theoretical context.*

Smith, Henry Nash, ed. *Mark Twain: A Collection of Critical Essays.* Englewood Cliffs, NJ: Prentice-Hall, 1963. *A collection of classic essays covering the range of Twain's works, ideas, and career.*

_____. *Mark Twain's Fable of Progress: Political and Economic Ideas in A Connecticut Yankee.* New Brunswick, NJ: Rutgers University Press, 1964. *A cultural and biographical study of the capitalist hero and the idea of progress in* A Connecticut Yankee *and allied writings.*

_____. *Mark Twain: The Development of a Writer.* Cambridge, MA: Harvard University Press, 1962. *A thorough study of questions of the style and structure of Twain's works within biographical and cultural contexts.*

Tenney, Thomas A., ed. *Mark Twain: A Reference Guide.* Boston: G. K. Hall, 1977. *A complete bibliography of writings about Twain and his works, updated annually in* American Literary Realism, 1977–83, *and in* Mark Twain Circular, 1987–current.